LAST TIME

*Labour's Lessons
from the Sixties*

LAST TIME

Labour's Lessons from the Sixties

Austin Mitchell and
David Wienir

Bellew Publishing · London

This edition first published in Great Britain in 1997
Bellew Publishing Company Limited
8 Balham Hill, London SW12 9EA

ISBN 1 85725 120 2

Typeset by Antony Gray, DTP Jungle, London
Printed and bound in Great Britain by
Hartnolls Ltd, Bodmin, Cornwall

For Archie, Maisie and Sykes
hoping they grow up under a
Labour goverment
to make theirs a better Britain

Contents

	Preface	9
INTRODUCTION	*A Time for Change*	11
ONE	*New Leader*	19
TWO	*New Labour*	32
THREE	*Swinging Britain*	50
FOUR	*The Promised Land*	76
FIVE	*To Govern is to Campaign*	117
SIX	*The Great Unmentionable*	140
SEVEN	*Parliament as Hustings*	157
EIGHT	*On to Victory*	178
NINE	*The Power to Fail*	193
TEN	*Epilogue and After*	218
ELEVEN	*A New Beginning*	236
APPENDIX	*Those Who Took Part*	241
	About the Authors	246

Preface

This book follows the techniques of *Election '45** in letting those who made history tell the story in their own words. Why impose retrospective frameworks or the views of those who weren't there when the people who were – all Labour in this volume, then if not now – tell it so much better? We've talked to all who would talk to us and we're deeply grateful to them for their time, their courtesy and their recollections. They bring alive a time when one author was in a happier land far away and the other wasn't even born (no prizes for guessing which).

We've concentrated on the two threads of the story of the second postwar Labour government which are most relevant to today's politics. How Labour can win and hold power and how Labour governments succeed or fail by their handling of the real economy. With hindsight the government of 1964–70 threw away a great opportunity. That's our perspective. Those who participated don't necessarily accept it. Indeed, several disagree, but all their views are represented so that thirty years later we can understand what happened and those who resume Labour's Sisyphean task of rolling the stone of progress up the hill can learn the lessons of last time.

A book is the tip of an iceberg of work and this as much as any. We did the interviews, mostly together but several separately. Pat Murray, Clara Bentham and Joyce Benton transcribed the interviews. They are reproduced here in edited form with the 'um's' and 'er's' and the meanderings of normal speech cut out to condense things to the essence of what was said. The names of those we interviewed are given as they were in 1964 though many have gone up in the world since then. Joyce, Pat and David did the editing, and Tim Grewal

* Austin Mitchell, *Election '64: Reflections on the Revolution in Britain*, Fabian Society and Bellew Publishing, 1995

and Dean Bullen waded through the proofs and helped shape the final product. Ib Bellew demonstrated the dynamism, flexibility, and the speed which only an entrepreneurial small publisher can contribute. We are grateful for his energy and faith in our project. We are also grateful to Antony Gray for his skill, courtesy and unruffled efficiency in setting the book.

We are indebted to the invaluable Hulton Getty Picture Collection for most of the photographs, to the Centre for the Study of Cartoons and Caricatures, University of Kent for providing the cartoons and Solo Syndication for permission to use them. Finally our thanks to the National Museum of Labour history and to David Kingsley who placed his own posters and research files at our disposal.

It's been a privilege to relive the hopes and aspirations, the disappointments and the defeats of what was, with all its fumbles and failures, a great adventure and an advance for Britain. Our hope is that learning the lessons of last time can make next time more successful, because Labour must do better at advancing the lot of the people of this country than it did then. It can by understanding the story told in these pages.

Austin Mitchell
David Wienir
January 1997

A Time for Change

Labour is ahead, commanding, riding a magic carpet to power. It's all wonderfully exciting after we've been in opposition for eighteen miserable years of heckling the Executive steamroller. Yet the last time we won an election was nearly a quarter of a century ago and the last time we were in the commanding position we hold today, poised to take power after a long term of Tory government, was a third of a century ago, in the marathon run up to a 1964 general election as long postponed as that of 1997. In political terms that's an eternity.

There are extraordinary similarities between then and now. Labour had an exciting new leader and yesterday's incumbent Tory government was failing and faltering almost as badly as today's. Yet Labour didn't come to power in one stride with a majority to rule, as Tory governments always do, for the electorate was more grudging to Labour, giving us power on the instalment plan, through a two-stage process: office in October 1964, real power only after a second election in March 1966. The same two-step ascent had to be repeated in 1974.

Even worse, the enthusiasm for change and another move forward, which underlay Labour's success in 1964–6, was soon dissipated instead of being built on to win another term. After 1951 the Tories held power for thirteen years and after 1979 Margaret Thatcher turned a seismic shift of opinion into a sustained counter-revolution, but Harold Wilson did not deliver on his mandate and the surge which brought Labour to power broke into a thousand eddies and ripples. The underlying promise of 1964 was not realised. Labour achieved much, but failed at the fundamentals: a second term and a British economic miracle generating the growth, the spending and the better society the people wanted. Labour's mission is to maximise the living standards of the people. It has not delivered on that since 1951.

Now New Labour seeks to break the chains of the past. It can only do so by avoiding the mistakes of old Labour. So we have much to learn from the last time we waited impatiently in the anteroom of power and from the mistakes which followed once we got there. Then Harold Wilson failed to turn his party into the NPG (Natural Party of Government) he wanted it to be. Tony Blair resumes the task of NPG creation and intends to pace it more slowly, over two terms of government rather than Wilson's one-shot wonder. To succeed he must learn the lessons of last time.

Today's is an age of younger politicians and leaders and their political folk memory is short, almost as if we are cut off from history and each decade and year even, is a *tabula rasa*; a blank canvas for new mistakes. In fact history has its patterns, and last time's extraordinary similarities to today's situation provide a fascinating test run for New Labour's hopes, prospects and mistakes.

Last time Labour had a dynamic attractive new leader Harold Wilson, elected in February 1963. A reformed and re-invigorated party had recovered from the Bevanite wars of 1951–7 just as today's has from its nervous breakdown of 1979–82. An opposition well and long ahead in opinion polls, council and by-elections faced failing incumbents. In 1964 the Tories had been in power for thirteen years then viewed as 'wasted'. Today's counterpart has had seventeen years, though these are now seen as a necessary learning process, even educative for Labour.

In each case it was, and is, 'time for a change', that most powerful of electoral dynamics, as government struggled to find a new course to be blown off after the failure of its central strategy, then entry to the Common Market, today membership of the Exchange Rate Mechanism. To improve the prospects each stimulated pre-election booms, bigger then, weaker now, but contrasting in each case with the deflation, scandals, dismissals and resignations which had gone before. In 1963 one Profumo Scandal was enough. A whole series has befallen John Major. Harold Macmillan had dismissed half his cabinet in 1961 (the 'wrong half' Harold Wilson said) just as John Major has jettisoned a similar number of ministers seriatim. The cumulative effect of scandals and changes was, and is, to undermine the authority of a party then born, these days brought in, to rule.

Both governments ran to the buffers of the last possible moment for an election: October 1964, and probably May 1997. Indeed the only real difference between the two situations was that in 1963 the Tories had changed leader less than a year before the election. Harold Macmillan, Prime Minister since 1957, developed prostate trouble in September 1963. Panicked by fear of cancer, he resigned and elaborate consultations well short of an election steered Sir Alec Douglas-Home into the leadership, giving more substance to Tory class stereotypes. A fourteenth earl who knew the working class well because he talked to the workers on his estate, described pensions as 'contributions' and did his calculations with matchsticks was a godsend for Labour, though 'New Leader, Old Stereotypes' also worked for the Tories and rallied the party. Change, any change, works wonders for political parties. Today's Conservative government needs it desperately but the trick was pulled last time when Mrs Thatcher was dumped for John Major. That was one reason (though not the only one) why the Tories won the 1992 election. Now that they need the boost of change more than ever it isn't available. John Major's still there. A leader isn't just for Christmas.

The parallels are numerous but the past is another country as well as another party. In 1964 Labour's stance and manifesto were more radical than today's. The agenda was change because Labour was opposing a do-nothing-very-much Conservative government. Today's Tories are raving radicals. The electorate in 1964 wanted a new move forward and a classless society after a decade of marking time. Today, after being buffeted by seventeen years of change, the electorate peers ahead nervously rather than optimistically. Today's electors are easily frightened. Radical new beginnings, equality, redistribution or tax increases are not on the agenda. Then change was accepted with equanimity and betterment widely desired. Even Conservatives such as Ted Heath and

Maudling offered themselves as modernisers. No longer.

Then a far higher proportion of the electorate, four fifths or more, had settled socially conditioned political allegiances inherited from parents and backgrounds. Electoral change came from the fluctuating, and looser, allegiances of a small minority of 'floaters' and the apathy and abstentions of those who didn't bother much. Thirty years of change, the destruction of neighbourhoods and industries, the growth of classless consumerism and exposure to a wide range of cases and arguments on TV have broken the conditioning process. Today's electors, pried loose from inherited loyalties, are more open to change. They flip TV channels, neighbourhoods, votes, even spouses in a way unheard of earlier. They choose as consumers where 1964's electors were like Pavlov's dogs. Then the aim of the campaign was to enthuse electors and get them out to vote. Today, it is to persuade them, offer a best electoral buy, and above all not to frighten them. All of which makes the media more influential in this, as in all, consumer decisions.

Tony Blair came to Labour from outside its essence, with neither history nor conditioning in party or unions. He is projected over and above a party from which he is different, holding out a vision and reaching the parts of the electorate old Labour couldn't reach. Harold Wilson was the essence of the party coming from the left after a long career in office and in the top echelons of a party he was steeped in. As Labour's white knight, Blair doesn't hesitate to take on his party, even bash it. Each time he does so his own standing rises. He represents a break with the past, a new start. Wilson, the wily fixer, on the other hand, struggled to hold it together and personalised Labour's old basics from its noble vision to its ignoble fudge and mudge. Blair looks less to the nation state, today seen as dated and less powerful. He seeks to co-operate with Europe. Wilson looked to Britain alone, to national instruments of economic management and to modernising a national economy then viewed as sluggish not failed.

By the sixties Britain was already experiencing 'stop go' and Wilson could refer to Prime Minister and Chancellor as 'Stop Go and Son'. Crises of confidence had hit the reserves at the time of Suez and in 1961. Yet external constraints were weaker, Britain's economy was more readily managed then than is possible in the days of fluctuating exchange rates, massive money transfers, looming balance of payments deficit and stubbornly high unemployment. In 1964 Keynes worked. So did Britain. Jeremy Bray, first elected in 1961, points out that the whole framework of policy was more predictable and manageable.

In 1964 there was a more or less fixed framework for economic policy. Its parameters were full employment and the fixed exchange rate whereas today everything is pragmatic. Now there is less definition and fewer clear objectives. Another difference is the task. In 1964 there was a clear distinction between policy on the one hand and administration on the other. Nowadays it's all management. In 1964 there were powerful external bodies who really could exert an influence on government – trade unions, local government, big British companies, universities. Today trade unions, local government, the big British companies are weakened. Multinational companies do not really know how to handle party politics and the government doesn't have a structure for policy or a right way of doing things. Then the acceptable approach to the problem was to set up a Royal Commission. What shall we do about Social Security? A Royal Commission. In 1964 we were spending a lot of time still losing an empire, we had a great many colonial situations such as Rhodesia. Nowadays we have lost an empire but we're still in the phase of trying to find a role. We are all orientated now towards international co-operation and all that.

Systems worked, though not well enough. The nation could control its own destinies though not completely. Britain was confident because it had yet to endure the long years of failure. All this made for optimistic policies, centred round a boost to growth and the end of Tory complacency. The mood was 'go', 'improve', 'expand', 'grow'. Today it is cautious, less confident and preoccupied with stopping things getting worse. The slogans today are 'as resources allow', 'no definite commitment', 'don't spend or tax', 'don't expect too much'.

Both manifestos put growth at the centre. Explicitly in 1964, implicitly but more crucially in 1997. With redistribution and higher taxes and borrowing ruled out, growth is now the only way to generate more public spending by putting people back to work at higher wages to widen the tax base. On both occasions Labour was festooned with supply-side policies: planning, education, training and investment and industrial reorganisation in 1964, investment, education and training in 1966. The missing element on both occasions was demand, taken for granted in 1964, a taboo subject by 1997 when Labour poses as tough on demand, tough on the causes of demand and talks the deflationary language of Maastricht.

In neither case was the serious underlying problem of the British economy faced, though it made growth difficult then, perhaps impossible now. Failure to tackle this in a manifesto is understandable. Failures to understand and prepare as happened on both occasions is disastrous for a party which aspires to betterment. Those failures arose, and arise still, from an inability to understand either the real dynamics of the economy or the exchange rate and its role.

By 1964 long comparative decline had made Britain vulnerable to balance-of-payments problems. These problems threatened an exchange rate fixed in 1949 but growing ever more out of line since. Demand could only be boosted if the exchange rate came down to channel it to British production. Without that Labour was locked in the Tory trap: low growth, runs on sterling, and then deflation. Today the problem is different but the same. Britain is in deficit even during deflation. The exchange rate floats but fixing it is back in fashion with enthusiasts for Monetary Union and it has been kept too high for far too long to defeat inflation with interest rates kept at historic, high levels in real terms. That pressure, sustained over twenty years, has left a smaller manufacturing base which is unable either to pay its way in the world or support present public spending levels without heavy borrowing. Again as in 1964, Labour has no plans to break out of that trap. Indeed attitudes on borrowing, taxation and devaluation show no indication of any understanding of the role of the exchange rate, the dynamics of competitiveness or the real constraints on growth. In 1964 the rocks on which British prospects are regularly wrecked were below the waves so to fail to see them was excusable. Today they stand well out of the waves but we turn our faces away. To propose to do anything might frighten electors, orthodoxies and financial institutions we want to conciliate or a European Union we want to get along with.

The past doesn't provide rules for the future. Similarities, striking as they are, don't determine what happens in a different age, to a changed society. Yet last time is interesting in itself as those who took part recreate its fears and hopes, and it does offer new insights on common patterns and similar problems. That analysis posts warnings and points pitfalls which can't be ignored by those who once again, and far too belatedly, tread the same yellow brick road to power, and face the same switchback after it unless the lessons of the great fall from the euphoria of 1963 to the forced retreat of 1967, as chronicled here, are learned.

CHAPTER ONE

New Leader

	1962				1963		
	Oct	Nov	Dec	Jan	Feb	Mar	Apr
Lab.	38	37	38	40	41	44	42
Con.	31	28	31	29	28	28	28
Lead	+7	+9	+7	+11	+13	+16	+14

(all polls from Gallup)

By the end of 1962 Labour was poised for power. It had eluded the party in the October 1959 election but Harold Macmillan's Conservative government, re-elected then with an increased majority and on an implicit promise of making an electorate which had never had it so good even more affluent, had run straight into major balance-of-payments problems. Macmillan's image as the unflappable actor-manager had then been badly dented when he abruptly purged a third of his cabinet: 'Greater love hath no man than this, that he lay down his friends for his life.'

Labour's leader, Hugh Gaitskell, the best prime minister Britain never had, grew in stature and popularity, taking on the unilateralists and winning, and reconciling himself with the left by rejecting membership of the Common Market – the centre-piece of Macmillan's strategy which was itself destroyed when General de Gaulle said 'Non!' in January 1963.

Labour looked impregnable: renewed, ahead in the opinion polls – standing nearly ten per cent in front of the Tories with Gaitskell even further ahead of Macmillan. That lead increased after Gaitskell's death of a sudden, mysterious, illness on 18 January 1963 produced a surge of affection and respect. Harold Wilson was elected leader on 14 February, mistrusted by the Gaitskellites because he had stood against their beloved leader, but becoming more popular and turning out to be a more vigorous and effective media manager and campaigner. Wilson did what Gaitskell had never completely succeeded at. He united the party and brought left and right together to win. The long years of exile became the exciting months of waiting for a victory which began to look almost inevitable.

✗ We were thirteen years in the wilderness and we'd gone through a lot of trauma, so the similarities are very real. You had the Bevanite group kicking up the dust then, like what I always call the loony bins kicking up the dust from '81, so you had a similar situation between the two. We were desperate to get back into government and we are now desperate to get back. Except it's seventeen years now rather than thirteen years. We were hitting them where it hurt politically in a whole number of ways. So the party was beginning to come together. The party was beginning to feel that we really had something. There was a tempo about it and things were beginning to hum.   RON BROWN

✗ A group of MPs, and others in the party, felt that the Labour Party was still backward looking. It hadn't modernised itself as the German Social Democrats had, our great models. What had happened in Germany with the Social Democrats was that they had really modernised themselves and got rid of all the socialist nonsense. We were very much supportive of Labour as a party of conscience and reform, dealing with practical problems that really worried people and not following outdated ideology. Our great hero was also Hugh Gaitskell, the leader, who we felt was a terribly charismatic figure and excited young people at the time. He addressed problems in an intellectual way. He was passionate too. But there was a practical idealism about him that was really very inspiring and I was one of those that was inspired by him. I had seen him at Oxford. He would come down and talk to students.

    This was the first great character who was trying to do important things with the party and modernise it and bring it up to date. He was under attack for this from the left and under attack from one of the most notorious lefties, Wilson. He was also under attack over the way the country was to be defended. The Campaign for Nuclear Disarmament became very vocal and took over a number of unions and dominated certain local constituencies. Wilson was linked in with these people. Whether he was really one of them is debatable, but he used them and it appeared to them and to everybody else that he was sympathetic. So he was always able to draw on the support of the left, in domestic politics and international affairs.

There were some very bitter fights within the party as the left increased its hold and it was felt that the Campaign for Democratic Socialism was a way in which we could fight back. I was a postgraduate student so I was involved in the student section amongst a whole range of universities. John Smith was part of it, from Glasgow; I was from the University of Oxford. A group of us got this going as the junior version to show that young people were not all mad lefties or all believing that you should give up your nuclear weapons and allow Russia to walk all over you. Our scheme was to make sure that young people with those views went to selection conferences. We were linked in with various regional organisers of the party. They made sure that our names were put forward.

GEORGE JONES

✗ Gaitskell's Common Market Speech certainly divorced him from the rest of us in CDS. We had great arguments with him over that and he did it because, as he said at the time, 'I can carry Frank Cousins on this. He'll come with us.' I'm absolutely certain that although I think Gaitskell was quite sincere in what he was saying about the Common Market, the reason why he was acting the way he did at that party Conference was probably to get the T&G on his side because he hadn't been supported by the left-wing trade unions. It may be a bit cynical but that's what he said, because I heard him say it. In the old Labour Party you had to think of about one million votes at the Labour Party Conference and its not cynical to say, 'I'm going to win the bloody votes.'

DENIS HOWELL

✗ I don't think Hugh would have been an ideal Prime Minister. He was one of those people who thought that anybody who disagreed with him was either a knave or a fool and he really didn't recognise the possibility of honest dissent and he was also hopelessly intellectual in his approach. He wanted always to argue problems through until he was certain everybody understood why he was right and as my American friend Dean Rusk who'd also been a professor used to say, the difference between academic life and the government is the difference between arguing to a conclusion and arguing to a decision. As many politicians have said the trouble about decisions in government is that you know you never have all the information you need when you have to take them, because life isn't like that.   DENIS HEALEY

✗ It was a disaster for the party when Hugh died. I responded to it primarily as this terrible, terrible loss, a personal loss not just a loss for the party; in the days before he died, each time I got home from work my eldest, Sheila aged six, would say, 'Have you told Mrs Gaitskell about my dream?' Sheila's dream was that if he had a mixture of pea and honey this would cure him. Then he died and the Italian mother's help, on whom I utterly depended, came running up the stairs at my home and said, 'I have just heard on the radio that Mr Gaitskell's dead.' Mr Gaitskell was this figure in our household, to the mother's help, to my children, certainly to me. He was a major figure in my life in this country. Tony's reaction was like that of all the people who had loved Hugh Gaitskell, they couldn't hand over their emotional loyalty to another leader just like that. No one, and Harold in particular, because Harold had been one who challenged Hugh. It was just like that, it wasn't rational. It would have been almost against human nature for the ones who had loved Hugh to welcome the man who had challenged him. In any case, Tony never understood Wilson.   SUSAN CROSLAND

✗ When Gaitskell died I said, 'It's bound to be Wilson.' I can't remember saying it but I seem to have said it to a sufficient number of people who have remembered it to make it true. About twenty of us began to meet to discuss what to do. It was, for the centre right, between Callaghan and Brown. One or two people, such as Tony Crosland and George Thompson and Christopher Mayhew, believed it had to be Callaghan, either because they liked him – Tony Crosland and George

Thompson were fairly close to Jim – or, like Christopher Mayhew, they thought George was impossible. Indeed George's liking for drinking too much was already apparent and put some people off.

So we met and discussed what to do and in the end decided that George Brown could beat Wilson but Callaghan couldn't. Therefore, even if we were rather divided between Callaghan and Brown the message was 'vote for Brown'. But those who didn't like Brown and preferred Callaghan voted for him. I predicted to within two or three votes what the outcome would be. I was not really very depressed by Wilson winning because I thought he was going to win. I was still running the Campaign for Democratic Socialism, on a very part-time basis, and I remember the key piece was written by Phillip Williams who wrote, 'An election has been properly held. The parliamentary party has chosen and we must now be loyal supporters of Wilson'– and on some very crucial issues, such as NATO, Wilson's record was impeccable. It was difficult for me. In a sense it's rather as though Wilson had killed my father and married my mother – that was the sort of feeling I had. I never really could adjust to Harold Wilson. I never settled down with him and only at the end, in 1974, when he came back into government with all passion spent and I'd become wiser and older, did we really begin to talk together very much.

BILL RODGERS

✗ The great blow obviously was Hugh's death. The question then was who was going to succeed. We had a meeting of the former Campaign for Democratic Socialism people rather than the MPs, because we were all going to have to take a decision, in Tony Crosland's flat. Roy Jenkins was in America so Jennifer represented him. The great question came up, 'Who should we back for leader?' because the obvious choice, Brown, had certain disadvantages. Callaghan was a possible and somebody said, 'Well what about Harold Wilson? We shouldn't just dismiss him, because Harold Wilson will be the most effective campaigner probably.'

The view, I don't know who first expressed it, but it was generally accepted, was that 'Harold won't put a foot wrong before the election. He will win us the election and then he will run us into the ground.' And that is precisely what he did in my view because he was not a good prime minister. He took the wrong decisions and eventually his failure to confront the left led to the split in the Labour Party which kept it out of office for seventeen years. So I think that judgement then was right.

Then came the awful question, 'Who do you back then, Brown or Callaghan?' George Thompson, Douglas Jay and Tony Crosland said, 'We must back Callaghan.' Well I didn't have much faith in Callaghan myself but the others said, 'Look, George is a neurotic personality. It's not his drinking which is the problem, the drinking is only an outward sign of an essentially neurotic personality. But he is bloody brilliant and I think in the end he is the person to do it.' That was the sort of view expressed. 'He is the one we have to back.' Well, I was a new MP so I was very much influenced by those who were better, wiser men than me. In the end I reluctantly voted for George Brown.   DICK TAVERNE

✘ The leadership election of '63 rather put us all back a bit because again that brought back all the bad feeling and ill will. Everyone thought at that time that George would take it and the people who let him down were our folks, our friends, our trade-union people who decided to vote for a don rather than vote for one of their own. Callaghan was brought into the game with Wilson's camp as a stalking horse. And he was daft enough to do it. Nevertheless, he put himself in the frame for later years. But fundamentally it was our own people that decided as working-class people they would rather vote for a don than vote for one of their own.   RON BROWN

✘ I was very fond of Hugh Gaitskell and I thought he was a very good egg. He used to say to me, 'That man,' meaning Harold, 'will only become leader of the Labour Party over my dead body,' and that was what happened. He had the utmost contempt for Harold. For example, at shadow cabinet meetings he would say nothing or support the shadow official line, then we'd go outside and he'd tell all the chaps whose support he was hoping to get, 'Oh, I fought like mad for our point of view,' and he hadn't said a bloody word. We always worried about him on defence and we were worried that he was going to be so soft on the left that this would bugger up the Labour Party quite a lot. And of course he was.

WOODROW WYATT

✖ We were all involved in the Campaign for Democratic Socialism which was organising nationally. Bill Rodgers ran the office. Dick Taverne was the treasurer. We turned the party round and then made it possible to win the election which Harold did quite brilliantly. It faded away pretty soon after, but it wasn't wound up until we won the election. They didn't trust Harold Wilson at first. Particularly Patrick Gordon Walker and also Tony Crosland and Jack Diamond, they were three senior figures in it. We had arguments in which we all agreed that there was now going to be a rapprochement between our part of the party and the centre left. Patrick Gordon Walker went out of his way to bring us together. He was a main messenger between CDS and Harold Wilson. The message was unity. We had won the argument and in the face of the enemy you unite.   DENIS HOWELL

✖ When Hugh Gaitskell died, George Brown was the only other alternative. Alf Robens had gone to run coal because he'd thought there was never going to be another Labour government, so George was the only alternative, and though he was without any doubt a brilliant fellow, with a very acute brain, he always had an inferiority complex in relation to these smart chaps like Tony Crosland and Roy Jenkins. I was always telling him, 'Don't be so silly, they're actually terrified of you because you've got a very sharp and acute brain, and you analyse things very well.'

I remember George Wigg coming to me and saying, 'Harold will give you a good job if you do back him,' and I said, 'I'd rather have George Brown drunk than Harold Wilson sober.' That didn't go down very well. The day after the first ballot, when George didn't do very well and obviously was going to lose the second one, I was sitting in the smoking room with him, and he said to me, 'What do you think went wrong?' I said, 'The trouble is, George, you are quite rude to people when you're drunk.' He said, 'What makes them think I'm only rude to them because I'm drunk?' He was a great man in his way. He then disappeared, for about a fortnight nobody knew where he'd gone, he was in a great huff, but nobody knew what had happened to him.   WOODROW WYATT

✖ I adored Gaitskell. When he died, I had no doubt. I'm a very red-blooded fellow. I liked and admired George Brown immensely. His alcoholism wasn't too apparent then. In fact I often thought he started two gins ahead of everybody else. He didn't drink all that much, surprisingly. He'd go mad, suddenly berserk on a couple of glasses of wine. Willie was made George's PPS to watch George's drinking. He used to say to me, 'I can't understand it. I am with him all day and he hasn't drunk a thing and then he goes to a reception and after two or three glasses he seems drunk.' It was down to his metabolism. Alcohol, no matter how small the amount, used to change him, change his personality so that he became very aggressive. In fact he was a very warm-hearted man. I did vote for George Brown. I didn't think he would win but I did vote for him. I liked Wilson. Wilson knew I liked George, so did he in a strange kind of way. Although he was a rival he got on very well with George, better than he got on with James Callaghan. They were much more in tune with each other. George was very strongly pro-market. Harold was secretly a pro-marketeer, but he was secretly so many things deep down.

DICKSON MABON

✘ George Brown was a bewilderingly good and bad minister. When he was good he was very very good and when he was bad he was awful. George Brown had great virtues and considerable faults, too. I didn't say vices because that's too strong a word, but his virtue was that he was in my view generally right on a big issue and he instinctively liked big issues rather than trivial issues. A lot of people loved to get bogged down in trivial issues. George Brown swept them away and was interested in the big and difficult issues, and was generally right on those.   ROY JENKINS

✘ I was naturally very disappointed. I had lost my old friend. All Gaitskellites were very antipathetic to Harold Wilson. He felt very much shut out by them. I think I'm right in saying that when he won that election only about two members of the shadow cabinet voted for him. So it was rather extraordinary that he came in. Not that he was really a lefty in the ordinary sense, it was just chance that had placed him on that side of things, and he was the younger generation. He campaigned quite well but, for all that, to the people of my age group who'd been at Oxford, he was very provincial, with a provincial accent. I don't suppose they thought so in Bolton

New leader, old pipe

but he did have one down here. He was also ten years younger so he wasn't in the Gaitskellite world.

Harold Wilson was very intelligent in the way he dealt with the old Gaitskellites. He backed up Gordon Walker who was a complete Gaitskellite and one of the first things he did was to give Dora Gaitskell a peerage. When he came to the cabinet, he brought people in like Roy Jenkins and Crosland (who were hostile to Wilson) and gave them cabinet positions. So he was very sensible about people. He did really do quite a remarkable thing in bringing the party together. You can't imagine how bitter the split was in the party in the old days, even in the Lords we could see that. It was quite apparent here.

LORD LONGFORD

✗ Harold was elected as a left-of-centre candidate. Gaitskell was much loved by the party machine so the establishment of the Labour Party, as the majority of the Parliamentary Labour Party, were right of centre, governed in the main by trade unions and trade-union money and when Harold came in as leader it came as a great shock to them that they had got a left-of-centre leader. I don't think Harold ever gained love and affection from, say, party headquarters. Respect is one thing. They respected him because he was the winner and he was also efficient and knew how to operate the system. He had worked out how to beat the Tories at their own game and this was the real reason he was a winner.

Everyone thinks that there was masses of time between Harold becoming leader of his party and taking them into an election. It was a very short period. It was sixteen months and the '63 leadership-election campaign was a very vicious campaign from which the party, in my view, never recovered. The right wing indulged in practices which were not really acceptable and used Tories to help them do it, and that sort of poison stayed. Harold never thought of himself as embattled because he was a technocrat really. I suppose you could say he believed in getting on with what had to be done and he knew the means by which he was going to do it and he was immensely interested in the mechanics of it all. He could actually lose himself in those mechanics. He loved to work out what the headline was going to be in the newspapers the next day and he had a gift for working out his press release for each speech because it would have a soundbite that would absolutely dominate the next day's headlines.   MARCIA WILLIAMS

✗ He had a problem in that he took office as a leader who'd been elected because there was nobody else to vote for. There were the Gaitskellites of whom I was one – he was godfather of my kids – and then there were the left-wing trade unions. Nobody was positively for Harold. I voted for him with tears streaming down both cheeks in the belief that once he had actually got in he would dump the left and run a centre type of campaign. I was fairly accurate on that too. Not only was he not trusted by the left, he wasn't liked by the right, and the guy who, in my view, would have won that election hands down, as leader, was Alf Robens. The slate was George Brown, whom everybody liked and admired but thought the possibility of

"... AS CHANGE THUS CIRCULATES THROUGHOUT THE NATION, SOME PLAYS MAY JUSTLY CALL FOR ALTERATION. — FROM SHERIDAN'S 'A TRIP TO SCARBOROUGH'

World War III was bad enough without doing it in a drunken haze, Jim Callaghan who really had no weight at that stage at all, and there was Harold who had so many enemies, and I don't think had any sort of solid enthusiastic friends. He wanted these new people who owed their allegiance in a way to him and he invented me and he invented other people, there is no question about that, he pushed us there.   RICHARD MARSH

✗ It was that curious kind of mixture in Harold of the vision, of the idealism, of the flair, coupled with a lack of confidence almost in his ability to ride this circus horse of two parties pulling in opposite directions, and the right wing, from the beginning, had far too much influence. They were plotting against him all the time. They hated his guts. He had succeeded their beloved Gaitskell. That was an unforgivable sin. Mind you, they knew perfectly well that George Brown would have been disastrous and the PLP rejected the idea of Jim Callaghan. They thought he was too lightweight. Harold, who'd been working for this all the way along, very skilfully, almost got it by default. And the first thing he did in that PLP meeting when he beat George Brown for the leadership was to say, 'I do hope George will be my deputy.' He knew he was taking a snake to his bosom but that was what he did. George's only reply was to stalk off the platform and sulk. Eventually his own right wing persuaded him not to be a fool.

BARBARA CASTLE

✗ Wilson was a good leader of the opposition. He was a terrible leader of government. He was not good. First of all, though he was a man of experience he actually had no experience of the sort of situation the country was facing in 1964, but he gave the appearance of being a man of experience. He'd been in the cabinet and he'd been a prominent public figure for a long time, so he gave people the appearance that here is a man of experience so we're not taking too great a risk in electing him as prime minister. But he was very bad as a leader.

One reason was personal character, another was that he didn't have any experience. He was always 'bouncing' everything on this group and that group and keeping the party united, as though this were, at that time, ever a problem. The problem was that fundamentally he did not understand the economic situation he had inherited, that was the main thing. Indeed if you look back over what he'd been saying up to 1964 it's quite evident he didn't understand the economic situation he'd be inheriting. He is perhaps less to blame for that in that it didn't appear the Tories understood the economic situation they were creating, but so far as Wilson was concerned the main point is that he didn't understand the situation he was inheriting. The irony is that people like Jim Callaghan thought that Wilson was a man of experience. Jim Callaghan used to sidle through the linking doors of No.10 and No.11 to ask Wilson what to do. There could have been no worse adviser. It would have been much better if Callaghan had stayed where he was.

EDMUND DELL

✗ Harold Wilson was being interviewed by Brian Hooey. He said, 'I was most impressed. I turned to Mr Wilson and told him we'd be going on the air in five minutes so I thought I should tell him some of the questions I was going to ask. He said that he didn't deserve to be leader of one of the two great parties if he had to know the questions in advance so I should ask him anything I liked, he would just like a thirty-second cue.' The studio manager said, 'Thirty seconds, Mr Wilson,' and Harold nodded his head and at twenty seconds his hand went into his pocket and out came a pipe which he put on the table in front of him. At fifteen seconds his hand went in the other pocket and out came the matches which also went on the table. At ten seconds out came a match. At five seconds he struck the match, and at zero the first attempted puffs were going up on the screen. Brian said, 'That was professional.'

ALAN WILLIAMS

✗ Clearly there were problems getting over the division and bitterness of that campaign. But they were almost completely pulled together by the time the 1963 conference came. That was the first time that this 'white heat', you know a new future forged in the 'white heat of the technological revolution', came out. Harold Wilson made that speech. The party was joined together. The Tories were clearly, at that time, running out of steam, and he had presented a new vision from the Salisbury clique. Harold Wilson was presenting something different and he was clever because a working relationship was forged with George Brown. The party got itself together. There was a sense of unity in the air, a sense of purpose, a will to win without any doubt whatsoever that things would be different and different in a way that was not appealing to opinion polls, or bowing down before them. That wasn't it.   BERYL URQUHART

CHAPTER TWO

New Labour

Modernisation was the great theme and the greater hope of the early sixties. Modernisation of the economy by hitching it to the faster growth of the Common Market and by national planning. Modernisation of society and industry as the 'classless' grammar-school technocrats took over and a new generation came in. Modernisation of culture by pop, fashion and an exploding generation of new talent which made this 'swinging Britain'.

Modernisation, too, of political parties. Particularly Labour. Gaitskell had attempted this, after the 1959 defeat, with an abortive struggle to change the name to Democrats and to modify Clause Four. Then he began the more patient work of policy development and organisational improvement. The new political techniques of polling, image building, advertising and sloganeering were brought in. Socialism and policy were updated to be relevant to the needs and aspirations of an affluent new generation. These processes started by Gaitskell were completed by his successor, a man fascinated by the media, by political techniques and organisation. He welded policy into a new blend, the 'white heat of the technological revolution', mixing science, socialism and hope in a way which allowed socialism to be sold as an entirely new product. Unlike today's leaders, Wilson did it on his own and instinctively, without a tribe of spin doctors and advisers stumbling all over each other and confusing the message. Yet behind the scenes Labour was beginning to gather advice and incorporate the new arts into its approach.

'I am trying to run a Bolshevik revolution with a Czarist cabinet' – Harold Wilson

✗ In '64 it was not like now. There is a greater hunger now than I detected in '64. I think Wilson had tremendous hunger and indeed I remember being told round about May or June by, I think, Tommy Balogh, 'It's so awful for Harold. He is so impatient. He can't wait and now this bloody election isn't going to be until the autumn.' Elsewhere, I didn't detect that hunger in people like Roy Jenkins, who very nearly went off to be the editor of the *Economist*. They were rather languid in those days, even people like Tony Crosland, who I knew quite well had a tremendous hunger for office.

I think Dick [Crossman] hardly believed it until the moment he got into his padded cell, as he called it. He couldn't believe it had happened. He'd been nineteen years on the back-benches

with just one period of three months as an opposition back-
bench spokesman and suddenly to find yourself catapulted into
cabinet, like Barbara Castle, they were still rubbing their eyes.
They didn't somehow believe it was going to take place. I
suppose there were people who were hungry but of course a lot
of them had just given up belief in a Labour victory. Look at Alf
Robens. If he had not taken himself off to the Coal Board in
1960 in my belief he probably would have been the leader of the
Labour Party and not Harold Wilson. It wouldn't have been a
very good thing but I think it might well have happened.
Kenneth Younger went off to Chatham House. It was like the
retreat from Moscow. So the people who were left didn't really
believe they were going to win.   TONY HOWARD

✘ Here was this man Wilson, who'd been absolutely treated
with contempt by Hugh Dalton, who used to call Wilson
'Nye's little dog', and they hated him. The chairman of the
party though was intent on getting rid of the 'penny-farthing
machine', modernising the party's structure and so on. It was
different from the modernisation today: (a) because it had
political substance and clarity and (b) because it wasn't about a
new Labour Party, it was about the historic Labour Party
bringing about a New Britain.

Hugh Gaitskell tried to amend Clause Four. His version
was much more radical than the new Clause Four, but the day
Wilson was elected as leader, the Tories said, 'Does the Rt Hon.
Gentleman believe in Clause Four?' and Wilson said, 'Of
course I do,' and that killed the issue stone dead from then
until 1994. Harold was very good at that. He never allowed
them to open up a side. He never apologised. He was proud of
what he was. He wasn't, in his heart of hearts, a radical, but
he'd been through the experience of the Board of Trade and he
was very proud of his work as a minister.   TONY BENN

✘ Harold was always a superb machine politician. He
understood how it worked. He had a feel for the electorate and
how they were going. He had a feel for the grass-roots Labour
Party (which wasn't expressed in those terms at that stage) and
he had this ability with the buzz words which we could put in
at the right time. I'm not saying it was a shambles, but it was a
pretty unfocused thing in retrospect, with an enormous lot
going on. A lot of it not our fault, genuinely not the Labour

Party's fault, it had inherited this appalling situation. I don't think there is any dispute about that.   RICHARD MARSH

✘ Harold was very largely his own speech-writer, at least during his days in opposition. There were a group of us who helped him to some extent because he had an enormous pressure of work and among those who were in that group were Dick Crossman, Tony Benn, Tommy Balogh and myself, and we did assist, but Harold had a remarkable capacity for doing his own speeches and an enormous memory. He was able to draw upon all of his experience in government and in opposition over the previous fifteen or so years. Spin doctors hadn't then been invented.   PETER SHORE

✘ Harold asked me if I'd help him and I went to see him in early 1963. I helped him with the famous New Britain speeches. My wife actually thought of the idea, New Britain. I worked with him throughout that spring, summer and autumn. It was very exciting. People laugh at Wilson now, but the Harold of 1963 was a very committed man, and there was a genuine air of excitement about it. Peter Shore was head of the research department at Transport House working on the manifesto, and Wilson made speeches covering every aspect of policy. I think the first one was about January 1964 and he went right through the summer.   TONY BENN

✘ Wilson took the view that the Labour Party, in those days still in Transport House, was absolutely no good at all. He coined the phrase 'penny-farthing machine'. There was an extraordinary man who had been national agent and became General Secretary, Len Williams. Wilson was always cruel about Len Williams. I once said to him about a photograph when he was wearing his plumed hat that I thought he looked pretty good as a new governor-general. Wilson said, 'Jolly well should have done, years of practice standing outside the cinema in his uniform.' He didn't think that Transport House was any good at all, with the exception of John Schofield-Allen, whom he brought in to write his speeches, and a little bit on the side, a boy called Terry Pitt, who was head of the research department. He didn't use Transport House.

I think it's only fair to say after all these years that the election was really run by two people, Harold Wilson and

Marcia Williams. Not only was he the performing artist on the stage, he was also the stage-manager, producer and director, and she was the assistant stage-manager, assistant producer and all the rest of it, and he was almost sitting there in the box office as well. It was an amazing feat. The last time it could have been done because British politics at that stage was still pretty amateur. I don't think simply in terms of human resources you could do it now – you couldn't get through all the marketing material, the research and all the rest of it. Then you could. He decided everything that was going to be done. He even elbowed Dick Crossman out of the way who was very hurt. Dick thought he was going to write the manifesto but he wasn't allowed to, Wilson kept it under his own control. It was Wilson's own manifesto and I think it was a remarkable achievement that the Tory Party, even in those unsophisticated days, had batteries of people sort of meant to be professional at doing elections and really they were just fighting this duo. And the duo won.

TONY HOWARD

✗ Everything we did from beginning to end was done on a shoestring because it was done in the days before public funding. There was nothing for a leader of the party. If he wanted to run a campaign, which Harold knew you had to do if you wanted to win, you had to have two campaigns. One that runs from party headquarters and the one that you run yourself. You couldn't do it unless you were very skilful or you had loads of money. But we had passion and belief, we had excitement and the absolute determination that we were going to win. We worked hours that really were, now when I think about it, beyond credibility. We went in first thing in the morning and I would leave often after midnight and Harold would be even later.

It was all hands to the tiller. We had to do jobs that were menial jobs. We all had to take our part and do what we could do. Harold would end up signing letters that we'd piled up all round the shadow cabinet table and he would sign them and Joe Slater who was Hugh Gaitskell's PPS (Harold kept him on) would put them in the envelopes and I would stick them down and put the stamps on and then at midnight I'd go trailing round and put them in the box, hundreds and hundreds. Two or three thousand letters were put out a week.

He was a one-man band and he had just me in the office to run the office. I did his publicity and his press relations. If anyone rang up from the newspapers I took those calls and gave the messages back. We had half a secretary who also worked for George Brown. She was provided by Transport House, and we had a girl clerk who could do the daily fetching and carrying. All the rest was done by himself and yours truly helping out. That's it. There was nothing else and no money.

If we wanted anything, even down to papers-clips and things like that, we would ask Transport House but they would always argue about the cost of it all and the leader's office shouldn't be using this. There has always been a sort of battle that goes on between party headquarters and the leader's office because they see the leader's office as the glamorous end and they're doing the nitty-gritty and working hard. If you take that into consideration and put on top of that the sort of context in which Harold became their leader – suddenly, after the very tragic death of a hero figure – then you can understand it was quite a mountain to climb and beyond that he had the mountain to climb of getting rid of the Tories. They had a very large majority so it required an extremely big swing to get them out. He also had a constituency which had to be nursed and wasn't particularly safe because at one point it had been an eight hundred majority. MARCIA WILLIAMS

✗ I was a member of the AEU candidates' charm school. A new Assistant General Secretary, Jim Conway, said, 'We are going to be very careful about the people that we endorse. We are going to have a properly constituted panel, people who are going to have to pass an examination to get on to our panel. Once they have got on to the panel we will then spend money on training them in speech-writing and policy, all kinds of things.' The party was doing nothing apart from running its old-fashioned summer schools and that kind of thing. The proper training of candidates was something the party did not do then. They had just started a scheme under which you could come down here to Transport House to be given a little bit of an insight into being televised, handling yourself in a television interview. But that was only insight of a perfunctory kind. HAROLD WALKER

✗ I'd been writing reports on the need for publicity from about 1956, and I'd sent them to people like Harold Wilson, Dick Crossman, George Brown, quite a number of people. Slowly, over the period, it got through to other people in the media. I was in Fleet Street, I had my own agency, also other companies I was involved with, and other people had come in from advertising and PR. David Kingsley was one. We managed to arrange a meeting, I think it was in '62, it took that long to really break through. Harold supported the activities of this group, and I think we got his and George Brown's weight behind us. George was very receptive, then, oddly enough. A meeting was set up at Westminster and quite a lot of us turned up, people who'd been trying to tell the party that if they went on with the old sort of poster campaign, in a disorganised way, they wouldn't win any elections, because it was done higgledy-piggledy. They didn't even work out their target audiences, who they were talking to.

Transport House was very disorganised and old time. We imposed a different structure so far as publicity and information for the campaign was concerned. We convinced them that it wasn't going to threaten them but it could win the election, for which they'd get the credit.   PETER DAVIS

✗ It was the first time the Labour Party used professional people from the business world and it was all very new and surprising to them. It wasn't until John Harris came around and helped move things forward, and George Brown was very keen on getting professional help in. I got together a shadow group because the party couldn't bear to be seen to be employing an actual agency. I think they were right at the time. It wasn't terribly popular in the advertising industry to be seen to be working for the Labour Party, but I was just starting my own business so I could write my own rules. The main thing was that Labour had no experience of professional handling of this kind, so we really had to start from scratch. We had, thank God, Mark Abrams, who was a marvellous researcher. He was one of these intuitive researchers who could give you the answers before he did the research – which I think is quite a good skill. So we were using market research when the Conservatives weren't.

We were adding on to polling research and looking at the character and attitudes of people, which hadn't been done before. That gave us a basis on which to work. The next thing was that there hadn't been any targeting. You thought that you just talked to everybody and the right people would hear. So another contribution we made was to look at who should be our real targets. It was quite difficult to persuade them but we started to use Conservative newspapers because a lot of our targets read the *Express* and so on. That was at that time innovative as well. Our targets were a number of different social groups but it was segmented. We wanted to go after women but at that time women's magazines, for example, wouldn't take political advertising, so we had to find other ways round it. We were very constrained. The only two media we could really use were newspapers and posters – posters we used a great deal because we could tactically put them in areas where we most wanted to have an impact. At that time the Labour Party still had a separate committee that ran the television broadcasting side and in '64 I found it very difficult because I wanted to get that as part of what we did. It wasn't until '66 that we finally achieved that and it was integrated.

DAVID KINGSLEY

✘ We were just outsiders. We were Labour Party people who wanted the party to win. It's one of the important things for publicity advisers to remember when they are outside the core of the party. You've got to make it absolutely clear you're not going to talk policy. You take the policy and then advise on how to project it. That's what we did, we stood right away from it. That's something we had to make very clear at the start because I think they really thought we were 'muscling in' and were going to start telling the party what it ought to be saying, which, of course, is no role for a voluntary adviser.

I was the press, Kingsley was advertising and Dennis Lyons was the PR man, and they laughingly dubbed us the 'three wise men'. We were total volunteers and we worked fairly hard, giving a great deal of our time because we were very keen Labour people. It was astonishing how much talent we could bring in absolutely free, because out there the party's view at that time tended to be that if you had a good job and were fairly well off you weren't Labour – which was complete rubbish, of course. Brian Murphy was very good at captioning and writing copy. Mark Abrams was there already, doing the head counting. We were saying to Mark that this is where we wanted to go, we wanted to know who we should go for; there's no point in wasting money, talking to people, producing publicity, about foreign affairs – they're not interested. They're interested in housing, in education and health. These are the matters we'd got to concentrate on, and we'd also got to find out what the mood of the people was.

PETER DAVIS

✘ We had a more stylised way of doing it, the presentation and the design. That was not anything to do with trying to look more respectable, it was trying to get a stronger single image through the campaign. We didn't have roses and things like that but the idea was to give a strong and clear identity. We were just trying to produce an identity which we could use. In '64 it was about the first time the Labour Party ever used the leader's face strongly. Harold didn't like that.

We didn't have the money. We weren't getting our case through on the media. So we decided any advertising or any promotion we did should always be related to issues and be case based. I wanted to see our case spelt out in detail in the *Mail* and the *Express* and papers like that. That's the way we did it. The Labour Party was highly suspicious, the public were very relaxed. We hadn't got spin doctors, and my approach to political promotion is that you've got to relate to what people feel and think already. You can extend it and reinforce it and clarify it, but you can't do something which is either in contradiction or alien to what is already being thought.

DAVID KINGSLEY

✘ He certainly looked at the Kennedy campaign because there were resemblances, great resemblances between the way the economies of America and Britain were. Both of them had slowed down and both of them had got out-of-date and industry was badly managed and there was the power thing and the rest, very similar, and their Kennedy campaign was to get America moving again and we used that blatantly, we just took it because it did actually serve the purpose our PR team came up with to get Britain going again, and it was a good slogan because it described how everything had suddenly come to a standstill and you needed to get some life back into the system.

So we did watch how that had been done and we had

THIS
£3500 HOUSE
can be yours
for only
£6520!

watched when Kennedy was elected so we knew the Kennedy campaign. Harold knew a lot of the Kennedy people. He had taught some of them at Oxford so he was on good personal terms with a number of them. But he knew a lot of the Kennedy White House so we did get a lot of ideas from them and we got speech ideas from them, but you can't actually translate America to Britain as it's not really possible to fight Blackburn and Bolton and Newcastle and Truro in the way that you would fight Chicago.   MARCIA WILLIAMS

✗ I think there were greater preparations for the '64 election than there'd been up to that moment, through all those meetings on policy in the Bonnington Hotel and all the rest of it. They did do quite a lot of work. Wilson had had a row early on in some book that he wrote about government and Whitehall. There was a series of talks, Bridges or someone like that. He'd given the sort of Civil Service view and Wilson got frightfully angry because it criticised what he'd said. He used this ridiculous phrase 'he was going to turn No.10 into a power house and not a monastery'. Burke Trend was probably the greatest influence upon him. In those days frankly it was considered improper for permanent secretaries to have footsie lunches or dinners with opposition spokesmen. I have no memory of that going on and Wilson had been a civil servant himself; being an old civil servant made him very conservative. Norman Brook, who had been a great panjandrum of the Civil Service, had been made chairman of the BBC in 1963. There was great fuss at the time saying that it was very improper for a dying government to give this five-year term. But we now know that it had been sort of trailed across Wilson. The friendship with Trend really helped Wilson when he became Prime Minister.   TONY HOWARD

✘ I'd put down a series of science questions and this pleased Gaitskell, who I had no idea had any interest whatever in back-benchers' questions. I became involved with speaking on science on any suitable occasion. When Gaitskell died Dick Crossman, who until that time had been firmly consigned to the back-benches, was promoted by Wilson, his colleague on the National Executive Committee of the party, to the Shadow Secretary of Education and Science. He was looking for a PPS and, rightly or wrongly, I was the young man chosen

So I then became the organiser of what was called the two-way traffic in ideas at science conferences, which took place up and down the country, and Bonnington conferences, so called because they were at the Bonnington Hotel. They were organised through the party but the donkey work was done by my wife and myself. The point of the technological revolution really came out of what had been happening. The phrase, as far as I know, was Harold Wilson's own and I don't think anybody else can justifiably claim it. He was marvellous in those days. A great deal of detailed policy was formulated. Crossman was marvellous at policy formation and a lot of it was extremely sensible.   TAM DALYELL

✘ You'd get one person saying one thing and another saying another. One of the things I tried to help them towards doing was speaking with the same voice, so there would be briefs going out saying, 'Try to talk, say, two of these subjects up this week in among the other things. Obviously we don't expect you to keep plugging this thing all the time but if you can mention it it will slowly come across.' To get the one voice, and the repetitive element in it is important when you are dealing in political slogans, and also it is very important to say what you are doing. The Tories do this the whole time and of course it's a complete pack of lies most of it, it isn't what they've actually done.

I think you have to do that, it's an essential part of any publicity; there is an element of repetition. The thing to do is to make the repetition acceptable so that you're not just saying, 'I told you, I told you,' but are saying something different but making the same point. PETER DAVIS

✗ He never had a speech-writer, I know there's been a lot of different statements but he never had a speech-writer, except at No.10, when he had official speeches which are always written for the prime minister. Political speeches were written for him then, in later years, but not in '64 and '66. 1964 and 1966 he worked on the whole lot and, he would take from the main speech the one or two pages that were given out as a press release and into those he would insert the main points which he wanted to cover in a catchy way, which is what they all do today. They were all written by hand in pen and it was quite an achievement. He loved to sit with a board on his knee, and the foolscap lined paper. He did it all by hand. He loved it.

He was an academic as well as being an administrator by training after being in the cabinet office during the war. He'd organised wartime coal supplies. He loved writing. He also liked journalism. When he first left college he would have liked to have been in journalism. He just loved the physical act of writing, not just writing in the creative sense. He liked that; so many words a day and then they would be brought back to him having been typed up.   MARCIA WILLIAMS

✘ I drafted the manifesto for '64 and I can remember presenting it. It was in itself the result of previous meetings of the Home Policy Committee, which included members of the NEC, some people from the PLP, the leader and so on. It wasn't, as it were, a suddenly produced manifesto. We had paved the way about two years beforehand with a document that just simply made the case for dealing with specific problems, like regional unemployment and housing shortage and educational reform, in a document called 'Signposts for the Sixties'. That had been strongly endorsed by the party conference and it was the kind of framework within which one was able to produce the manifesto two years on. It was really very easy. It almost wrote itself.

The theme of the whole thing may sound almost ironic in the light of more recent developments, but was really the need to correct the imbalances in our society, to correct the imbalance that had occurred with a very substantial increase in people's private incomes and private acquisitions of consumer goods and the neglect of public services. So it reflected in some ways the sort of Galbraithian analysis of the affluent society. The theme within it was quite clearly that the public community sector had to be expanded in order to make tolerable even the enjoyment of the private possessions people had. Take education, it began with the quite specific pledge that we would abolish the 11+ and introduce a system of comprehensive education. Absolutely plain. No reservations, equivocations. That's what we were going to do.

Secondly, we would deal with the problem of urban land prices which were so high that they prevented an effective housing policy in our big cities. We were going to tackle that by bringing necessary inner-city urban land into public ownership. Thirdly we were going to introduce a national plan which would address the macro economic problems and also the imbalance between exports and imports. We were worried, and had every reason to be, by the size of the current deficit, though it was not revealed fully until we took office. We were

determined also to develop regional planning to a point where the great differences between the levels of unemployment between the South, Midlands and North and Scotland and Wales would be really reduced. After all we had suffered thirteen years of Conservative rule and there was an enormous amount to do and put right. It was radical. It was aimed to change society. PETER SHORE

✗ A lot of policy committees had been set up under Gaitskell. One of the most important of these was the Science Committee which in fact provided the basis for that first speech Harold ever made: the scientific technological revolution speech was based on the work of that committee. They had a number of distinguished academics like Patrick Blackett and Harold sat on those committees with them. He actually attended those committees and the Home Policy Committee of the party. He kept a very tight control as a function of the leader's office over policy and the way it was going and he took the Science Committee's work as his main theme because he could see that we were moving out of one age into another – which we were, rapidly, into a technological age – and for him that made the most sense. MARCIA WILLIAMS

✘ I wrote the defence part of it. What we agreed in that was not to abolish the Polaris programme but to reconsider it, which we did, and we decided to go ahead with four submarines rather than five and we got rid of the ludicrous American idea of the multilateral force. The thing went fairly smoothly after that. We didn't have an absolute commitment to get rid of our own nuclear weapons without a two-thirds majority at conference because we put what our view was, that we had to look at the whole thing again when we got in.

DENIS HEALEY

✘ The manifesto was a great cost. Actually manifestos are not necessarily read by candidates. One thing about the manifesto that was absolutely absurd was the creation of the Department of Economic Affairs and the Ministry of Technology. All this was based on the theory that what had been missing in previous years and the great contribution that Labour was going to make to the great future was industrial policy. Wilson as Shadow Chancellor or as Leader of the Opposition would say in the House, 'The reason why we won't have to resort to all these devices the Tories resort to is because we're going to have an industrial policy.'

They knew nothing about industry. They didn't know what an industrial policy should consist of. They didn't know how long it would take an industrial policy to take effect. They imagined that if they had an industrial policy they would be able to get away without devaluation even though we were in a state of fundamental disequilibrium. So the manifesto was also a cost in that it committed the party to things which in the actual situation of '64 could not be afforded. The essential thing about the manifesto was that it encapsulated an illusion. The illusion was that industrial policy, technology, was going to transform the economy so that we could get away without rectifying in the only way that was then possible the fundamental disequalibrium in this country's relations with the rest of the world.   EDMUND DELL

✘ I think for the first time George and Harold got the agreement of Douglas Home on a friendship basis that we could go and talk to the top civil servants about the proposals we had on the economic front. George and others of us were discussing it and felt that we ought to get away from the money side, which was the Treasury side of it, but the economic side ought to be developed as a separate adjunct. So that only when you've got the things in place you marry the two things together. George had developed the concept of the economic side being different.   RON BROWN

✘ Jim Callaghan's going to Nuffield College was very much a one off. That was a Nuffield College bit of enterprise that was a good thing to do but it's the only one I know about. It's certainly very different from today when even before the '92 election regular contacts were authorised by the Prime Minister between the Labour front-bench and the heads of the various Civil Service departments. I think then we were in a very old-fashioned vein and it would have been considered to have been virtually conceding the possibility of defeat if you allowed these talks to take place.   TONY HOWARD

✘ The party had been out for thirteen years, but remember it was much better then than it is now because the turnover now is more rapid. There were a lot of people with, at any rate junior, experience in the Attlee government. George Brown, Jim Callaghan, Patrick Gordon Walker, Harold himself had been a cabinet minister. Remember, Harold had sat in the Attlee cabinet; Tony Blair has not put his feet as a PPS under a ministerial chair.   TAM DALYELL

✘ I expected a Labour victory and had been to some extent involved with the Labour Party in its internal arrangements. Two of the people who had contacted me while I was defence correspondent for *The Times* and tried to draw me more closely into political life were George Wigg, who was Harold's so-called intelligence guru although George hadn't really a deep understanding of intelligence, his understanding was of military matters of a fairly low-level kind. He was a very loyal man, especially loyal to the army, but he wasn't a profound thinker about intelligence or other matters. The other person was George Brown, who had written to me whilst I was writing about strategy and defence policy in *The Times* and asked me to come and talk to him about it. Which I did.   ALUN CHALFONT

✗ There was much more emphasis then on making sure that candidates really were fully informed about policy, and the publication that the candidate had wasn't as encyclopaedic as the book that comes to candidates now in general elections. It was much more manageable. We weren't overfaced with commitments. But the commitments we were making we were able to argue in depth, and to justify in detail, much more than I can remember in 1959 or in 1951.   ALFRED MORRIS

✗ Doreen Stainforth was the first broadcasting officer that we had. The first real one. It was round about that time that a little studio was being fixed up at Transport House. But the image makers weren't there. There wasn't all this nonsense, it was just very elementary, basic coaching. People were told things not to do, how not to look dodgy and very sly in front of a camera, but it was very basic.   BERYL URQUHART

✗ He was very nervous all that time that things might slip away and he didn't want that to happen. It was a struggle. There were other things about that period which people also tend to forget. It was the period of the Cold War and I don't think people in this country actually understand just how deeply ordinary people believed that somehow being left wing was the same as being a Communist. I remember clearly in the election campaign going down to Cornwall with the girl who worked with us and was half George Brown's secretary. She was a very cultivated and well-educated woman, but when we got to Truro we were disembarking and she was shocked beyond belief because the porters shouted at her, 'Why don't you go back to the Kremlin?' It wasn't shouted as a joke, they were really fierce. They really meant it and that for me just describes exactly what that feeling was. We were in a situation that was very cold and everyone was suspicious and we had only just got over Burgess, Maclean and Philby and the rest so that sort of stuff was in the system.   MARCIA WILLIAMS

✗ Wilson I think did prove to be a brilliant campaigner. He made that great speech at Scarborough, the 'white heat of the technological revolution'. It inspired me. I thought, 'God, I've got this man wrong. He really is good.' And of course it meant bugger all. He just thought it up in his bath the night before. It sounded very good. He hadn't thought about it in very much detail. He never did anything about it when he was in power. It was just hot air. Typical Wilson. It was all for show, all for party management. 'How am I going to get votes out of this?' A very, very good campaigner.   DICK TAVERNE

✗ It all fitted together very neatly. The white heat of technology, the planning, the competence, this whole modernisation fitted Wilson's apparent personality very well, very neatly. Even his own person seemed to encapsulate this. The fact that he was fighting Home who encapsulated the opposite on the Tory side, fuddy-duddy, backward and incompetent, etc. I mean if the Conservatives had had a different leader or hadn't been so easy to caricature as being antiquated, and the Labour Party hadn't had somebody who seemed so neatly to fit the slot of the moderniser, if either of those two things had been different, the result might have been different. I think there was a mood of feeling that Britain needed modernising. There was a modernisation theme. In a way the question was, 'Who is going to modernise the country?' The Conservatives might have been able to capture that theme and get away with it, if the Labour Party had remained divided as it was immediately after the '59 election. But they didn't. This sort of sense that there was a need for a new government that would modernise the country was there in the background.   DAVID MARQUAND

CHAPTER THREE

Swinging Britain

		1963			1964				
	Oct	Nov	Dec	Jan	Feb	Mar	Apr	May	June
Lab.	39	42	39	42	42	42	42	47	4
Con.	29	31	32	32	33	32	32	30	34
Lead	+10	+11	+7	+10	+9	+10	+10	+17	+12

				1964					
	July	Aug	Sep 1	Sep 9	Sep 21	Sep 28	Oct 4	Oct 12	Oct 15
Lab.	43	42	44	41	40	38	43	42	41
Con.	33	36	37	38	38	39	39	37	38
Lead	+10	+6	+7	+3	+2	-1	+4	+5	+3

(all polls from Gallup)

Governments lose elections, oppositions don't win them. Harold Wilson set out to disprove the second part of this assertion just as the Tories themselves were well on the way to proving the first. The Macmillan government's central strategy collapsed in January 1963 when General de Gaulle slammed the door of the Common Market in his face. The Profumo Scandal and the Rachmanite rent scandals produced a moral shock that made the Edwardian impresario look out of touch. Macmillan's resignation, followed by a bitter, closed-circle, fight for the successor, and the ascent to power of a former fourteenth earl to preside over the emerging classless society, all reinforced the decline.

Labour's lead in the polls grew as that eventful year, 1963, unfolded. The public wanted change, modernisation and a new move forward. Labour looked, and was, confident and eager for power. The government had to hang on and let the new prime minister settle in the hope that the boom, timed for an election late in 1963, could be sustained through 1964. Sir Alec opted for a run up to the buffers. In March 1964 he announced that there would be no election until October, the last possible month.

This was to be the longest election campaign Britain had known. Opposition widened the fight outside Parliament. Government campaigned as it governed. Labour worked to keep the excitement alive through the nerve-testing cycles of hope and disappointment. Government struggled to keep the boom rolling.

✗ I was selected in 1962 and at that time Doncaster had a Tory member of Parliament, Tony Barber. Doncaster didn't seem a very attractive prospect to some folk but I got selected and from then on it was one long hard slog because I was living in Manchester, up on the Pennines. Imagine my agony going from there to Doncaster to nurse the seat, working in a factory all the time, having to work overtime to earn the money to pay for the petrol to get to Donny.

By hell that was some slog that was and I was yearning for the election to come. The Tories kept stalling and stalling waiting until the last minute and of course the last minute came when they couldn't stall any longer. I was still living on the Pennines, married, a new baby and still having to go to Donny.

HAROLD WALKER

✗ Labour won in '64 because of thirteen years of Tory rule. It was very largely time for a change. That normally does determine an election. Wilson was a first-class candidate. We had our views on him as a prime minister but as a national candidate I think he was extremely good and the Tories made this colossal error by taking Alec Douglas-Home in succession to Macmillan which meant they'd had three old-Etonian prime ministers on the trot. The Liberals in a sense let Labour in as they came basically from the Tories.

Another person who I think might have won, but the Tories

being the stupid party could never see it, was Iain Macleod, the
Tory Wilson was scared of. There was never really any chance
of Macleod being leader, especially after he refused to serve
under Alec Douglas-Home, but he certainly would have been a
powerful national candidate. A better orator than Wilson;
better use of sarcasm. Reggie Maudling would have been a
much more difficult candidate. So in a way the Tories set
themselves up by choosing Home. I've always believed that
Wilson was disappointed. He wanted his opponent to be
Macmillan because he thought he represented the old regime.
When Macmillan resigned he was very upset.   TONY HOWARD

✗ Just before the 1964 election, Alice Bacon said on the
National Executive, 'Do we want British politics to become a
battle between two Madison Avenue advertising agencies?' By
the 1966 election, Alice, who was chairing the publicity
committee for the party, was one of our strongest advocates to
the National Executive. Our research and copywriting began to
shape the priorities and visibility of the party's policies in a
way that was a foretaste of what happens to both parties in
abundance today. As a group we were starting from the
electors' (customers' in today's jargon) point of view, whereas
the politicians were seeing things from the point of view of
internal political priorities and, as our research showed, the
two didn't match. As we translated policies into language that
electors could understand, wrote ads and developed literature,
not only the tone changed but the emphasis and relative
weight of policies did too.

In the 1964 election we had to focus on a very few key
issues. The top ones were 'overcrowded schools' and
'housing'. They got played up much more strongly than other,
equally important, elements of the party programme. In 1966
we played up the 'continuity' and 'give the Labour
government a chance to deliver' message. Inevitably other
issues had a lower profile. But the biggest difference between
then and now is that there was more content in terms of actual
policies and positions then. Today we seem to have publicity
used for slogans, and little opportunity for the elector to get
down to the content and the actual policies.   DAVID KINGSLEY

✗ I had a great deal to do with the party political broadcasts,
trying to get it away from talking heads and getting something

'Cheer up. We're still going to win!' – manifesto launch, 1964

interesting that would hold people's attention so that they might actually not go out to make a cup of coffee but might hang on for a few minutes. Harold preferred talking heads, but then that's the don in him, as it were, the lecturer. In 1963/4 we did get film in, so they weren't all talking heads. We presented different people; to that extent, talking heads, I suppose, but we did present younger people. We had a lot of fights with the Beeb, the continuing row between political parties and the

Beeb is nothing new. I can remember personally stopping one broadcast, walking straight on to the set, and another occasion when Harold just packed it in, he just said, 'No, no, we're not going that way,' and they had to start again. It was a bit iffy, a lot of the television. I think they found it difficult to accept that they were in the party political area and they almost had to switch off and leave it to the parties either to make complete fools of themselves or to put on a decent broadcast.

PETER DAVIS

✘ The first campaign we did was not very focused. That was called, 'Labour's Got Life and Soul'. It was a positioning in that we were being characterised as not being very active or progressive. It wasn't until just before the '64 election that we developed the 'Let's Go with Labour and Get Things Done'. That was invented by Peter Davis and myself. We presented our ideas to Harold. I remember the first thing he said was, 'I've heard of these fancy advertising-agency presentations . . . ' Just trying to put us off. I made the presentation and he made a remark about, 'What do you mean *let's go*? In my part of the world that rhymes with po.' We laughed that off and that was the campaign we went with.

There were two parts to it. One was to be positive because I think you owe it to the electors to try and make it very clear what it is you stand for and what it is you are going to do. If you look back at it you'll find the subjects have hardly changed since that time. It was health, schools and housing. So we had a positive campaign and then we just had this positioning of 'Let's Go with Labour and We'll Get Things Done'. We came on to this thirteen wasted years. That was very effective. It made people think. Most of our battles were in getting the party to agree to do this. The first budget they gave us was £120,000 for six months. Then we got a bit more money but the ratio of Conservative spending against Labour in that campaign was something like nine to one. We had no money and the party spent perhaps £20,000 on market research.   DAVID KINGSLEY

✘ The government was in a worse state than the present government's in. They were rudderless. There was old Alec Douglas-Home counting his matchsticks and no sense of going anywhere at all, so we built on that, the sense of inactivity, nothing happening politically. All successful slogans reflect the mood of people. You are not just imposing them. 'Let's Go with Labour and We'll Get Things Done' encapsulated how a lot of people were feeling. It summed up the political mood. No one person wrote the slogan. People felt after '64 that things were happening, things were changing and being driven along under Harold's leadership.   PETER DAVIS

✗ We weren't playing it cautiously, we were playing it challengingly in saying that we were going to have an expansionist economy. And we had the big advantage that Maudling's 'Dash for Growth' had ended in this catastrophic, record deficit. That was a great card for us because the country was uneasy and of course the retirement of Macmillan from the scene was extremely important because he'd buoyed everyone up with the, 'You've never had it so good' though I must say I had a sneaking admiration for this actor-manager prime minister. And Harold was absolutely lost in admiration of him. He used to say that he was the best prime minister he'd ever known, partly because of the panache, the insouciance, the carrying it off. Macmillan was a genuine expansionist because as a young MP, Stockton-on-Tees, he'd seen, in the thirties, mass unemployment in all its horrors and misery and he really was not going to have it any more. So he sacked any hair-shirt ministers, like the Treasury boys who wanted to go back to balancing the budget, and he got a compliant Reggie Maudling to carry on the expansionist policy. He was prepared to introduce import controls, all sorts of controls to carry on the expansion period until British industry had caught up with the possibilities of expansion. The Profumo Affair just knocked the guts out of him, so when he got prostate trouble he absolutely panicked, assumed it was cancer, and resigned. Reggie on his own hadn't the stuff to stand up to the Treasury and the Treasury big boys moved in in a big way.   BARBARA CASTLE

✗ I don't think we had an exciting manifesto then, I think above all it was the country wanting to get rid of a government which had clearly outlasted its welcome, a prime minister who had very limited ability, and put in a clever young fellow who seemed to understand the 'white heat of technology', which is incidentally the one area which Wilson conspicuously failed to deal with at all.   DENIS HEALEY

✘ Labour had this record of being split and tearing itself to pieces, the Bevanite rump and all that sort of thing, and on the whole the government had not been too overtly unsuccessful economically. Indeed, if it hadn't been for the Profumo Scandal in the autumn of '63 they'd have gone on on the basis of a carefully engineered economic boom that Maudling had brought about, but the timing went askew. If the election had been in '63 the Tories would probably have been re-elected. Gaitskell made a terrible mess of tax in the '59 election, but the whole point was that although there was suspicion of Labour in many ways, Labour wasn't feared. I think it was Benn, Scargill, Livingstone, all that terrible crew, who were responsible for the fear factor which the Labour Party has not entirely succeeded in living down even now.

GERALD KAUFMAN

✘ We had a good lead and it was OK and suddenly in the summer the British government decided to sell three or six frigates to Franco of Spain. This was awful for us. What could you do? You couldn't criticise it but you couldn't say, 'OK fine no harm done.' If Harold had done that the Labour Party would have been up in arms because a lot of leading people in the party had actually fought against Franco. They'd been there in the Civil War. So we knew from the public point of view it was a very difficult one and we just had to sit almost with our mouths shut and nothing was said at all that would rock the boat. Thus the change came with those frigates, at that moment when there was argument, because not all our people kept quiet, some were out in print almost five minutes later to say how disgusting it was. It did have a reaction in the country.

There was obviously some sort of swing back because Alec Douglas-Home actually did fight a very good campaign considering he came from a very aristocratic background and it was a past that everyone wanted to get rid of. It was the bit that people were trying to say goodbye to in order to say hello to the science and technology of the future. He had already started to regain a bit of the advantage and with the frigates it slipped for us badly. I remember going round to the Scillies to talk to Harold, because we had to decide what we should do.

I remember we walked up and down the quay and he said, 'We won't panic,' and I remember thinking I wish he wouldn't walk up and down quite so quickly. It seemed to me he was panicking just walking up and down. But he didn't, in fact, panic when he got back to London. He just took it in his stride and fought the campaign as he would have fought it anyway.

MARCIA WILLIAMS

✗ Harold was at his most dynamic at that time and he had this vision of a fresh start, the white hot revolution in technology and all that kind of thing, and I think that theme had a positive appeal. After thirteen years of Conservatism there was a mood that it was time for a change and I think in some ways that's the most fundamental mood in producing a shift when an election comes – and, of course, it will be a powerful mood on this occasion.　　　GEORGE THOMSON

✗ I think it was won by Labour, but I have to say that I think that it wasn't during the campaign. During the whole period leading up to the campaign, there had been a progressive disillusionment with the Tories and that obviously moved not just into our solid working-class supporters but also embraced many professional, middle-class people as well. There was undoubtedly a very important process that went on prior to the election in which Harold Wilson was in the forefront and thanks to which we won the electors beforehand. Obviously when the election campaign took place we could still have lost, but the foundation work had been done beforehand.

STAN NEWENS

✗ Staff attitudes were somewhat different from those at present. For one thing, whilst some hopefuls actually joined the staff – in the research department of Transport House in particular – with the idea of moving into a parliamentary career, there was at that time a ban on anyone gaining nomination as a prospective parliamentary candidate and remaining on the staff. Fair enough when one considers that the total complement of PLP staff, including the offices of the leader and deputy leader, was less than the number of the present leader's staff. At Transport House and in the regions, the staff numbers were substantially lower, and all were needed for essential general election campaign work.

BERYL URQUHART

✘ He had a press conference every morning at Transport House and he used to give a little WEA [Worker's Educational Association] lecture on the subjects that he dealt with, whereas Home was going round the country with the same speech, saying the Tories had built up Britain, don't let Labour ruin it, and keep the bomb. He made the same speech again and again. You used to see him on television, under a street lamp with a dog listening and the rain destroying his press release, but it was rather like 1992 where both Major and Kinnock had gimmicks but Major's gimmick was the right one. He was out – and Harold tended to be in. Home was a very much underestimated political figure.   TONY BENN

✘ I rate Harold's contribution to the '64 election very highly. He worked with what they referred to as the 'kitchen cabinet'. There was no such a thing as a 'kitchen cabinet' because we were not talking about policy. We used to meet all through the campaign every morning at the crack of dawn, and go through Harold's speeches for the day, the main things that he was going to do, and then he would go on to the party meeting prior to the press conference. He played a very full part and was very supportive. He was very good, and had a good sense of humour. I liked Harold. He could make you laugh. He had this funny sort of deadpan sense of humour which made working with him very agreeable. But every morning we would meet and we would review the day in terms of speeches projecting the party, publicity and so on, and then he'd just go on straight through a blinding day. This was one of the things about George Brown as well. He was astonishing. We'd go on these caravans of his all round the country and come back to Transport House having done about two thousand miles, innumerable speeches and meetings.   PETER DAVIS

✘ I had been in charge of the '59 campaign and I was on the campaign committee in '64, keeping in touch, I probably had permission to get away from Bristol and be in London most days. Harold was always available and you pumped ideas into him, and it was innovative in the sense that there was a clear message. New Britain was a fairly clear message, technological revolution was a clear message, and all the ones that went with it, like full employment. Harold said to me at about that time that in a technical age social expenditure would be the engine

"THIS IS ONLY THE TRAILER!"

of economic growth. So all the attacks on public expenditure and everything were years before Hayek and monetarism came in and destroyed the core of Labour thinking. There was a real choice and a real difference. There was modernisation there as well, but it was a genuine modernisation. It really was about changing British industry, putting support back into British industry.   TONY BENN

✗ We were incredibly excited because we were going to win after so long of being in opposition and we were going to change everything and everything was going to be better and we weren't going to live in slums any more and for me that was important, coming from Liverpool, because I did my undergraduate thesis on housing in Liverpool. You had this tremendous desire to change things. Personally, having come from Liverpool and seen all this poverty, housing was what I wanted to do. We wanted to change lots of other things as well. Everybody had their own thing at that point that they were keen on.   ANN CARLTON

✗ The 1964 campaign was great and exciting. Fred Mulley
was, in name, head of the unit which looked after Harold's
correspondence and office at Transport House. At that time,
we had no access to the House after a general election was
convened, so the PLP staff were accommodated at Transport
House. In fact, Fred was in the office on only one occasion, and
I was in charge. Most of Harold's time was spent on the road
with Marcia, Brenda Dew, Phyllis Birt (PLP), George Caunt
(PLP) and Alf Richman (ex *Daily Herald*).

The correspondence was a hell of a chore for me and for the
PLP's clerical staff who were assigned to me. Pensions and
racial issues were far and above the most dominant subjects.
In the early days of the campaign, Harold was insisting on
signing all the replies, but as the numbers grew from a couple
of hundred a day at the start to many times that as the
campaign progressed, I persuaded him not to sign them all
personally in case some error which pressure of work made
likely managed to creep in. Remember, our staff did not have
word processors at that time, and even when standard replies
were appropriate, they had to be individually typed. I
confined Harold's signing chore to those from party members
or wavering voters in marginal constituencies.

                                                    BERYL URQUHART

✗ He did a total tour of the country. There was a morning
press conference wherever he was. Percy Clark was director of
communications in those days. Morgan Philips was the
General Secretary. We went round to Labour headquarters at
Smith Square – in those days it was a couple of floors in the
T&G headquarters – so the Tories and ourselves used to use
the Marquis of Granby. We all used the same pub and
everybody was very careful to listen for other people's gossip
without saying anything indiscreet themselves – but there
were more stories that developed wings from the Marquis than
from anywhere.

It was all train travel, no planes or helicopters. We went to
Glasgow, Edinburgh. I remember there was an open-air tour of
South London that took in Clapham, Peckham, down to
Lewisham, where he spoke at open-air meetings all the way
along. They were traditional soap-box meetings with plenty of
questions and hecklers, and he was just brilliant. We would
follow round in cars and get lost, we didn't know where to

park. Going round after an open-air tour was really a
nightmare because you just abandoned your car and ran.

ANN WARD

✘ We had wonderful meetings in Birmingham. I took charge
of the Birmingham campaign and it was a splendid affair, full
of triumphalism. It felt like '45 because this time we were all
certain we were going to win. Of course, we didn't win by
anything like as much. But there was this feeling in '64, the sort
of feeling we had in '45. The late euphoria. In '64 there had
been thirteen years. So there's this cycle. It's healthy in a
democracy that people say, 'We can't have a government in too
long,' which is what happened in '64. The great rallies that we
had in Birmingham for Wilson – I think he came twice to us –
were absolutely superb.

DENIS HOWELL

✘ I think the fact that we'd been out of office for a very long
time, thirteen years by then, had created a kind of question
mark in people's minds. Maybe it was better the devil you
know than the devil you don't know, and will the Labour
government be able to handle affairs as well as the experienced
Conservative government? It was a much more formidable
government than the present one. You had people like Reggie
Maudling, substantial people like Edward Heath, Iain
Macleod. So they were quite a serious lot.

During that six months leading up to the October '64, the
summer had been very good for everyone. Indeed the
Conservatives were embarked on a kind of breakneck growth
policy in the last year of their government so the feelgood
factors were swinging their way very strongly and they did
make quite some progress in the areas of defence and nuclear
policy. We were not then unilateralists but nevertheless we
were much less committed to the independent deterrent than
were our Conservative opponents. But it's still difficult to put
a finger on what moved opinion because by the end of the
parliamentary session in July we were well ahead in public
opinion and yet very much affected by this feelgood factor.
People had a reason to feel good in the summer of that year.
Very full employment, the economy bounding forward and
so on.

PETER SHORE

✘ There was tremendous enthusiasm because we all thought things were going to be different. The country thought things were going to be different. It's terribly hard now to recall this feeling of optimism with which Labour was welcomed.

SUSAN CROSLAND

✘ He was giving some very good speeches with very good text. What we did was we looked for the gems and we used them. We attributed them to him. We felt that that would build the dimension of what he was, and I think it worked quite well. In '64 and '66 John Harris got this brilliant idea of timing all Harold's speeches with the nine o'clock news. This was an absolutely brilliant idea because the BBC loved the idea of being able to go live into a speech. As soon as the light went on Harold slipped into the bit we wanted to go out on the news. In those days this was absolutely fantastic. The real thing that happened in that period was trying to change the way the Labour Party thought about this sort of thing. They were scared out of their minds. They thought it was unholy, the old sort of church ethic, that advertising was dishonourable.

Harold was very good at that time. I think in the '64 and '66 elections he did a very good job; '70 was a different story because he'd developed an agenda which was really moving apart from what we knew.

Don't forget we had some other good people. There was a good team at that time, some of the giants. They were very good presenters and they came over very well. Everybody liked George because he was nice and rough and tough. That was good for the core of our voters. I liked George very much and we did a lot of good things together. I would say that Harold worked well and came out well and looked good. Am I allowed to compare it with today? I think that there was less political campaigning, which meant that you could keep hold of what was going on rather better. The scene is now so busy that it's difficult.

DAVID KINGSLEY

✘ It was frenetic but it was also much more relaxed, there was none of the protection. The journalists who were in the group that travelled with him everywhere had very easy access, and he knew them all well. I suppose that happens today but I'm not sure if it's quite as relaxed now. There were very few press officers in those days. Harold was such a brilliant communicator that he did it all himself, more or less. It was the first general election that had substantial TV coverage, and this was one thing he was brilliant at.

At public meetings in the evening he would know exactly when they were going 'live'. He would keep an eye on the red light on the camera, and even if it meant switching the speech slightly because he hadn't got to the part that he wanted to broadcast, he would switch into that bit and he would know when the camera was turned off. They didn't record continuously, they just had this 'live' interlude.

There was far more heckling in those days and he really welcomed it. He came alive with the heckling. The heckling was terribly unimaginative and you knew exactly what was coming up, and he gave what looked like totally spontaneous answers. It wasn't cheating, it was just that people always repeated the latest Tory slander so he'd got a pretty good idea if there was going to be any heckling and what would come up, and the answers got slicker and more well timed – the put-downs were brilliant. He was really good at that. It was great fun. It was one mad dash.   ANN WARD

✘ Tax was one issue that frightened Wilson. I remember him saying to me once that there were three things he didn't care about. One was nationalisation, I can't remember the second one, but the third one, and he said this was not going to be a problem for us, was the cost of the programme. What he meant was the very good remark by Home that the Labour programme represented a menu without prices. It was a good phrase and I think they were a bit frightened of that.

                                                    TONY HOWARD

✘ We were very doubtful. There is such a natural conservatism in the British people that it almost takes a Holocaust to shake them out of their dull acceptance of things they don't like. But, the most encouraging thing was Harold Wilson. He really gave people the feeling (a) that he believed in socialist solutions and (b) that they were highly relevant. He played very brilliantly on the nature of his opponent, this country landowner, this landed aristocrat who couldn't add up without an abacus, against the bright grammar-school boy who had got to the top by his own brains. The country was ready for that. But it ought to have been far more ready than it turned out to be.   BARBARA CASTLE

✘ It got very bad until 27 September, during the campaign itself. Two or three polls had the Tories actually leading on that Sunday and I think at that moment even the most professional politicians like Dick somehow thought it was slipping away. The great crisis of the campaign came on 30 September when those very bad trade figures came out. Wilson had been rather pussy-footing around and the question was did he take the gloves off and did he say we are now facing a real economic crisis? The man who at that time was as close to him as anyone was an odd Hungarian named Tommy Balogh who had been his economic adviser all through the days in the wilderness. Balogh from the beginning of the campaign was saying to Wilson, 'You've got to bloody go for them.' Wilson didn't want to because he was frightened that if he exaggerated the dangers to the economy it would affect his inheritance when he became prime minister

Finally, I think it was at Norwich on the evening of the 30th, he did say there was a serious economic crisis and the Tories had tried to cover it up. I think from that moment on because he made it their crisis he had to some extent neutered the attack on him of 'where's all the money coming from?' to pay for all these programmes. I think he made a calculated decision but it worked out that he gave the Tories a week or ten days to run with the thing about 'they'll ruin the country'. Then he hit back with 'fine ones they are to talk. Look where they've got the economy.'

People say campaigns don't matter. I think that 1964 campaign mattered quite a lot. If it hadn't been for the new offensive after the speech at Norwich on the 30th, if it hadn't been for some mistakes, bad mistakes, that the Tories made about calling pensions 'donations', they might have won. But Wilson also slipped up over Hardy Spicer's, which everybody's forgotten now, but which did look very dangerous for the Labour Party until the boss of that firm started talking about his workers as 'poor dears', not of very high intelligence, this kind of thing. I think the campaign did turn round then.　　　　　　　　　　　　　TONY HOWARD

✘ Tax wasn't really an issue. People wanted us to do things. I think our problem over tax now goes back to John Smith. He did two things together which was fatal. I don't think in the last general election that the nation would have worried too

much if he had just said he was going to have a fifty-per-cent tax limit. The other thing he did was to say he was going to bring back into the national insurance surcharge a lot of people who suddenly felt that weekend that they were going to be pushed off to fifty per cent which John, with his great legal mind and clear logic, thought was absolutely right in principle. Which it is. I think we are making a bit of a mistake now in thinking that the tax issue is totally dominant so we shouldn't say anything about tax this time.   DENIS HOWELL

✗ I had an exciting by-election in 1962 and in a way the 1964 election was a slight anticlimax because I had realised that we weren't going to do as well in '64 as we had done in the by-election. It was a curious campaign because one had doubts about how well it was going nationally. Alec Douglas-Home was not a bad campaigner. He had quite a lot of appeal. In retrospect people say, 'This silly old earl who came back from the grouse moors of Scotland.' But he was quite an impressive man. He was very direct on television. He was rather appealing and after all he did extraordinarily well. The Conservatives, mainly because of the economy, pulled up tremendously after he became leader. One hopes it doesn't happen again! His directness and candour contrasted quite well with Harold, although the public didn't see it that way. I was never a Harold fan.   DICK TAVERNE

✗ Around about a week before polling day, Quintin Hogg made his famous adultery attack on Labour's front-bench in a speech at Plymouth. Dick Crossman came into the office and asked me whether I thought Harold would wish him to make a rebuttal. This slur on the Harold–Marcia relationship had started well before the campaign, but anyone who knew anything at all about it knew that it was then and remained totally groundless.   BERYL URQUHART

✗ I suppose the small majority was because of the phenomenon which perhaps we now face that after a party has been out of power for a long time people get very cautious, however bad the government they have. 'Better the devil you know' – I think that sort of thing actually applies.
                                        PETER DAVIS

✗ Tax wasn't an issue. The tax and spend argument only came about later. It certainly was not an issue in '64. It would be strange if we went into the next election saying we were going to increase public expenditure (which I personally would like to do, although for five years as chief secretary I said no to every bit of increased expenditure), but if we don't then I don't know what we're in politics for. I want to see improvements in public services and we fought for that in '64. We weren't attacked on the grounds that we were going to increase taxes in order to use money on public expenditure. That wasn't one of the issues of the day. It's strange, looking back on it, that it wasn't. Yet there we were, determined to spend more money.

In my kind of area there would have been a lot of people who didn't earn enough money to pay income tax, so it was not a big issue. I suppose it became a bigger issue later with the growth of incomes through inflation, not necessarily through real earnings but through wage inflation. More and more people were paying income tax so naturally they became concerned about levels of income tax, indeed, you could argue that income tax and national insurance – which is the same thing – is in many ways why we lost the 1992 election, because so many people on fairly modest incomes, not high earnings, were going to be faced with higher tax and national insurance and they didn't like the idea. So tax has grown as an issue. But it certainly was not an issue in 1964 or even in '66.   JOEL BARNETT

✘ People do believe that Labour will raise taxes. They assumed we would raise taxes and indeed I don't think we went around promising that we wouldn't because we had a number of commitments which required an awful lot of money. But then they had years of Labour Government thereafter where taxes were increased and we have to face the fact that Income Tax was through those '74, '76 and '79 years. It was not our fault, but the result of Middle Eastern crisis oil problems and the rest which made it difficult.   MARCIA WILLIAMS

✘ I don't think tax was an issue, not like now. In those days we were for social justice and the idea that it was going to cost more didn't deter Labour people. Now everybody seems to concentrate on this terrible thing, tax. I once shared digs with Hugh Gaitskell and I was what's called a Gaitskellite – though not one of the old Hampstead 'sherry on Sunday' set because I was away on Sundays. He was a very straightforward, passionate but academic sort of socialist. He would set out everything very clearly, and Wilson I suppose was too clever to do that. So I suppose Wilson may have avoided the issue a bit more cleverly than Hugh Gaitskell did.   LORD LONGFORD

✗ In 1964, the big argument we were fighting in Birmingham was immigration. My by-election in '61 was the first time ever as far as I know the immigration issue was raised. We had a Conservative going around the constituency with his loud-speaker talking about the invasion of coloured people. We'd hardly got any coloured people! As it happened, my father was dying during the course of that by-election. In fact he died about ten days before the poll. We stopped campaigning. All sides did until after he was buried. So I was able to say as I was asked questions about immigration, 'My father is in a hospital where every single nurse is coloured, but he is getting as much attention there as anybody could ever wish to have, as are all the other patients in that ward.' I found that a very effective answer in that campaign. It shut them up straightaway.

The '64 campaign was really the start of the immigration thing. The party never got to grips with it properly. I remember the late Gerry Reynolds, a great mate of mine. He was very much against the Labour Party line on immigration. He and one or two of us who came from the Midlands would say to Hugh Gaitskell, 'Watch what you are doing on this because it is all right having policy, but if you get a policy where you disturb the social and racial mix in the constituency, there isn't a maturity there amongst the constituents to take it on board.'   DENIS HOWELL

✗ It wasn't that clear that we were doing that well. I was pretty nervous. There were very nerve-racking polls just before the election. Our lead went down pretty dramatically and at one stage it was down to two or three per cent. So one didn't know quite what was going to happen. I found it a nervous campaign, not a great, exhilarating campaign. The election night was a real nail-biter, at first to see that you were OK and then gradually to see this majority going down and down. We were saved by the skin of our teeth – a curious bloke in Brighton getting a majority of seven.   DICK TAVERNE

✗ What I do remember is on polling day in Dundee coming down by our local newspaper office about 4 o'clock in the afternoon and seeing the headline that Khrushchev had gone and I thought to myself my goodness if that had happened a few days before it might very well have helped the Conservatives, Alec Home was the prime minister then and he had a reputation in foreign affairs and if the people are frightened of events they stay with what they've got for fear of something worse. So it was remarkably narrow but it's a mystery to me as to how after thirteen wasted years when we were very confident and all the public opinion polls of the time were very much in our favour that the gap closed at the time and in that sense I suppose it's like a cautionary tale for the present time.   GEORGE THOMSON

✘ I would say, before the death of Gaitskell they had confidence in the economic management, because Gaitskell built up a great feeling of competence, and Harold Wilson was really at his brilliant best as Shadow Chancellor of the Exchequer. I think it seeped through to the country that a lot of his own colleagues were less than enamoured of Harold Wilson, who was brilliant and sparky and amusing but I think it came through that he wasn't exactly to be trusted, and Alec Home, in a curious way, galvanised the Tory party in those days as few other people could have done. This was the kind of man that they really rather admired and took pity on, and the Tories worked extremely hard in the 1964 election. There is no doubt whatever about that. That was part of the reason they held seats that nobody had imagined they could hold. One other thing. I think it is much more difficult to winkle hard-working Tories out of seats where they have fought ferociously – whatever they've done at Westminster – partly for social reasons and partly for reasons of face. That's totally different from a by-election or an opinion poll.   TAM DALYELL

✘ Harold was still the dominant political figure and the exciting politician but there was this gradual re-rallying of the Tories and Home nearly pulled it off. For a politician of no outstanding merit it would have been a singular triumph to have done that. We underestimated the impact of Douglas-Home simply as a new face, and hadn't taken on board the effect of the honeymoon period.

The analogous situation is not Major now but Major at the last election, after Thatcher. Although Home came over as a decent, nice man he also came over looking quite skeletal and became a sort of cartoon-type figure, but in an affectionate, not an unpleasant, sense. This fresh face, this clean record in no way tainted with government experiences because he'd been in the Lords and out of the main political stream – we didn't realise the extent to which he would, in the honeymoon period, rally the Tories.   ALAN WILLIAMS

✗ I expected we'd win in 1964, but I'd expected we'd win in 1959 so I think we were all very much more cautious and wary in 1964. The indications right through the campaign were that we'd win but the surprising thing is we won with a tiny majority. I always remember that polling day because I was up until early in the morning as the results were coming in and it looked as if we had a pretty good majority, forty maybe. When I drove back to London the next morning it melted away with the results from the scattered constituencies which, of course, were mainly Tory rural constituencies, and, of course, we finished up with a tiny majority. So Wilson's overwhelming objective when he got in was to keep alive until he could fight another election and get a good majority.   DENIS HEALEY

✗ *The Times* newspaper published a full-page map of the political pattern of Britain. It was set out in blues and reds and there was this great swathe of red, South Yorkshire, with this blue dot in the middle, Donny. The whole of South Yorkshire Labour Movement, trade unions and party, were determined that they were going to wipe that blue blot off the map. I've never experienced anything in a lifetime of politics, and I've been involved in nearly every general election since the war, like the way people from the whole of South Yorkshire poured in on that day to make sure that we got every Labour vote out. 'We've got ten here from Rotherham, where do you want us?' and then, 'We've got a party of twenty from Worksop.' It was like that all evening.

Came the count and of course we made it and I'm bound to say the one reason why we did make it was that there was a nice man, Gerald Broadhead, who had decided to contest the election on his own account, standing with a label that stood for everything in the book – National, Liberal, Conservative, Labour, etc. etc. He picked up sufficient votes (2,500) to put Tony Barber out and me in. I remember the Corn Exchange at Doncaster at 1 o'clock in the morning. My wife flung her red hat down from the rafters and they carried me shoulder-high from the Corn Exchange to the Labour Club and I wondered how we'd ever get in. The walls seemed to be bulging from the people who were there, and altogether it was a quite fantastic and unforgettable night. Then, of course, came the reality of coming down here and realising that we were only in by a whisker. HAROLD WALKER

✗ We thought we were going to have a safe margin. But as it got down to polling day, we began to wonder. Things seemed to be flowing against us. Agents were reporting in window bills being taken down. Were they being taken down purely so the poor lady could clean her windows, or were they being taken down because they no longer supported us? We tried to find out, but not very successfully. I think in the main it was that people had become disillusioned over some issue or another. We were getting all sorts of funny reports like that through from agents in the field. If you looked at the canvas records you found that so and so street was very good. It was about sixty-per-cent Labour. But much to our horror these records were purely fictitious and had been marked up by the canvasser in the local pub. He knew everybody. He knew Labour supporters and these workmen and the rest of it. When we tried to check, it just didn't tie up at all. Nowadays, there is very little of that sort of thing; much of the canvassing is done by telephone. That is a great improvement. WALTER BROWN

✗ There was an apprehension amongst the voters that Labour was still wedded to socialism. Socialism was still expressed by many of the leading Labour figures. There was the association of Labour with trade unions and the narrow sectional concern with promoting trade-union interests. There was the fear that if you did vote Labour then you were going to vote for more public spending. They had many imaginative schemes that all involved public spending and that could mean taxes and you would probably be hit hard in your wallet. There was a general apprehension. I suppose in the end a lot of people came back to the Conservatives because better the devil you know than the one you don't. Labour, after all, had been out of office for so long. Its people were new and there was apprehension. Wilson failed to drag the party far ahead. GEORGE JONES

✘ On polling day I did a tour of certain constituencies. The regional organiser did a different group. The women's organiser, she did some as well. We went round to see how things were going, and could we jolly it along, get them out canvassing. For the last couple of hours I went on the doorstep myself. I sensed a reaction from the electors. Working in a street which had been canvassed as Labour, you knocked on the door and said, 'Are you coming out to vote?' 'No, I don't think I'm going to bother today.' You felt deflated. 'I'll go tomorrow,' one said. All sorts of silly things were being said. You had a devil of a job to knock them up in '64. We were failing rapidly over the last twenty-four hours or so before polling. That applied to '66 as well.   WALTER BROWN

✘ In '64 I was on the political staff of the *Daily Mirror*. John Freeman, who was the editor of the *New Statesman*, had asked me to do a series of pieces, and one piece he'd asked me to do, which was published the weekend before that general election, was to try to extrapolate on the basis of overnight results what a final result would be. In those days there were fewer overnight results – I think there were just on three hundred at that time – and I did a whole series of tables and extrapolations, constituency by constituency, trying to provide people with a measuring tool of what a final result would be on the basis of the overnight predictions, and I got the final result almost exactly right on that basis. I think I forecast that, on the basis of the figure that Labour did end up with on the overnight declarations on 15 October '64, Labour would end up with an overall majority of eight.

I was sitting in the newsroom, taking a prominent part in the way in which the *Daily Mirror* was covering the results, when on the basis of the very substantial gains that Labour was getting, they showed me a mock up of the front page, which said, 'Landslide for Labour', and I said, 'Don't do it. On the basis of the results so far it's not going to be a landslide and, indeed, Labour will be lucky to win at all.' They changed the front page from 'Landslide for Labour' to 'It looks like Labour'. So I wasn't surprised, it always looked dicey to me.

GERALD KAUFMAN

Harold, Mary and panda arrive from Liverpool – 16 October 1964

✗ The last week was in Liverpool with the Adelphi as the base, and we all went up and stayed there. The night before there was a huge indoor rally, and at the end of the rally they walked to the Adelphi, with thousands of people thronging behind them. It was a great march, very informal, it hadn't been organised, and they'd been presented with this panda for good luck and Mary was clutching it. They were at the head of this great procession and when they got to the Adelphi they went up to their room and opened the window. There was this massed throng of people outside, all singing and shouting. It was a fantastic night. They stood in the window looking out over the mass of people there. In the morning it was the usual thing, going round the committee rooms talking to people, and then going to the count. Then we all went back to the Houghton Labour Club which was in his constituency, and had a few drinks and celebrated, and then we went back to the Adelphi. It was quite a night.

In those days there were no TV sets in hotel bedrooms, and either Peter Jenkins or Ian Aitken had arranged for a television set to be put in his room – they were massive rooms in the Adelphi which is an enormous Victorian railway hotel. He'd got plenty of booze in and invited all the travelling circus of journalists to come and watch the television for the late-night results coming in. We were all relaxing and there was a knock and Harold's face came round the door saying, 'Can I join you? They've all gone to sleep in my suite.' He came in and stretched out on one of the beds. I can't remember what we talked about but he was very relaxed. The important thing about that night was that he really let his hair down and shared a lot of political stories. When they closed the television results programme down we all went off to bed. It was about three or four in the morning. We all had to be on the eight o'clock train to Euston.

The train journey down was amazing. Harold kept saying to me, 'Ann, don't get excited, it's not enough,' because when we'd gone to bed there was a huge lead but all the rural areas were still to come in and with his memory for figures, he knew. There were no mobile phones and we were out of touch for four hours – it was an eight o'clock train getting into Euston at midday – and there were people standing on stations on the route with blackboards with the latest figures chalked up (I think the station staff organised it for us) and we could see that the majority was getting smaller and smaller all the time, and Harold kept saying, 'It's not enough.'

We'd lived in our own cocoon of informality and very easy access and all being together, and it didn't hit us until we got to Euston, what had changed. When the train drew in, we were at the back behind Harold and Mary, and we looked up and there was this enormous crowd, and a red carpet, and a station master with a top hat, and banks of cameramen all there. I did a picture looking over their shoulders showing the scene. The result still wasn't final at that moment, and it was still very tight. Harold got into a car and got whisked to Smith Square to Labour Party Headquarters, went up to the first floor and stayed shut in there until Sir Alec Douglas-Home conceded.

We were all hanging around waiting for Sir Alec, and Harold had on a formal suit, black jacket and striped pants, I'd never seen him dressed as formally as that. One very nice touch was to spot his father and sister, who were so thrilled. He was an enormously generous person. He wanted people to share in his success, and he arranged for a second car for when he went to the palace to accept and though they didn't go into the palace they followed in the car and sat waiting for him so that he could include them.   ANN WARD

CHAPTER FOUR

The Promised Land

Britain's transfers of power are quick, brutal and total. Prime ministers concede immediately the result is clear, successors drive to the palace to 'kiss hands' and the furniture vans arrive at Nos 10 and 11. So it was on Friday 16 October 1964. Harold Wilson went to No. 10 a little bewildered, more than a little lonely, but above all else conscious of our small majority and the utter unpredictability of his immediate future. He then put his new government together – six major appointments that day, then the rest over the weekend and Monday. The new cabinet was dominated by the right. It included two others who, besides Wilson, had had previous cabinet experience: Patrick Gordon Walker, who had lost his seat but became Foreign Secretary pending election for another, and James Griffiths. Several other appointees had held ministerial office below cabinet: Lord Longford (Lord Privy Seal), Arthur Bottomley (Commonwealth Secretary), Michael Stewart (Education), George Brown (at Economic Affairs), Jim Callaghan (Chancellor of the Exchequer) and Frank Soskice (Home Office).

On the Friday night Harold Wilson, his Chancellor, Jim Callaghan, and the Secretary of State for Economic Affairs, George Brown, were told that the trade deficit was eight hundred million pounds, double their expectations. Next morning and again in the evening the three tired principals met to consider the three options offered by the Treasury. The crucial decision not to devalue was taken. The unprecedented balance-of-payments deficit and the crisis of confidence Labour had inherited were to be met by deflation, discipline, higher interest rates and, a few days later, option three, an import surcharge.

This was proclaimed as eschewing easy options. Labour was to tough it out and show that it could be firmer and more rigidly orthodox than irresponsible risk-taking Tories. The decision, taken without real discussion, almost as if ratifying the inevitable, seemed natural, even right at the time. It was to have disastrous consequences, vitiating the hopes and the optimism with which Labour was coming to power. Yet none of this was seen, or even considered, in the heady days of October 1964.

✘ I think he was so convinced that we would win that he was switched in to win. I wasn't switched in to win because I had to pick up the pieces if we lost and had to work out what would happen then; but the moment we knew it was a majority he just rattled off what he wanted doing and he wanted his old driver back from when he was in the cabinet before. So the man was summoned to Transport House to drive him to the palace and the family were rung up and put in an appearance so that we could all go off to the palace together and with our little tiny five majority we went off to Buckingham Palace to shake hands with the Queen and receive her permission.

We went straight to Downing Street from the palace. Douglas-Home never lived in Downing Street or worked in it in the sense that people have before and since. He did three-day weeks in London and went back to his house. It was an integrated building – Tory Central Office was integrated completely with the rest of the officials there so they all worked together. So there wasn't really any packing up.

I remember in the small dining-room upstairs in the private flat there was some Tory posters on the wall so they'd obviously used that as a little political room. But Douglas-Home didn't use it or think of it as a work place, and certainly not as a home. When he was there he lived in the state rooms downstairs, not in the flat upstairs. Harold didn't move in straightaway to live there. He still went out to South Hampstead. But for working we had to go to Downing Street.

MARCIA WILLIAMS

✘ First thing he did was to put out an order that the Foreign Office must be made clear – and the Defence Department – that no arms would be sold to South Africa. It was his first priority, no arms for South Africa. Then he set about calling in the people to appoint and it takes a very long time because while you're doing that you are being briefed about the state of the economy and you are being asked what measures you wish to be taken. They go in and see you individually. The cabinet secretary sits with you and goes through it with you and in this case it was the Governor [of the Bank of England] who was brought in immediately because of the sterling crisis problem.

There could have been a decision there and then to devalue. It would have been rather disastrous. If he had done that he would have had to go back to the country because the slippage would have been so great and sterling would have gone into freefall. The crisis would have been even bigger and he couldn't possibly have faced it on a five majority. He would have had to have gone back to the country.

Those decisions were not easy for him. Reggie Maudling told us endlessly what a good condition we were in and that Britain was doing rather well compared with the rest of the world. It seems familiar now, doesn't it? So if there is a nasty something or other in the woodwork, it's not a surprise, it's an experience we've been through already and one that may well have to be gone through again. A campaign puts you in a fighting mode so you are prepared to take it on and see what you can do and fight it through. George Brown was a great fighter and very good election campaigner and he was ready to take anybody on. So they were not going to be downcast by it, but what was heart-rending was that they knew that the National Plan, for instance, which George was given the task of implementing, might not be as easy to put into practice as we'd thought.

The top people knew what they were getting. George Brown did and there had been quite a lot of preparation for the setting up of the Department of Economic Affairs. I think he'd had talks with civil servants and had got a scheme for the organisation of the ministry. I think he and Callaghan, Healey and Gordon Walker all had quite a clear idea what they were going to do. I think one surprise here was that everyone thought that Crosland was going to get Education because he had had Housing and Local Government and Michael Stewart came from Education. But he wasn't one of the top six.

ROY JENKINS

✘ After every election, every possible person is hovering about at their phone for a call to No.10, and in 1951 when the Tories won, Randolph Churchill left messages for all his friends saying Mr Churchill phoned (and, of course, Winston was the Prime Minister) and they all rang No.10, only to be told, 'I'm awfully sorry, there must be some terrible mistake!' So you sat there. Then you were called and I went in and Harold said, 'Will you take the Post Office?' I said, 'Yes.' At the Durham Mining Gala earlier that summer, he'd said, 'I'd like you to take the Post Office and then when I have my major reshuffle I'll bring you properly into the cabinet.' I'd written an article in the *Guardian* about the Post Office because he had said you should use nationalised industries to advance technologically, which was what I did.

I came out of No.10 and the journalists were all there. They always say, 'What have you been offered, Mr Benn?' and I said, 'Well, I can tell you one thing I haven't been offered a peerage.' Of course, the press were very different in those days. They were much more respectful of leaders and respectful of answers. I got home and I rang the Post Office and I said, 'Can I speak to the private office?' and they said, 'Who are you?' So I said, 'Mr Benn.' There was a long pause and a very nervous voice said, 'Postmaster-General?' They sent a great big Austin Princess with my private secretary. As we got in the car he said to me, 'How do you intend to play, minister?' as if it was a game of cricket!   TONY BENN

✘ It was not his cabinet. It was a cabinet that he felt he had to appoint and he felt it was just and right to do it and they had the ability – but one of the awful things was that there were not as many talented people in a sense of being qualified to be Secretaries of State on the left as there were on the right. There were obviously Barbara and Tony and people like that but after you've been through Tony Benn, Dick Crossman and Barbara Castle things are coming a little bit more difficult; there were not that number of people on the left as highly qualified to be in government jobs as there were on the right.

Harold was very fair and he formed the government he thought would do the job best not the government he necessarily would have found more supportive of him. He knew he had to win another election and so our sights were set on the next election date – when it would come and how we would get there – and, of course, we had a lovely hiccup in the autumn when Patrick Gordon Walker decided to lose two seats for us. So that was quite a blow and then we arrived with a one majority really.   MARCIA WILLIAMS

✘ Harold argued that he was keeping the wings of the party together. Because he started off in the left wing whatever he did he nevertheless had to give ground to do it. It came out in the making of the ministers. George had to fight like hell to get Crosland and Jenkins and all these people because Harold was desperate not to see too many of that kind of person as against the left wing being brought in. In many cases, left-wing people were brought in with no brains, and they got parliamentary secretaries and all that kind of thing when there were much more capable chaps, but Harold kept them out because he argued that he had to keep this balance.   RON BROWN

✘ In those days you didn't get any briefing until you went into your department and, of course, it wasn't guaranteed that you would have the job in office that you'd been preparing for as a shadow minister. Pretty likely but by no means certain. I think if you take our government, George Brown under Wilson was certainly going to be in Economic Affairs in this ill-starred experiment to divide up the Treasury which was a total disaster in practice. So we had to end the economic and financial separation.

I had been very well prepared. Gordon Walker was going to be the Foreign Secretary and he'd worked very hard at it, but of course he had lost his seat and then he lost the by-election after the general election. So he was out for good and nobody had been preparing themselves to do the job. But as I say the nature of this job was changing very fast because of the Chinese bomb, the uncertainty in Soviet policy following the fall of Khrushchev and the white backlash against anti-colonialism in Rhodesia.   DENIS HEALEY

✘ The top six were announced the first day. I remember I'd come down from Birmingham that day. I went and did a television thing – I think it was Maudling and Edward Boyle on the other side, with Crosland, I think it was, and myself on the Labour side – and in the course of that interview or just before we were about to go on air somebody came in with a bit of paper which had the top six appointments in order right down to Healey as Minister of Defence so that we were all settled and done on the Friday evening.

I was slightly on tenterhooks, inevitably, but I didn't expect to be in the top six. When the full cabinet list came out, which I think it did on the Saturday afternoon, I was beginning to get a bit jumpy though there was no reason why I should because I didn't expect to be in the cabinet, but I remember we went out for a drive in Richmond Park or something and when we came back our youngest son, who in '64 would have been only just ten, said, 'By the way, 10 Downing Street rang up, but I expect it's too late now.'   ROY JENKINS

X In 1964, we came back from Grimsby Friday morning in a state of such excitement you can't imagine. From then on the telephone almost didn't stop. Tony didn't know if he would have a job at all because he'd been very outspoken earlier in his criticism of Wilson, when Wilson challenged Hugh. Certainly he wanted a job in the government but he didn't know if he'd get one. But he knew that there was talk that he'd go as number two to Callaghan. Friday night, that's when the deed was done. I didn't know that until subsequently, Tony didn't know it. Nobody knew it, except the three men who took the decision at the top. On Saturday morning comes that mellifluous voice saying, 'Number two, the Department of Economic Affairs. Can you and Susan come along this evening?'

So we go round that evening and there is George Brown in a velvet smoking jacket. Almost at once Tony said that he'd spoken with Jim on the telephone an hour earlier to discuss the division between these two economic departments. George shot right up out of his chair and shouted, 'Traitor! Traitor! How could you do such a thing? Traitor!' – and so it went on. His two main supporters then arrived, Jenkins and Bill Rodgers, and their wives. We all settled down again, but each time the conversation would turn to the serious detail of what the new DEA would do, Tony who was by then distinctly nettled would say, 'You'll have to excuse me for a moment while I go and telephone Jim to tell him about this.' George would go right up in the air again. It was very unpleasant and quite a baptism into seeing what politics was like at the top.

At that time I smoked with an eighteen-inch-long cigarette holder, and I put my cigarette in and looked up at the ceiling,

really because tears of outrage had come into my eyes and I
didn't wish anyone to see them. I found the whole thing very
unattractive. On the way home, however, when I voiced that
view, Tony wasn't interested in that, he was utterly depressed
by the private conversation they had had, George and he – at
some point they had gone off into the garden or somewhere for
a private conversation and George had told him that the
decision had been taken the night before on devaluation, and
that under no circumstances was devaluation ever, ever, ever,
to be mentioned again.

Tony said to me – he was so depressed and thoughtful – 'I
have to consider my whole position and clear my mind.' In the
morning he told me that he would become a number two at the
DEA, and within a week he had circulated the first of his
papers to the Prime Minister saying why he, Tony, thought
that his entire economic policy could not be achieved unless
we had devaluation soon.   SUSAN CROSLAND

✗ George Brown I saw that evening. He summoned Tony
Crosland and me round to his flat near Marble Arch and he
had just come back from agreeing to what was probably a
mistake – a decision not to devalue. Certainly economically it
would have been better to devalue straight off but I could see
there were political arguments against it. At any rate he and
Callaghan and Wilson took that joint decision that evening and
George came back home and announced that to us and
announced to me that I was going to be Minister of Aviation.

I was both surprised and pleased so perhaps that slightly
took the edge off my annoyance with him for having agreed to
no devaluation. But it didn't take the edge off Crosland.
Crosland spent the rest of the evening abusing him. Tony was
quite good at that. That was the Saturday evening. As a result,
when I went in to Downing Street at about 10.30 on Sunday
morning, Wilson offered me the position of Minister of
Aviation not realising that I knew the whole time what he was
going to do. As I say, it was a better appointment that I
expected. Wilson had no reason to keep me remotely above my
market value.   ROY JENKINS

✗ I knew I was going to be Defence Secretary and I had two
enormous advantages. First of all I'd been in the services for
six years in the war, so I knew the ground problems very well,

'Just off to work, dear' – Hampstead, 17 October 1964

and secondly my main interest in life as well as politics since the middle fifties, that's to say for about ten years, had been how you deal with the impact of nuclear weapons on both strategy and foreign policy. I'd really become one of the very, very few Europeans who took an interest in that and I'd been arguing it through with some of our best soldiers, sailors and airmen with experience of the previous war so that that part of my job I was extremely familiar with. So I was able to go into the Ministry of Defence and in effect take control because I understood this problem better than any of my advisers, as I think they'd admit now.   DENIS HEALEY

✗ Harold, on the morning after the election, took a view that his government could last at most eighteen months, possibly much less than that. Therefore, they had to make an impact on something. That something could be housing. You will remember that it was the time of Rachman, the Rent Acts and really appalling housing situations. He reckoned that education and science was very much a long-term, five-year effort, therefore, thought Wilson, I will put the dynamic Crossman into the Ministry of Housing and put the somewhat more sedate Michael Stewart, who'd been shadow housing, into Education. The upshot of this was that Michael Stewart, who was at that time a very self-important man who thought that he knew more about education than anybody else, took not a blind bit of notice of all the policies that had been worked out in the two-way traffic in ideas. So we got the Secretary of State for Education, who resented what had been done by his shadow predecessor, and we got the Secretary of State for Housing, who wasn't at all clear what the grant systems were and had to be educated from the word go.

If you look at the Crossman *Diaries* you will see how far down the learning curve Dick Crossman was when he entered the ministry. There was one level which was funny but there was another level which was absolutely tragic because a great deal of the work had been done in opposition and expectations were raised in the scientific and education fields. They said, 'Why were we doing it, going to all these conferences, listening to Crossman and his team, contributing ideas, and then he doesn't become the Secretary of State?' That had a very bad effect.   TAM DALYELL

✗ I wondered about office because Hugh was going to put me in the cabinet. I thought if you go into Parliament when you are young it is rather a waste of time if you never get into the cabinet. If Harold Wilson, with whom I was obviously at loggerheads, had said, 'Would you like to go in the government,' and it had been a decent post I would probably have said, 'Yes,' even though I didn't admire him very much. But no offer came. The papers didn't arrive!   WOODROW WYATT

✘ I did expect to be called. I'd come back to London where I had a flat because I worked in a hospital. I got a call to come on Monday morning and as the various appointments were announced my hope of this, that and the other were dashed. I never expected any more than being an under-secretary. I would have been very disappointed if I hadn't been invited to be an under-secretary, but I didn't expect to be offered a higher appointment than that. So Harold sent for me and I turned up at No. 10 Downing Street. I thought there'd be a committee of them or something, but there was just him. He sat there smoking his pipe and said, 'OK, Dick, Scottish Office. Willie would like to have you in the Scottish Office.' I said, 'That's fine, I get on well with Willie. But Harold, our housing target in Scottish terms is to be 50,000. Houses take eighteen months to plan and build. How long have we got with a majority of only four?' Harold said, 'Eighteen months.' OK, so he was guessing, but you could see that he had made up his mind that he couldn't function on a majority of four. He was determined that we should have another election quickly.   DICKSON MABON

✘ It wasn't an experienced government at all. Mind you experience is very far from being everything and I think it was probably a better government than the Labour government that came in in 1974, which was dripping with experience and which had five or six major figures who had a lot of experience in senior office but which was very divided. I think the '64 government worked better than the '74 government, but it wasn't strong in experience. There was Wilson himself who had been President of the Board of Trade. There was Gordon Walker who didn't last long. The only other person who'd ever been in a cabinet was Jim Griffiths who was a rather sort of veteran figure brought back as Secretary of State for Wales. So all the key jobs, Callaghan, Brown, Castle, they'd never been in the cabinet. It wasn't a rule in those days but in fact he did appoint nearly every member of the elected shadow cabinet. I think Dick Mitchison and Fred Willey were exceptions, members of the shadow cabinet who did not go to the first cabinet. But I regarded it as a temporary cabinet and of course it did turn out to be a very temporary cabinet because poor old Gordon Walker who had lost his seat in the general election then lost the by-election so he only lasted as Foreign Secretary until January and that caused a reshuffle.   ROY JENKINS

✖ I didn't come down but the truth of the matter is that they came in their hoards. They thought it was a great advantage to be present, I think, around the Palace of Westminster, and many were the cabinet ministers who were importuned. When Crossman was made Minister of Housing he got various requests from old friends to be his Minister of State, but actually his Ministers of State were imposed on him by the Prime Minister. He was taken aback that the Ministers of State were Bob Mellish and a man called James McCall. Bob Mellish, previously, had thought Crossman to be the intellectual devil incarnate but, subsequently, they got on extremely well. With Jim McCall rather less so. He was a very prominent, decent Fabian, who actually was very competent.   TAM DALYELL

✖ I'd helped to run George Brown's election campaign against Harold Wilson. Gerry Reynolds and I ran George's campaign. George was appointed Secretary for Economic Affairs on the Friday and he rang me up on the Saturday and said, 'Have you had a call from Wilson?' and I said, 'No' and he said, 'Well you will do, so stay by your phone.' So I stayed by the phone and late on the Sunday night I got a call. Somebody said, 'No. 10 Downing Street here, the Prime Minister wants to see you at 9.45 a.m.' which caused me some problems as it was difficult to get from Birmingham to Downing Street for 9.45 a.m.

So I had to get my old Morris Minor out and travel overnight. He had asked a series of people to come in every quarter of an hour. I was number two. When it got to 11 a.m. people were beginning to stack up, waiting to go in and see him. We were all outside the cabinet room in that little area. When it got to 12 noon, out came a secretary and said, 'Well I'm very sorry, the Prime Minister and other ministers have very serious matters to attend to this morning. So will all those people who were asked to come after 10 a.m. please go away and we'll send for you again.' Well I've never seen such a collective drop in morale in my life.

Anyway I was all right. Jenny Lee was one and I was two. There were going to be ministers for the arts and sport which of course was Harold being extremely far sighted. What the cabinet meeting was doing, it turned out, was discussing whether to devalue the pound or not. It was the Chancellor and George Brown and Harold. Just a small group. So I went in and Harold apologised profusely and said, 'Sorry I kept you waiting, but I want you to be the first Minister for Sport and go to the Department of Education. You'll be one of the first men in history to have the pleasure of creating his own ministry.' So I said, 'Thank you very much.'

As I was leaving the room I suddenly thought of the 1966 World Cup and I said, 'By the way, you do know, Prime Minister, we've got the World Cup on our hands in 1966?' And he didn't know what it was. 'What's that?' he said. So I said, 'It's the sixteen top nations in the world playing football here.' And I said, 'What's the point of having a Minister of Sport with the World Cup on his hands and no money.' And he said, 'Well, how much do you want?' Of course I hadn't seen a civil servant or anything, I didn't have the faintest idea how much I wanted. But I thought if I miss this moment, then it's gone. So from the back of my head I produced a figure which sounded then a lot of money. Half a million. I said, 'I want half a million pounds.' And he sucked his pipe and he said, 'You can have half a million pounds and not a penny more.'   DENIS HOWELL

✘ I didn't expect anything. I was out of London. We had an eve-of-poll meeting in Manchester, in the Victoria Hall, Manchester, and I was speaking and of course Harold was there. The first inkling was when he said out of the corner of his mouth, 'Don't go far from a telephone tomorrow.' But neither Dick nor I had ever been ambitious plotters and I was in my dressing gown, getting up lazily on the Saturday morning and the call came. Could I come to No. 10? So I hastily put on some clothes; my hair was a mess, so I borrowed my dead sister's hat and stuck it on my head and we went. Harold was enjoying enormously handing out the sweets of office. When we came in he said, 'Minister of Overseas Development.' I'd worked with the Fabians to produce a blueprint for a Ministry of Overseas Development which snatched powers from anybody who had a bit to do with aid – from the Foreign Office, the Board of Trade, Technical Assistance Bureau, Treasury even – and it all came in my hands. Then he said casually, 'In the cabinet, of course.' He kept his word.

BARBARA CASTLE

*'The Prime Minister? Good heavens, no . . . it's the only
back-bencher who isn't a minister!'*

✘ I wasn't in the top echelons of the party at the beginning of
that government. I got a rather better job than I expected to get.
I became Minister of Aviation, the first government job I ever
had. I always thought I was very lucky to avoid being a junior
minister. Not the most rewarding occupation. I don't think I
had a clear view that I was going to get Minister of Aviation;
indeed, I got it mainly because I had written three long articles
in the *Observer* – the sort of thing I sometimes did in those
days. Investigations in depth. Three articles on the front of the
review section about the British Overseas Airways
Corporation, as it was called then, and why they were flying
Boeings and not DC10s, and I did quite a major feature on that.
It caught Wilson's eye and he decided to give me that job. I
don't think I had that in mind at all.

I'd had quite a long talk with him about a year before
because I was then being offered the editorship of the
Economist. I had to make a decision so I had a talk with him but
we certainly didn't mention a specific job. Electorally, as you
know, I've not all my life been a tremendous Wilson fan and he
behaved both skilfully and well in that September 1963
interview because he encouraged me without specifically
saying, 'No, don't go to the *Economist,*' but turned my mind
away from it. Going back to that interview I had with him in
September 1963, I remember admitting in spite of myself that

Harold treated me much more skilfully than Gaitskell would have treated Barbara Castle. He was quite good at doing that. His footwork was always extremely good. He was better at balancing the left and he was better also at balancing the right than Gaitskell would have been at balancing the left.

ROY JENKINS

✘ Looking back, what strikes me is how little we knew about what government was going to be like. I'd been in the House of Commons for two and a half years. I'd never been in a government department in my life. So I had no idea what it was actually like to go into an office which was going to be mine. Although I had one or two friends who had been civil servants, they were really very, very careful about what they said to me. I hadn't really had any contact with civil servants as such before I went in. So it was all very strange and new to me. Friday night it looked very dicey indeed. On Saturday night I went over to Roy Jenkins. George Brown telephoned and said to Roy, 'You're going to be Minister of Aviation and Bill Rodgers is going to come and join me as Parliamentary Secretary.'

Nothing happened on Sunday, on Monday, on Tuesday. Then on Wednesday I had my call to No. 10 and it was the first experience I had ever had of going within No. 10 and sitting alongside the cabinet table. I remember Harold Wilson said that Patrick Gordon Walker had also asked me to go to the Foreign Office but I was going with George. We had a very friendly conversation. I felt the biggest man in the world at that moment. Harold knew I didn't like him very much, but we'd won an election, we were both in the same party and he was very excited at his level and I was very excited at my junior level. He said, 'It's in Storey's Gate,' so I walked out of No. 10 and along Storey's Gate. I couldn't see anything that looked like the DEA. I went into the pub and I said, 'Could you tell me where the Department of Economic Affairs is.' They didn't know. In the end I went into the Treasury in Great George Street. A woman said, 'Can I help you.' I said, 'Yes I wonder if you could tell me where the Department of Economic Affairs is?' She looked up and said, 'We haven't got any list of it here. Why do you want to know?' I said, 'I'm a minister.' 'Oh,' she said. 'Are you?' And she picked up the telephone and she rang someone and said, 'There's a gentleman here who says he is a minister in the Department of Economic Affairs. Where is it?' She said to me, 'You go down Great George Street and you turn right. It's not in Storey's Gate at all. It's overlooking the park.' So that was my first experience of government.

It had been the Ministry of Defence before it was cleared out. So all the lavatories were marked 'officers' and 'men'. I decided I was an officer for the first time in my life so I used one of them. It was a curious department. We'd got one major division from the Board of Trade and then we had one or two other good people. We had quite a lot of cast-offs. I couldn't do anything about it because I was very junior. What the permanent secretary says to every department is, 'Will you give us your best people for this new department?' 'Oh yes,' they say to the head of the Civil Service and then they find the people they least want. So we had some very good people but we had some people, very nice people, who were not very good at being civil servants.   BILL RODGERS

✗ We won in Dundee. Dundee has two constituencies and we won both of them comfortably and I expected to go into government because I had served on the front-bench for a very long time. I was basically the number two in Commonwealth and Colonial Affairs, which still existed at that time, so I rather expected and hoped that I would go into perhaps Overseas Aid or the Commonwealth side of things. In fact, I went into the Foreign Office as a Minister of State. We'd had all the jokes and all that and then suddenly the reality came that day in 1964. I hung around at home waiting for the telephone to ring and to be called down to London. Then finally it did in fact ring – on the Saturday or maybe on the Friday, I can't quite remember. Anyway, I went down on the night train and I had this appointment with the new prime minister, Harold Wilson, at 10.30 in the morning and I remember walking round and round St James's Park in a state of total nerves as to what on earth I was in for. Then having been asked to be part of the Foreign Office team I went in on Monday morning to the Foreign Office, and I had only been in the Foreign Office – although I'd spent years being a shadow spokesman – maybe three times on deputations, that kind of thing.

                                                    GEORGE THOMSON

✘ I was hoping for a job, yes. Everybody hopes for a job. But I didn't realise until I read Crossman's *Diaries*, how much Wilson hated me. I didn't get a job but I became PPS to Dennis Healey and that was fine. Then a vacancy came up as a junior minister for the army. I was wondering whether I might get that. Merlyn Rees got it. I met Harold Wilson in the lift and he said, 'Not this time, Dick, but you're high on the list.'

DICK TAVERNE

✘ After thirteen years there were a lot of people who expected office. Harold decided quite a number of them from the beginning weren't going to get it and this was one of the features which will happen again. The National Executive and the TUC people tended to be people you really had to find places for on the front-bench. You had to invent more jobs, you couldn't ignore them, and in the same way with the trade unions. As far as Ray Gunter was concerned, Ray's career was dependent solely on the fact that he was a member of the General Council. He was never a particularly great parliamentarian and he certainly wasn't a natural administrator of a ministry and that was just typical. So Harold had decided that he had to balance his government. It happened very quickly because I suddenly got a call from Harold on that wondrous Monday morning and I was offered a brand new job. I don't think it was total flattery because he made it very clear he wanted to get in a number of young people and left me in no doubt at all that, come the next election, if we won it, he would be moving those young people up into the cabinet.

RICHARD MARSH

✘ At that time Dicky Mountbatten was the Chief of Defence Staff, the senior military chap, and the Chief Scientific Adviser at Defence was Solly Zuckerman. Now I'd known Solly even before the war; he was a brilliant young fellow, wrote a book on the sexual life of the primates – not the Archbishops of Canterbury but the monkeys – and that sort of thing. As soon as he knew I was appointed, which was on the Friday the second I got back from Leeds, he rang me up and asked me if I would have dinner with him on the Sunday night and Dicky Mountbatten. To give you some idea of the confusion, we had dinner at Solly's flat in Westminster and while we were eating there was a call from Harold Wilson who asked if Solly would agree to be Minister of Disarmament and he said, 'No,' and I advised him strongly against it because I knew he would have no real power. In the end it was given to Alun Chalfont who had no party allegiance of any sort and spent his later life largely selling arms to dictators in the Middle East and elsewhere.   DENIS HEALEY

✗ It was a Friday, shortly after the Labour Party came into office. As defence correspondent at *The Times*, I was taking Friday off and I went to have a drink in a club in the West End. One of the waiters came over and said there was a call from No. 10 Downing Street. I immediately thought that this was to do with defence matters. Very flattering. So I went along to Downing Street but it was clear as soon as I arrived that this was something rather more than a little discussion about a *Times* article because I was met by a private secretary and taken straight into the cabinet room.

There was Harold sitting at the cabinet table in the prime minister's usual position and he motioned me to come and sit alongside him. Then in the space of what seemed to me about fifteen seconds he said, 'I'd like you to consider the possibility of coming into my government as Minister of State at the Foreign Office. You would have the title of Minister of Disarmament. Because of the kind of material you would be dealing with I should have to recommend that you be appointed to the Privy Council and as I am not anxious to invite any by-elections at the moment given the balance in the House, I shall want to recommend that you go into the House of Lords.' I was for once speechless!

I said, 'There are two people whom I will clearly have to consult: first of all my wife – it will come as a great surprise to her – and secondly the editor of *The Times*. I can't suddenly leave Printing House Square just like that.' So he said, 'There's a telephone next door. Go and consult them now.' Puff, puff, puff. So I did. I went and spoke to William Hayley and to my wife. They both, in different ways, said that they thought it was a challenge that I couldn't possibly turn down. William Hayley made that famous remark of his that when you leave Printing House Square and go to Whitehall you will miss two things. One will be your freedom of action. The other will be your influence on government policy. My wife was a little less profound. She simply said, 'Well, you know, I'll have to leave it to you. Whatever you decide to do, I'll back you.'

That evening, my wife and I were going to Covent Garden to the ballet and we went off. I thought this will probably emerge in a few days and I've got time to prepare for it. When we got back to my flat in Chelsea after the ballet, the place was surrounded by press photographers. The announcement had been made that evening. I became a member of the Chelsea Labour Party which was only sensible because to have been a member of a Labour government and not a member of the party would have been rather perverse.   ALUN CHALFONT

✗ Harold invited me to become Chief Whip about three months before the election. We'd talked about many of the ministerial jobs beforehand. So I knew I was going to be Chief Whip. I was then the Deputy Chief Whip, of course, in opposition. I didn't want to be Chief Whip. I didn't want to be a whip at all. It's a horrible job anyhow, even if you've got a good majority, because you're the dogsbody. He asked Herbert Bowden – he was the Chief Whip – and myself to go through the whole party and make suggestions for people who were suitable, not for specific jobs in most cases, but people who were suitable for the three stages, full minister, cabinet minister, the minister of state or parliamentary secretary. So we went through the whole party and gave our view on what we thought people were suitable for.

I didn't really think we could govern when the results came. I thought we could make a good try at it but I hadn't much confidence inside. But I exuded confidence to everybody, the press and the party, etc. I said, 'Of course we can.' But it didn't need much of an accident to slip up.

Wilson was very good. He consulted Bowden and myself about a lot of them (and we violently disagreed with some of them and agreed the rest) at the beginning of his government but as time went on he didn't and when it came to the second lot, after the '66 election, he didn't consult us at all. He knew the party, of course, but we knew it better than he did, but he did know the party.   TED SHORT

✗ There was some very careless casting. For example, it was mad, to think that C. P. Snow could conceivably be of any use at all as a minister, and the last thing that you wanted to do was to set up the Ministry of Technology under Frank Cousins, which had a lot to be said for it, and then give him a thoroughly incompetent, extremely vain, lazy peer. If he'd been given some ambitious technical politician, like Dick Marsh was in those days, or Gerry Reynolds, the whole story would have been different. In higher education the situation was not improved by the fact that one of Wilson's favourite scientists was appointed to the Minister of State from the Lords, and he was Vivian Bowden, principal of the Manchester College of Science and Technology (UMIST), because Harold Wilson actively favoured scientists. The real heavyweight, Patrick Blackett, refused to go to the Lords on a matter of principle. So Vivian Bowden was appointed. In March 1965 I met Vivian Bowdan in the corridor. He said, 'It's awful. I have just sacked my secretary.' So I said, 'Was she incompetent?' 'You don't understand,' he said, 'I've just sacked my permanent secretary.' My jaw dropped. I said, 'You have sacked Sir Bruce Frazer?' 'Yes,' he said, 'I got rid of Frazer this morning.' Sir Bruce Frazer was one of the mightiest mandarins in Whitehall. So I said, 'But, Vivian, what did Michael Stewart say about this?' 'Stewart?' he said, 'I haven't consulted Stewart.' 'Vivian, what about the Prime Minister?' 'Harold,' he said, 'Why should I talk to Harold?' Within a fortnight Frazer was reinstated and Vivian had gone. He had not the slightest notion of how the government machine worked.   TAM DALYELL

✘ I was appointed on day two as the senior appointments were going on involving the Treasury. Harold called me to No.10 and said, 'This is the job I want you to do, the job that Boyd Carpenter has done. You'll be very unpopular. I think you'll do the job very well.' Harold and I were good friends and because of that we were open with one another and he knew that my politics and his were not the same. He was then a left-winger and I was very much centre of the road and so if he had chosen not to give me a ministerial job I would have gone back into business, but he did and I give him full marks for that. He later on put me into the cabinet. I gave him a hundred and one marks for that. He behaved supremely well. Then a telephone call came through. Would I go to the Treasury and somebody would be there to meet me? I went over and there was the daughter of a good friend of mine who happened to be a civil servant in the Treasury. She met me upstairs and said, 'There's your office.' You get thrown in head first.   JACK DIAMOND

✗ We came down here and I can remember the euphoric mood when Harold Wilson started to form his government. Here is a significant lesson for Tony Blair. There were a lot of people who'd been junior ministers in Attlee's period and even younger ones, PPSs. They'd been looking forward to a fulfilling period in office. But of course they were all a bit long in the tooth and they were overtaken by a new generation of bright young intellectuals, people like Shirley Williams, Bill Rodgers, Dick Marsh, David Ennals, all of whom could reasonably expect a place in the government.

These were the people who were to build our new society, the intellectuals. That meant that a lot of others were out who had thought for all those years before that they would have fulfilling ministerial careers. So they were bitter. One thing that added to their bitterness was that Harold Macmillan had sprinkled knighthoods around his party like confetti at a wedding. Harold Wilson said that he wouldn't do anything of the sort. He wouldn't exploit the honours system for political ends. So there wasn't even that little bit of emollient to placate these fellows, who could have gone home and told the missus, 'Well, love, you'll be Lady Brown,' or whatever. That added to the bitterness to sour an otherwise good atmosphere.

HAROLD WALKER

✗ The shadow cabinet that he had inherited very much reflected Hugh Gaitskell's wing of the party which was on the whole somewhat more right wing than Harold's. He dished out portfolios to people who had been prominent in the shadow cabinet. I think there was only one who didn't get a cabinet post, he went to the Lords. Harold had sufficient room because in those days we only had twelve on the parliamentary committee. Since there were something like twenty-one or twenty-two cabinet members that gave him some room for manoeuvre. Straightaway he brought in Barbara Castle as a cabinet minister, Dick Crossman as a cabinet minister, Tony Benn just below cabinet level to begin with and very quickly brought into the cabinet. So he was able to get a better mix than the elected shadow cabinets.

PETER SHORE

✗ The trouble with Harold was that he wasn't, like Callaghan, the sort of prime minister who was prepared to say, 'So this is what we've got to do,' and push. Harold always wanted a majority for his ideas. So he used to appoint people to jobs who really weren't worthy of it just so that he could top up the majority. The serious discussions tended to take place not so much in the cabinet as in cabinet committees. The Defence Policy Committee, which deals with defence, foreign policy, Commonwealth policy, that discussed the issues in great detail and thrashed them out with big disagreements. The same was true of economic policy. In the end, when Wilson recognised that he couldn't refuse to allow a discussion on devaluation, we had a very important little committee on sterling which finally came to the conclusion we ought to be prepared to go down.

DENIS HEALEY

✗ We had thirteen years of Conservative government with their own particular emphasis on policy. Perfectly straight-forward and basically disinterested civil servants after a long period of one-party rule get the impression that this is really orthodox thinking. Yet the incoming government has to try and turn things round. I think one or two permanent secretaries found that difficult to handle, but they very quickly adapted to it. There were changes at the very top and Harold was very keen to have a new Governor of the Bank of England, which was effected very quickly, and the head of the Civil Service was changed. But generally speaking the remarkable thing was the ease with which the new departments were set up – like the new DEA with George Brown in charge.

Really it was extraordinary how the Civil Service responded to that and to the Civil Service Department set up a bit later. These two departments directly and consciously challenged the power of the Treasury. It was Harold's strong belief that the Treasury was too powerful so he had to create a department of equal power to the Treasury. That was the whole purpose of the DEA – but the people who manned the new DEA were plundered from the Treasury and all over the place. They very loyally backed the DEA. The Treasury had total charge of the economy until '64 and they also determined the movement of the senior civil servants. They were the personnel department. What the CSD did was to take from the Treasury that command over personnel. These were real challenges to the Treasury and the fact that George was created First Secretary was absolutely deliberate, making him

one above the Chancellor of the Exchequer in the pecking
order of the cabinet in terms of chairing committees and inter-
departmental committees and so on.   PETER SHORE

✗ When you get there they offer you a deal. They give you
this thing called a brief for an incoming minister, huge thick
thing. You're exhausted afterwards. You arrive there to find all
these decisions waiting since the last government ceased to be
operational, and you're given this fat brief which I don't think
anybody ever read except me. That told you what the officials
wanted you to do. During an election, officials take the two
manifestos and dress up what they want to do to make it
compatible with the two manifestos. They then offer you this
deal. If you do what we want you to do, we will brief the press
that you're an incredibly able minister. If you don't do what
we want you to do, we'll undermine you.

I won the support of the private office and they became
very warm and friendly. I issued masses of minutes which
used to infuriate them because the role of a minister is to sign
the minutes they'd drafted. It was said of Reggie Bevins that he
used to come in on a Tuesday and Thursday. There was this
huge table and the minutes were there and he would walk
round and sign them and have a glass of sherry and go off.
During the first recess at Christmas, my officials said to me,
'We take it we shan't be seeing you till Parliament meets.' But I
was there every day. And I had my blue mug of tea, Mr Parrot
and Mr Rice used to bring me a mug of tea on the hour, and we
had a very matey atmosphere.

A minute from a minister in the main in Civil Service
language is the final word. So if a minister writes a minute
himself, without having consulted, it destabilises them. I
issued about a hundred and fifty minutes. Why don't we do
this? Why don't we do that? When are we going to do this? I'd
talk to the unions and they'd say well what's going on in
this? – so I'd do a minute on it. In a funny way in the end I got
on well with them because they felt here was a minister
committed to the Post Office. Permanent secretaries told me
later that if you don't keep at us we'll be like a clockwork
motor that slowly winds down. Therefore they wanted an
injection of energy at the top. But they didn't much care for it
at the time. Or some of them didn't.   TONY BENN

✘ I think the Foreign Office had been working away at Labour's policy statements and trying to prepare themselves to field them but on that first morning Patrick Gordon Walker was the new Foreign Secretary and I went into the office and the permanent secretary at the time, a man called Harold Catcher, took me along to the office I was going to occupy which is what's called the Parliamentary Office in the Foreign Office.

It dealt with and processed all the parliamentary questions, amongst other things, and there I was introduced to my new private secretary who'd been the private secretary of my Conservative predecessor. He turned out to be an extremely able private secretary and a very good one altogether but at that moment he had a slight tendency to pomposity and he drew himself up beside the desk at which I was sitting for the first time and said, 'Welcome to your new office, Minister of State, it is my duty to tell you that if you wish our resignations are entirely at your disposal.' I didn't know quite what to say.

GEORGE THOMSON

✘ I found at the Treasury a private secretary, and the private office was large in terms of numbers – I think five. I thought, 'What a waste,' but I realised afterwards how wise it was. They take over every concern, every activity in your life. If your wife rings you up they listen in in the outer office: they listen in in case your wife says don't forget we're going out to dinner tomorrow night and I hadn't told them I'd got a dinner appointment. The whole of your waking life is at their disposal, and they do this job supremely well. But the important thing to say is I was totally ignorant of the way we went about it, of the departmental responsibilities and how the department went about it.

After a very short time the head of the Civil Service gives you a piece of paper saying these are your responsibilities. That took about a fortnight and we had big discussions and I was given my responsibilities – the control of public spending with responsibility in terms of taxation. Overall the Chancellor is number one so that the whole time you're making decisions you're thinking two things, you're thinking what you think is right and you're thinking what the Chancellor would think is right and it is very rare for there to be a conflict between the two.

You depend on your private secretary and I was very

fortunate. He was absolutely superb and other people are going to say they were worried about the problem of the switch of Civil Service loyalty but let me tell you there was no question over the whole of the six years I was doing my job, no question whatsoever. I don't believe there is any strong minister who is entitled to complain about disloyalty among his civil servants, they are superb. My private secretary told me all that went on. He started off by saying he regarded ministers as very important people. 'May I tell you the sort of things that you'll be required to do?' JACK DIAMOND

✗ When I arrived we had had no communication at all with the Civil Service, unlike today's shadow cabinet members who now, I think, are being briefed on the Civil Service. The two briefs are lying in the office. There isn't a third one for the Liberal Democrats. The two briefs are not dissimilar, but you don't see the one for the Conservatives. You are not allowed to see the papers of the previous administration, so if the same problem reappears and the minister before you had postponed it, you will not see his comments. You will know that he's postponed it, or you will guess that he has, and if you are on good terms with him you might go and talk to him, otherwise you are at the mercy of the Civil Service.

You are very short on legislation. It takes so long to cook up bills in government. You decide you will now instruct draughtsmen. The draughtsmen can take from nine to fifteen months to come up with a bill. Then the poor guy has got to fight for his place because all his comrades have got their bills, and there is a natural rivalry. We had one space, in the '65/'66 session. We inherited some bills, not many, and in '65/'66 there were some gaps I stumbled over. There was one very shy civil servant who had obviously been worn down by years of disappointment at trying to get his bill through. It was the Water and Sewerage Department and his bill was always being turned down. DICKSON MABON

✗ I had big books about everything, about weapons problems, defence, NATO, Far East and so on. Immediately, the moment you're appointed. They're indispensable because there are a lot of detailed facts there is no chance of your knowing in opposition. But as far as policy is concerned, my personal opinion is that, even in defence, an intelligent guy outside government can learn all he needs to know to decide policy. There may be problems on weapons, for example, where you need a lot more information than you can get outside, but the major policy issues you can learn enough if you work at it and I'd been working at it for ten years.

The first job I had to decide, and I think it's the most important single appointment any minister has to make, was the choice of the right private secretary. He's the chap who decides whom you see and what you see. One secret in politics is to try to judge people well and some politicians, even prime ministers, are very bad at that. I didn't accept the chap who was suggested to me. I asked around and I decided to keep on the chap who'd been working for Thornycroft who was very able. By the time he was due to leave, because normally private secretaries only do the job for about two years, I had quite a good idea of the field and I chose a chap called Pat Nairn who got to the very top of the Civil Service later on.   DENIS HEALEY

✗ Jim Callaghan must have got the piece of paper on day one (I only came into the Treasury on day two) showing the fantastic, totally unexpected deficit which was facing us and which determined the whole of our policies from then on. I won't say everything went into reverse but you had to adjust everything to that new hard fact. We shouldn't have been surprised because the talk on the Labour side before that was that a Labour Party only gets in when the Tories have made such a mess of the financial situation that they are prepared for somebody else to have a go.

It was a terrible mess and really meant that you had to focus all your thoughts long distance as well as short distance on doing something about it. Particularly in the Treasury where I was responsible for public expenditure. The size of the deficit was a complete surprise. The size of it. The fact that there was going to be a deficit was clear but the size of it had not been indicated at all; they had never come clean. There wasn't the same openness in disclosing Treasury figures then as there is now, nothing like it, and there had been no indication that it was anything like that and it was a total shock. It's the only thing that remains deeply ingrained in my mind. It altered all the arrangements; we had great difficulties as you can imagine with social ministers wanting to carry out a social programme against this new background.   JACK DIAMOND

✗ I really don't think that the civil servants had kept their side of the bargain. They had read the manifesto. They knew what Labour's programme was and therefore when the minister appeared they were able to say they had drawn up this paper – 'Minister, there may be differences you do not appreciate,' this kind of thing – and that side was done, but it was the ignorance on the side of the incoming ministers that was really pretty horrific. Being a minister very soon separates the men from the boys. You can tell almost instantly who's going to be a success and who's going to be a failure.

I think that from day one Barbara Castle, who had what is in many ways a very simple ministry, ODA, was going to be a success. Somebody like Tom Fraser with Transport, absolutely no good from the word go; Soskice, the Home Office, absolutely no good from the word go. Antony Greenwood was really pathetic: attractive, popular at conference, a left-winger, but they found him out. Office does tend to do that. I hesitate to say much about Dick Crossman. Dick was in some ways a very bad minister but I certainly think he was a strong minister and I think he took a hold in his department. He may have made terrible mistakes but he was certainly the best Minister of Housing and Local Government they had in that period of six years, even though he may not have been a glorious success.

Other people who I suppose were pretty good were Roy Jenkins and Dennis Healey. Fred Willey was an absolute disaster. A very sweet man but I remember going to see him at Gwydir House, Whitehall. He really hadn't got a clue, poor chap. He'd been landed this absolute dog's breakfast of a ministry and he didn't know what was going on. It was a total shambles. That was an indictment of not doing your homework before coming into government. We had all this nonsense of the Land Commission and development tax but it just hadn't been thought out and it was never made to work. The ministry was closed down in 1968.   TONY HOWARD

✗ I think the Labour Party in this election is trained for government in a way that we were not, and could not be in 1964. In 1964 only Harold Wilson and Patrick Gordon Walker had previously been in a cabinet and of course Patrick Gordon Walker sadly didn't last very long. None of the rest of us had ever been in government. To some extent that is the same now but there are very big differences. In those days we had no research assistants. In those days there were no select committees within the parliamentary system. Nowadays Labour MPs, whether they are on the front-bench or not, are accustomed in select committees to cross-examining ministers and civil servants.

In our time you weren't allowed to get near civil servants, there was a great *cordon sanataire*. I don't think I ever knew civil servants closely until I walked into the Foreign Office as a brand new inexperienced minister in 1964. Now the Labour Party is much better equipped to face the possibilities of government. They'll still find it very strange. It is a lot easier to be in opposition than it is to face the decisions of government but I think they are much better equipped for it now than we were in 1964.   GEORGE THOMSON

X I quickly discovered who were the civil servants that could move, and who were the indolent ones, and who were the ones who couldn't care less. It had nothing to do with being anti-Labour or pro-Labour, that had nothing to do with the Civil Service really. Of course there would be natural biases but it doesn't follow that the civil servant who is obviously pro-Labour is going to be the best civil servant available. I remember asking for something and I said to the head of the department, 'Why is it that I'm getting advice from you? Why don't I hear from Ronnie Cram and people I know at the university?' He replied, 'This is the settled view of the department.' I said, 'Do you mean that you've consulted every single civil servant in the department during that short time?' He said, 'Well, not exactly everybody.' I asked him, 'How many principals and under-secretaries and so on are there?' He replied, 'Thirteen.' I said, 'Let's consult the whole thirteen. I want to know all of their views.'

So we called a meeting. This was much against Willie's way of working; if he was having trouble he'd just say, 'Send them to me and I'll knock the hell out of them.' He didn't care what the trouble was, he just was not allowing ministers to be subjected to civil servants. Willie had a healthy disrespect for civil servants. He took it to the point of being personally offensive sometimes, which could be very awkward and there was no need for it, but he did get them into line.

                                                          DICKSON MABON

✘ Some of the old guard really were quite awful. The calibre of a lot of the Labour ministers who came in then was pretty poor – Tony Greenwood, Fred Lee. An awful lot. Callaghan wasn't a bad PM but he was a bloody awful Chancellor. He was a slightly less bad Home Secretary and Foreign Minister and then he was quite a good Prime Minister. Later I went to the Treasury and John Harris, who was Roy's aide, told me, 'I saw a note dated 5 November: "Can somebody please explain how forward market works?" So I presumed that was 5 November 1964, immediately after Jim Callaghan came to office. No it wasn't, it was 5 November 1967, just before he resigned.' He still didn't know how to do it! He just wasn't up to the job. He listened to the wisdom of the City, rather like the man in the pub, and the City was much worse, much less professional than it is now. He never understood the papers before him. One of the mottos in the Treasury was, 'If you've got a bad case you can always appeal to the Chancellor. Anything might happen. He won't understand the issues.' He really was a bloody useless Chancellor.   DICK TAVERNE

✘ Some of the people becoming departmental ministers were quite overawed by Whitehall. You know, the limousine when they had been used to coming to work on the tube. Some were overwhelmed by that. There were certain areas where permanent secretaries may have had an undue influence on the direction of policy. Remember at that time only one or two people took political advisers with them. One of them was Tony Benn. Later on, Ann Carlton went to Local Government. There wasn't this business of political advisers. That all grew up later and became bigger and bigger through the Thatcher administration. Maybe it's necessary with so much inexperience but Whitehall is certainly not going to be able to accommodate all of the people now. I think the Civil Service is still strong enough to be quite obstructionist.   BERYL URQUHART

✘ First of all it became clear that George Brown was going to be a loose cannon whatever job he had, and he was, both as Economic Secretary and when he produced this great National Plan which was worthless really. It was good idea if you could do what it told you to do but only a totalitarian government can plan like that. A democratic one can't.

I still think that the type of plan that George wanted in

which you set targets for various areas of industry doesn't make sense in a democratic society, and particularly in one which was beginning to be even then and is totally now subject to international forces. It was a manifesto commitment but it was a silly one.   DENIS HEALEY

✗ We had the idea of producing, like any good company does, a five-year plan. No company runs without knowing what it's going to do in the future. So, we thought it was a sensible thing to do although nobody had ever done it. The object of the plan was to make quite sure that everyone was in on the decision-making circle. So all these regional bodies had to be in on the decision-making circle. The trade unions had to be in on it, the employers had to be in on it. You couldn't keep anybody out. They all had to be a part of it otherwise it wouldn't work. George suddenly discovered what he thought was going to be an absolutely dead-easy doddle – calling out people anxious to make decisions, people wanting to be in on decision-making – wasn't. George had enormous trouble trying to get the trade unions to come forward to the TUC as a party to the plan. But he got it. He knocked heads together.

It was a problem with his drinking life, because he was having to drink with all these chaps, and these chaps didn't have orange juice and milk for discussions. But he did it. He got the leading industrialists and employers in and he got the trade unions in and he got the government in. So for the first time in our country, you had these three groups setting about putting together a 'National Plan'. I still believe it was right. George tended to believe in the end that we'd made a mistake. I don't think we did. But of course immediately, having got the employers, who were Tory supporters, having got the trade unions, who were now smarting under things they wanted and couldn't have, we had to cut back on the building. So that got kicked out. Within a year or so of it being published it was denigrated and held up to ridicule and the Tory press really really tore it apart.   RON BROWN

✗ I think Jim was not well prepared for the Treasury job and Lloyd did a much better job there than Jim was able to do partly because Jim for virility-symbol reasons was so attached to not letting sterling depreciate at all. But, of course, and this is what I used to argue with my colleagues, devaluation won't work unless you control the unions or the unions have no power. If the unions take in extra wages the inflationary effects of devaluation, then the value of your currency in international trade is no better. I think Michael Stewart was a very good steady minister, what you might call a safe pair of hands, but I think he was a little too influenced by Harold. I think prime ministers have a tendency to want to run foreign policy and are often quite good at it because they don't think the people they have to negotiate with are after their job. Wilson had persecution mania as far as domestic issues were concerned; he thought everybody was after his job and of course he was right about Jim Callaghan. DENIS HEALEY

✗ A number of outside advisers came in and contributed very greatly. Balogh was actually in No.10 and had direct access to the Prime Minister. The Civil Service swallowed that with great reluctance but they had to. Nicky Kaldor came into the Treasury and among his many ingenious proposals was the Selective Employment Tax. Nicky was one of the most creative men I've ever come across. He really was a marvellous economist and a great help to us. So was Tommy, who at No.10 helped to organise quite a group of academic economists who had sort of been seconded from various universities and who were helping to produce economic advice which was a supplement and sometimes an alternative to what the official advice was. PETER SHORE

✗ I will never forget, on election night of 1964, seeing the pictures from the Adelphi Hotel in Liverpool, and there glued to Harold's shoulder was the ominous visage of Tommy Balogh. Some of us knew that he would give advice that was bound to cause trouble with the Civil Service. Very unlike Nicky Kaldor who was well received in the Treasury, full of good ideas. Many of the best ideas that the Labour government had came from Nicky Kaldor – for instance, the Regional Employment Premium and the Selective Employment Tax – and Kaldor was very tactful when it came to the civil servants who, anyhow, regarded him as one of the great economists of the century – which he was. Tommy Balogh was another matter, he was not well received in the Civil Service and that was a disaster. He also occupied an unconscionable amount of prime-ministerial time. As, indeed, did George Wigg. George

Wigg used to ring Crossman every morning, right from the start in '64. I stayed in Vincent Square and we would just be ready and the bloody telephone would go and here was Wigg on, recounting at length the forty minutes he'd just had with the Prime Minister. The Prime Minister couldn't even get his breakfast because Wigg was in. It really was a serious problem and Harold was very bad at saying, 'Boo.'   TAM DALYELL

✘ I came away from No. 10 and went straight from there to 8 St James. A minister! Jesus! I thought, we've done it, we're here! and I went straight up and was met by my private secretary who said, 'The Minister would like to see you.' There was Ray. I said 'Well, Ray, this is fantastic.' 'It's good to have you, boy. Very pleased to have a good trade-union lad.' I said to him, 'Well, what do you want me to do to start, it's all new to me,' and he looked at me and he said, 'Damn, boy, I haven't even found out who makes the bloody tea in this place yet. I don't know any more about it than you do.'

This was literally how we started. We had all these little working parties but, looking back on it, it was a farce. We didn't know how the machine worked at all. Harold had given me specific responsibility for manpower planning and industrial training. Ray's only advice to me, it wasn't advice it was a command, he said, 'I want us to be quite clear, boy, that in no circumstances will you get involved in industrial relations. That is my field. Any other paper, boy, that you can take, that's fine.'   RICHARD MARSH

✘ They didn't want to know about Harold's political staff and of course there had never been a political office there before. That's something that I started when I got there because Harold had strong views that a leader of his party when he becomes Prime Minister must remember those dual roles and keep them going and maintain them, relaying things back to the party so the party would understand what he was doing and could have access to him through his political office. That's why we set up the political office.

That was a battle because one had to get the room to sit in first and then there was a terrific struggle where you put the rest of your staff and in the end you got them into a housekeeper's room or cook's room or somewhere you could manage to find places; and then they didn't want you to use the notepaper with No.10 printed in black on it, they made us, *made us*, have it reprinted in red so that when we sent a letter out across Whitehall they'd know that this was the mark of Cain.

We were not happy bunnies in there I can tell you. We felt under siege. We felt we weren't very welcome. Harold knew that his staff were unhappy and that didn't help him. Then all his ministers were busy finding their way round because most of them had never been in a Department of State before and it's one thing for people to tell you what it will be like and sit with you outside a Department of State and say you will do this and that – it's not how it works when you get in there. There are specific items that you have to make decisions on and plans to be put into operation, and if you don't know how you stand or whether you are doing it right or wrong or whether it's going to meet the requirements of your cabinet colleagues and your party, it can get very difficult. MARCIA WILLIAMS

✘ My particular interest at the time was the nuclear deterrent and the possibility of setting up some serious organisation to deal with arms control because I didn't think it was being treated particularly seriously in the Ministry of Defence where arms control and disarmament were regarded as being hostile concepts to the whole business of defending a country and there was hardly recognition of the issue at all in the Foreign Office. How you conduct a foreign policy without a defence content is beyond me. I'm not suggesting that the Foreign Office was ignorant of defence matters. It had a department dealing with defence but it had very little intellectual effort going into that grey area between defence and foreign policy which is to do with arms control and disarmament.

At first there was a certain amount of suspicion as to what I was going to be up to, but they regarded it as a normal Minister of State appointment. They regarded the term Minister of Disarmament as a piece of political PR. I think, with hindsight, you can say that it was. There was never really any idea of my being the minister to preside over the reduction of our own military potential. What I was meant to do was to represent the United Kingdom in the disarmament negotiations in Geneva in what was then called the Eighteen Nations Disarmament Committee and on the first political committee in the United Nations. For the Foreign Office this seemed to be a routine piece of diplomacy. They didn't regard it as anything very startling. But they wondered whether I was going to bring any new ideas, which they were always slightly wary of because they thought that new ideas in diplomacy and foreign policy should originate in the Foreign Office not outside. But they very soon got used to me. They accepted me.

ALUN CHALFONT

X Later when I came back from an overseas trip, I got a message would I go immediately to No.10. It was one of those dream calls. I went to see Harold and he puffed his pipe and said, 'I've got a challenge for you, boy,' and I said, 'Challenge? Good.' He said 'I want you to become Parliamentary Secretary to the new Ministry of Technology.' I said, 'What?! Frank Cousins is a wild left-wing trade-union official and C. P. Snow's a bloody novelist!' He said, 'That's why I want you to go there, because we have got to have a parliamentarian there to set up a brand new ministry.'

Frank's first meeting was with a table. He had one table, a permanent secretary, a private secretary, and a remit to set up the Ministry of Technology. When it was eventually wound up I think it had 37,000 employees. If you put your mind to it you can create anything, but you had this situation where Frank loathed the House of Commons, couldn't handle it, didn't like it, it wasn't anything like he'd expected. C. P. Snow spent the whole time, when he wasn't asleep after lunch, having meetings with all these industrialists who loved an invitation to come and have lunch there, after which he went to sleep.

RICHARD MARSH

X I came to London and I got a message two days later from Fred Peart who had just become Labour's Minister of Agriculture, Fisheries and Food. He asked for me as his PPS. I said, 'I don't even know my way from the Members' Entrance to the Strangers' Bar, never mind knowing my way about the House,' but within two days I was PPS to the Minister of Agriculture, Fisheries and Food, who was taking over from Christopher Soames. He said to me, 'Find out where the Sergeant at Arms is, get the key to Room 56 on the ministerial floor. That's my room. When you get in the room pick up the phone on the desk and it will come straight through to me in Whitehall Place, the ministry.' They gave Soames that room because Churchill was then very heavily disabled and they'd put him in what was about the best room in the House of Commons in terms of access to the chamber. Fred pointed out that if you become a PPS you have virtually your own room because he only used that room to 'hang his coat in'. So after four days in Parliament I had Churchill's room. Lady Churchill said, 'We've been here all this century. Please thank Mr Peart, because always before they would just have thrown our things out.' She gave me a box of these Havana cigars. I didn't smoke. So Fred was smoking himself to death for a few weeks.

ALFRED MORRIS

✘ When I walked into my room, this all-English figure as he was rose from his chair and said, 'Minister, we've been waiting for you. Allow me to greet you on your first day in office.' I said, 'Thank you very much. Who are you?' He said, 'I am Sir John Lang, your principal adviser.' He said, 'I've got a few files here you might like to read tonight in bed and I'll come back in the morning and perhaps have a talk with you.' They were the thickest files I've ever seen in my life, about three files filled with stuff about the World Cup and things like that. He said, 'I have, of course, been reading all your speeches in opposition. And I know that you are committed to having a sports council.' I said, 'That's right.' He said, 'I hope I may be permitted, sir, to have three weeks to put the arguments to the contrary before you reach any such decision.' So I said, 'Oh no, you can't have three weeks. We've got to get a move on. You can have two weeks.' A fortnight later my secretary said, 'You're due to see Sir John tomorrow to discuss this sports council. I've been able to secure an advance copy of his paper. I thought you might like to read it over lunch.' So I read these two pages of argument as to why we shouldn't have a sports council. Sir John came the next morning. And I said, 'Notwithstanding all the excellent arguments in your paper, I've decided in fact that we're going to have a sports council.' 'Very good, sir,' he said. 'In that case allow me to tell you the best way to proceed in the matter.' Which is a classic example of how the Civil Service ought to operate and the relationship that ought to exist. DENIS HOWELL

✘ Ministers don't go into a department and suddenly invent legislation. They go into a department and there are always at least three or four major issues which are on their way. In most areas you are changing the direction and the emphasis, you are not changing the method of governing the country and we had so many things going on. We had this wafer-thin majority which was very vulnerable at any time and nearly went down over the steel nationalisation. We had this continuing battle over Polaris and nuclear deterrents and a number of these other issues. The National Executive was split. There was a personality split. I have never worked in such an unpleasant atmosphere in my life. People loathed each other, a hatred which you don't meet in any other business because there isn't any other business to go to. Anywhere else you say, 'Stuff you,' and you go and work for the other widget engineering manufacturer. There is only one Labour Party and one Parliament. So everybody who is sitting at your level is a threat in the real world.　　　　　　　　　　　　　RICHARD MARSH

✘ In January when he became the Secretary of State for Education the psychological difference was fantastic. Education was the mainspring for the greater equality that he believed was necessary for the well-being of this country as well as for individuals. He was in a position to change policy. As a number two you can do your best to influence the number one and he was probably frustrated as well being in an economic department that was crippled by not having devaluation. This was a daily problem because if you couldn't surmount it how the hell did you deal with it. Whereas when you went to education you were focused then on something where everything that you do isn't already obviously crippled by devaluation. So he could stop thinking for some of the time about it; he never stopped thinking about it on the whole because he went on writing those papers and Harold Wilson later said of Tony in cabinet, 'The Secretary of State had muddied the waters,' when Tony had raised the question of devaluation.　　　　　　　　　　　　　SUSAN CROSLAND

✘ There were very few chocolate soldiers in 1964. John Harris, now Lord Harris, was really brought into the Foreign Office originally by Gordon Walker, being the last of the old Gaitskellites, and he hung around in the Foreign Office, though never happy, with Michael Stewart. Then, as soon as Roy became Home Secretary, Harris happily moved in with him. But I think Harris is about the only person who was a political aide and for that reason he was very deeply resented, especially in the Foreign Office.   TONY HOWARD

✘ I said, 'One of the things to make absolutely clear, I've got to start from somewhere and I would like you to fix a level of briefing. We have to take this documentation which consists of party documents on these areas of policy and work our way from there; its going to take some time.' He said, with a cynical lifted curl of the lip, which only Wykehamists or Scottish intellectuals are capable of, 'Well that's very helpful, Parliamentary Secretary, but I've already got all those documents, and I've got these few papers that I think you would find interesting to read through.' They had done their analysis of the whole document six months earlier and he said, 'This is your private secretary, a very well-informed young man, and he will do anything you want, he will lay on anything. I really would suggest that you spend some time working your way through these papers and then I will introduce you to all the rest of the people in the departments.' I remember he said, 'Yours are rather brief, if I may say so.'

They had done costings for the Treasury. I rang Douglas Houghton, who was co-ordinating social policy. I said, 'Douglas, I don't know where to start because, looking at just the conclusions, we will never be able to afford it.' 'Well, old boy, you've learnt lesson one,' and I said, 'What's that?' and he said, 'It's your responsibility to make up your mind what you do yourself,' and he laughed and he said, 'If I were you, the thing to do is go through it. These guys are much more experienced than anybody else you are going to meet. They really understand what they are saying. Then get as near to the documentation as you can, certainly in the introductory words and the conclusions.'

That opened up this new machine which was very efficient. We had had no serious contact with the machine at all. Indeed we had entered with a lot of naïve prejudice, that all these guys were closet Conservatives desperately anxious to get us out of office, when in fact of course they were intensely nervous because they had not dealt with this Labour Party directly. They desperately wanted the minister to succeed because their careers were latched to him. If they have got a dumb-bell it doesn't help them shine. They will work all night. I've never been anywhere where you sort of look at your watch around seven o'clock and say I think it's getting a bit late tonight and off you go and they say, 'Well we can't because, after you go, we've got some serious work to do.'   RICHARD MARSH

✖ No one would give us anywhere to work, we had to fight our way into every room. Looking back, at the time I assumed that it was (and I still think this was a strong element) that after thirteen years of being with Conservatives and working so closely with them the advent of a Labour Government was something that was not really palatable or nice – they didn't like the thought of all these socialists coming in and taking over the building and there was an atmosphere. Usually you are clapped in when you win an election. Staff line up and clap you in. When we went in in '64 no one clapped us in because no staff lined up. When we went in in 1966 with a ninety-six majority they clapped us wildly, because ninety-six is much better than five. Five is not good and, thinking back on it, five is so bad that I wouldn't wish it upon anyone.

Civil servants are judging, how stable? how long? Looking at us they might have thought, 'Well, these people might not be here more than a couple of months so we might have to do it all again and then our former people will be back and we might have done some awful things and get into trouble,' so they remained neutral. I don't think they were hostile but they were not going to move, their faces were expressionless; it was an unpleasant atmosphere; no one will convince me other than the way I remember it – it was cold, unfriendly and not very helpful.

You are walking into a monastery, in No.10 terms, the moment you go through that door; the silence is the first thing that strikes you, almost as if there is nothing happening and there is no one there. Exactly like it is in a monastery or a convent, and it's very intimidating. If you go into a religious house at least there is an air of godliness, an air of spirituality about it, but in there it is quite threatening, that silence, because you are not quite sure what is going on behind all the closed doors that you are walking past. And you quickly find out that it's not as happy and pleasant as you thought it would be. The campaign was so exciting, it was a crusade. We were going to get Britain moving again, we were going to change the face of Britain. We were going to get working men represented.

Suddenly you enter a door and it shuts behind you and you can't just say, 'Help let me out!' you're there and you make the best of a bad job and you try and work out day to day what you are going to do. I regard myself as a sort of pioneer. I had to trailblaze for them and I had to suffer an awful lot of indignity and a lot of insults along the way. Nevertheless, my political office is still there, it's still functioning and nobody's said we don't need it. They kept it and I think it's been one of the most valuable things that's happened at Downing Street.

Harold was brought up in the cloistered atmosphere of Oxford; he'd been an Oxford don, he'd taught at University College and New College; he'd been in the cabinet office which itself has a cloistered atmosphere. So he knew he was going to feel like that and he therefore was not fazed by it. But we didn't know it was going to be like that. We didn't think it would be quite so cold and so quiet. MARCIA WILLIAMS

✗ Harold Wilson said to me, 'I want you to be responsible for regional development.' So I was not dealing with the mainstream economic issues. It was absolutely fascinating to see what was called the 'creative tension' between George Brown and Jim Callaghan. I remain one of those who believes that the DEA was a good idea, but I'm in a minority, not quite of one. There was a concordat agreed with the Treasury and I think there were many ways in which the DEA did a good job. The things that people look back on the DEA for are things like the National Plan which was undermined before we began to prepare it by the decision not to devalue. But where I found the DEA made an important contribution was in another way. The Treasury was concerned with short-term economic policy. The job of the DEA in respect of both the National Plan and regional planning was to take a much longer view and we were represented at virtually every cabinet committee. George's policy was that we should be on every committee which the Treasury was on and this had very interesting results because in bilateral talks with the Treasury a spending department came away with perhaps, if it was lucky, one third of what it wanted. We were now there and made it trilateral. We took a long view. Sometimes we agreed with the Treasury but sometimes we agreed with the department. Wherever we put our weight, the decision was made. BILL RODGERS

✗ George had to set up the DEA to carry out the policy that had been agreed. In those days people at the top who were doing all the decision-making didn't necessarily tell everyone down below what the total score was. When George tried to set up a department he had a row with Jim. Jim had gone into the Treasury and anyone who goes into the Treasury becomes a big man looking at the wall, seeing all the great Treasurers of years gone by. Jim succumbed to that kind of thing and, rather sadly, he started attacking George on the economic thing. George had his new department in Storey's Gate and the title of First Secretary for Economic Affairs, identifying him as the deputy to Wilson as well as Secretary of State for Economic Affairs.

The Treasury didn't like it. The Treasury felt, and in a way rightly so, that there was an attack upon their autonomy and they would no longer be totally in charge of the economic issues. Therefore there was war. The troops get to know this, and everyone will then take sides. So you've got the pro-Callaghans, you've got the pro-Browns. If you're running a Labour government, that really isn't the best thing. In fact, the little man loved to see this going on. It suited him fine and whichever day it was, Tuesday he was supporting George and on Wednesday he was supporting Jim. So life was all right for him.   RON BROWN

✗ The DEA was very troublesome and invented by Wilson to make sure that George Brown and Jim Callaghan, who he quite rightly regarded as the two people who might have toppled him, would always be at each other's throats. He called it, or had the impertinence to call it, 'creative tension'. I never understood how that was going to work out if it goes on day by day, week after week, but it was done deliberately.

A job had to be found for George and it was originally going to be called the Ministry of Production and at some stage the title was changed to the Department of Economic Affairs, which meant a much greater threat to the Treasury. A Ministry of Production you can deal with if you're Treasury, but not a Department of Economic Affairs. So I think it was doomed. The Treasury set out to kill it from the beginning. I got into trouble once writing an article in the *Sunday Times* called 'Clash has been arranged', or something. All hell was let loose because I think I quoted one or two mandarins saying that this thing ought to be strangled at birth. Effectively it's what they did. I think it was bad luck on George that very early on he lost Tony Crosland who I think might have managed to form a bridge with the Treasury economists. He took in his place someone like Austin Albu who wasn't in the same kind of category at all, and also he wasn't terribly lucky with his civil servants. They tended to be blowers and not doers and they weren't up to much. TONY HOWARD

✗ I had no guidance. When it was government policy it was nothing to do with me. I had no connection whatever except that I was working in the building and knew what was happening and had to be told for the purposes of political liaison. I didn't have any role within the private office in that sense. My work was to make sure that the link with the Labour Party was preserved, that MPs, when they wanted, could have access to the Prime Minister and could come and complain as they had in his eighteen months as Leader of the Opposition. This was something Gaitskell had never done, Gaitskell did not have an open-door policy for MPs. Harold had a totally open-door policy. They could wander in and if he was not free then they were given a time to come back and see him. They were never refused. We wanted to keep that going afterwards, so that they had the same feeling of being able to approach him, and we wanted to make sure that the party could too. So I organised all of that. I actually got a new room equipped and fitted out in the House of Commons so that it could be done in the Palace of Westminster as well without having the Civil Service take over and not knowing people keep them out.

One of the problems for the Civil Service in a takeover is that they are very familiar with the party in government but they are not at all familiar with the people in opposition so when a whole lot of new faces start turning up they turn them away. They say things like, 'This funny man came in today . . . ' and you discover it is the chairman of the Parliamentary Labour Party who's just been sent packing. MARCIA WILLIAMS

✗ I was rather surprised and shocked at how much I succumbed to the infantile disease of departmentalitis. But such things are inevitable when one has been in the House a long time and never been in office, and it so happened that Aviation produced a vast amount of attention-attracting issues. So I was very very occupied with these right through that winter, particularly in the first two months or so. I hardly had time to draw breath from mid-October well through into late November or early December.   ROY JENKINS

✘ I once asked Harold, in 1965, what it was like to be Prime Minister. He said, 'It's much easier being Prime Minister than Leader of the Opposition, and it's much easier to be Leader of the Opposition than Shadow Chancellor.'   TAM DALYELL

✘ We had great opportunities. It was the last chance for opportunities really. There'd been this managed decline of the British Empire and the state of Britain and there was a feeling that this really was it. We'd seen the European Community countries going up and so although we had a standard of living which was higher at that time than that of almost any other country in the Community we were now perceiving this was under threat. Our superiority, which we'd taken for granted for a couple of centuries, was beginning to be questioned. We'd seen expansion in other economies and we weren't getting that. So there was a feeling that things had gone so bad that we really had to take a grip on the whole thing. People were prepared at that time to take all sorts of unpleasant short-term actions in order to overcome those particular problems. There was a mood for really tough action. So I was looking forward to a great expansion in manufacturing industry. The white heat of technology was what it was all about. You could have done things then.   ROBERT SHELDON

CHAPTER FIVE

To Govern is to Campaign

		1964					1965			
	Nov	Dec	Jan	Feb	Mar	Apr	May	June	July	Aug
Lab.	50	50	42	39	39	40	36	35	36	33
Con.	39	40	35	41	37	34	37	40	40	42
Lead	+11	+10	+7	-2	+2	+6	-1	-5	-4	-9

(all polls from Gallup)

Election victory brought two immediate problems. An exhausted party came out of a thirteen-year opposition to face an unprecedented balance-of-payments deficit and a consequent collapse of confidence in sterling. It did so without the majority to govern for any length of time. Labour had received only a first instalment on real power. Another election was essential and soon. The economic crisis had to be tackled in the light of that. Labour succeeded brilliantly at its political task but failed in its economic ones, in each case for the same reason. They tested the strengths and weaknesses of the new prime minister.

Harold Wilson's skills were political. Ever resilient, ever active, ever calculating, and master of the media, he was in his element and played the game like a master. A hundred days of dramatic action and announcements began, despite the precarious majority – which became more so after the loss of the Leyton by-election in the attempt to bring Patrick Gordon Walker back into the House, and the selection of a Labour member, Horace King, as Speaker. The 'hundred days' ended on 24 January 1965 with a majority down to three.

Government skated on as vigorously as if the ice were two feet thick. Decisions, a constant stream of announcements, news, visits, activity and initiatives kept government in the headlines and on the box. An opposition bereft of the authority of power was constantly outwitted as it embarked on its own reappraisals and leadership change. To take on Wilson there emerged his grammar-school conterpart: Edward Heath of Heath & Co.

✘ Harold Wilson was a brilliant politician, but we never quite regarded him as much on the left, and when he resigned with Nye many of us were rather surprised. He managed the leadership of the party with great skill and he led us into the '64 election with great skill. I think if we hadn't had him as the leader we very likely wouldn't have won. But his greatest political trick, his accomplishment, was how he conducted the party in the House of Commons between '64 and '66, preparing for the great victory of a hundred – nearly a hundred – almost restoring Labour's position to what it had been in 1945, not quite. Harold Wilson deserves I think a great deal of credit for that. I thought he was going to be able to translate those qualities into a full-scale Labour Party government that was going to do work comparable to that done by the 1945 government.   MICHAEL FOOT

✘ I think looking back there was a feeling amongst a lot of my colleagues that we were, I won't say a caretaker government because that would give the wrong impression, but people felt that it wouldn't be long before there would have to be another attempt to gain a proper working majority. You couldn't go on like that. Ministers couldn't go abroad and the government couldn't properly be conducted with a majority of that kind. So I think there was a feeling that it was going to be a very short time before we went to the country again. I don't think it had much effect on morale. I think everybody was still fairly euphoric over having won the election and everybody was confident that we could win another and win it better. So morale was good.   ALUN CHALFONT

✗ We did carry out important pledges fairly quickly. We carried out the pledge to old people. We did quite a bit on the social causes. We were in a much better position after Jim Callaghan's first budget in the spring of 1965. In Harold Wilson's first hundred days he believed that little things meant a lot. There's a great deal governments can do at no great expense, and sometimes you may get as much publicity from the mass media for introducing a nil-cost measure as you'd get for introducing something big. Wilson believed that there were some very small measures that could attract a great deal of publicity.   ALFRED MORRIS

✗ Doing the popular things first was very much what Wilson wanted to do and this alas set the alarms bells ringing among the Gnomes of Zurich. The result of doing that and one or two other things, like bringing on the pension, was the tremendous run on the pound. Therefore we had the fifteen-per-cent import surcharge in flagrant defiance of the rules of GATT. That was imposed very much against the advice of Douglas Jay who was then President of the Board of Trade. This was entirely a Labour invention. There was some argument with Maudling saying here is a remedy we could take if the pound goes on tottering and there was a Treasury paper saying this was a possible remedy, but basically Labour did it straightaway. We had to stem the haemorrhage on sterling. The only way to do it was to say if you're going to have a French cheese it's going to cost you fifteen per cent more. The rules of GATT in those days expressly prohibited this kind of thing. What we did was illegal under international agreement and against the rules of the club. We made ourselves terribly unpopular. It was just an effort to try and prevent the balance of trade looking so terrible.   TONY HOWARD

✗ We started with his 'first hundred days' and each day there was a separate announcement so that although you weren't actually doing things the announcements were coming day after day, right up to the hundredth day, new announcements of initiatives and policy proposals. It was a great way of keeping going the excitement of the new government during that fallow period when you are getting your bills drafted. There is always a shortage of drafting lawyers in government, it's something that you tend not to think about. Drafting lawyers are a scarce resource. So an incoming government with all its bills and all its priorities is actually going to find that the more complex the legislation it wants to bring forward the longer it's going to take just to get it drafted.

ALAN WILLIAMS

✖ Harold took over on a disappointingly small majority, thinking and scheming how he could make a go of the country and get a bit more of a majority. He said, I think at the first cabinet, how we all us had got to think in terms of an early election. Everything we do must be geared to that.

BARBARA CASTLE

✖ We had to keep up the pressure, with a majority of five. We had to have political rallies and meetings around the country on almost the same scale as we had when he was in opposition in '63. So that had to be organised, his journeys around the UK had to be organised and we were landed with a lot of girls from No.10 who came as his secretaries to do his official work who were not fully-paid-up members of the Labour Party and the fully-paid-up members of the Labour Party who came to talk to him would be sent packing because these people wouldn't recognise them. If there was a trade union they certainly wouldn't recognise it.

In that short period between those two elections I was very nervous that we would lose ground if we couldn't keep the connecting link between us; I was very anxious. We took people with us on that campaign round the country. We would know everybody in the local Labour Party and would know whom to contact and made sure the MP knew and would keep up the liaison and it was hard work and I don't think I had easier hours until after 1966. We had no press officer. We had Lloyd Hughes as his official press officer but that was with government information. Those two roles were never allowed to run together. I handled it all until Gerald Kaufman arrived like the cavalry in the middle of 1965, and I heaved a sigh of relief because by that time I was non-stop running hither and thither. Even down to being in charge of family weddings. It was non-stop and I was very relieved when Gerald came. Gerald then took over that side of things. MARCIA WILLIAMS

"... THE GOVERNMENT IS TAKING TOUGH, UNPOPULAR DECISIONS WITHOUT THOUGHT OF ELECTORAL GAINS" — MR WILSON, MAY 12.

✗ Harold was very clear-eyed on winning the next election. He also had an enormous confidence that we would. We thought we would. Harold insisted that people went out on stump around the country, cabinet ministers, everybody. That we did concentrate on.   RICHARD MARSH

✗ The first Queen's Speech had promised an awful lot of commitments to an awful lot of people; basic rate of retirement pension was raised straightaway and so were a lot of other benefits. We had brought all the old workman's compensation cases on a par with industrial injuries benefits. There were a whole load of commitments that were made an early priority. Income tax had been raised by sixpence in the pound in Jim Callaghan's first budget, two and a half pence in today's terms. Harold had had this first one hundred days' programme and there was a feeling that there was a surge – that there was something new.   BERYL URQUHART

✗ In the early period we all knew the important thing was to keep the ship afloat and take advantage of any favourable tide to increase our majority. So from '64 to '66 we were focusing in the short term on winning the election we knew was essential if we were going to survive. We assumed there would be an early election. We couldn't assume we would get a majority but the objective would be to get one and we did. Harold was extremely quick on his feet. That was his great virtue and he was a good tactical politician. It was really a tactical situation, a matter of just weaving through events until you got to a situation when you could win, and he chose his time right and he did win. DENIS HEALEY

✗ It wasn't going to be long before there was another general election. Any government, even if it is a minority government, can govern. It may not govern for very long, but it's like a self-sealing tank, our political system. The bullet goes through the tank and makes a hole, but it seals over. You can cope. So I don't think there was any worry. Harold Wilson was regarded in quite a different way from Hugh Gaitskell, as the new type of politician. Whereas, in fact, Harold was the old type of politician, and there is nothing wrong with that. I don't think there was any great feeling of crisis about governing, but there was a realisation that it wasn't going to be long. MERLYN REES

✗ I rated Wilson's short-term leadership as very good and medium-term leadership as fairly bad and his long-term leadership as bloody awful. He had other virtues though. He was jolly good to work for. He was polite. He was considerate and he kept his nerve well in a crisis and on the whole he didn't recriminate when things went wrong. He recriminated with you much more when things went right in your department. He would have had every reason to resent the Gaitskellites because the Gaitskellites were brought up to be very suspicious of him and no doubt he certainly wasn't mad about Gaitskellites as such. But he didn't, to a remarkable extent, discriminate against Gaitskellites in forming his government or in his promotions, and as time went on he became disillusioned more with the left than he did with the Gaitskellites. He was a very pragmatic politician. ROY JENKINS

✗ He was a very clever man and he developed his own parliamentary style. I have a great theory of parliamentary performances. Practice makes perfect! If you are there at prime minister's question time all the time you become good at handling that sort of thing. If you are constantly winding up at 10 o'clock, you turn in a rumbustious performance. You may be good at some other thing where you are at the maximum of performance. Harold's closest personal friend, I mean apart from cabinet people, was John Fulton. Fulton told me about that time that Harold had said to him after the honeymoon period, 'What people don't realise is that I'm the first political prime minister since Lloyd George.' Lloyd George was a manipulator and Harold was a manipulator, a perfectly good tradition, but manipulation only carries you so far and can't provide the basis for leading a country.   JEREMY BRAY

✘ I decided I will visit every large city in Scotland, on Fridays, and I will try to go on Mondays to the counties, thirty-three counties. I did that and it was great, it really went well, having ministers going around hadn't been done for ages. We had one place that hadn't been visited by a minister for the last fifty years. We had a hundred and thirty small boroughs. The others couldn't keep up with me because everywhere I went I was asked about housing, planning, water, sewerage, roads – I was in charge of roads. All these little departments wanted to send somebody with me but they couldn't, they couldn't keep up this pace of every Monday, every Friday, they had to form a deputation of seven, plus the minister, and they couldn't do that.   DICKSON MABON

✘ Immediately '64 was over, as a group we said, 'You've got to start preparing for the next election.' It took us six months to get people to accept that because once you go into a new Parliament you get very busy and people don't really want to know about the next time. We had a majority of just four so we knew there would be another election in the near future. After about six months they agreed and we actually started planning almost immediately for the '66 election. We managed to go round the country and to get the local parties interested in knowing what we were doing. We had done some of that beforehand but not very much.

We did research on what was going on in the local parties. The research indicated that on the whole there were more 'resolutionaries' than revolutionaries in the party. In a lot of local parties we were keeping new, young people out. They were comfortable and they actually liked the process of putting up their resolutions and they had their roles and they didn't want change. So we started before '66 to work in the constituencies to educate people and to help them understand what they needed to do and how they needed to change their organisations. We hadn't been brought in to do that, but we knew if you didn't change the inside you'd never change the way we acted or what we did.

We also managed to get much more linkage with television. We didn't get complete linkage. At that time Tony Benn was chairman of the television group and he was helpful. We managed to start to integrate our messages and what we were doing. We managed to integrate television with the other things that we were doing, and we knew very early on the kind of campaign and the kind of positioning we wanted to get, which was essentially a reassurance to give us more time, to increase the majority and give Labour time to get down to doing the job, because two years wasn't long enough. I think the importance of that '64/'66 period was that there began to be a change in taking election publicity and promotion seriously, and research seriously. That was the beginning of the way things have been running ever since.

DAVID KINGSLEY

✗ We all kept on after the '64 election. One or two people fell away, otherwise we kept right on and I have huge files of all the things we were doing, bringing publications up to date, introducing new publications, trying to organise the local parties, trying to improve – something which a new Labour government has to be very careful about – co-operation between the members of the party; although they've all disappeared into ministries they mustn't just forget Transport House, or the link through Transport House to local parties. It was quite a thing actually to tighten this all up and produce a report on the need to totally restructure Transport House and move it into different premises.

We did organise a whole range of things such as polling within the party. I set up one poll which worked very well although it wasn't continued, using the women's sections as a polling organisation. In '70 it told us we were going to lose! As did Mori. Everyone else said we were going to win. The publicity machine was kept running from '64 to April '66. We never stopped, we were going full steam.

Harold kept as far away as a prime minister has to do. He was really very busy and handling a hell of a lot of things and at that time he did face a terrific task. I'd go down and discuss things, and this would be at twelve o'clock at night or one o'clock in the morning and he was absolutely going full blast while we were all dropping by the wayside. He had enormous energy. As time went on we corresponded through Marcia, his political secretary, but we didn't bypass Transport House. We made sure that they knew what we were doing and we'd take them along with us because we didn't want to antagonise them. It was a pretty rickety organisation and it wasn't difficult to upset people so we had to play it very carefully.

PETER DAVIS

✗ I joined it in '65 which was in the run up to the '66 election which we were all convinced we could win. We had all this thing about when we opened the books we couldn't do this, that and the other but in fact we were spending quite a lot of money I think and we were trying to win the election that followed. There was the most dynamic feeling and there wasn't any of the hatred that there'd been before, the left-right thing had gone, and there was a great love for Harold Wilson as having won us the election. But he was Harold. He wasn't a god, he was Harold, which was different.   ANN CARLTON

✗ Harold wrote his own speeches. During my entire period there nobody but he ever wrote his speeches. I know that Joe Haynes later claims to have written speeches for him and I can't challenge that because I wasn't there in later years, but in all my time with Harold, which was nearly six years, he wrote his own speeches. He would dictate to a relay of typists. They would go out and type it, very laboriously in those days with manual typewriters, and then they would come back and bring him what he'd done and then we'd all go through it and he'd sit down and correct it in his own handwriting in the green ink which he'd always used ever since he was President of the Board of Trade.   ·   GERALD KAUFMAN

✗ I don't think the opposition was a particular problem. They were demoralised. They had been in thirteen years. They weren't used to living on a parliamentary back-bencher's salary. So they were looking for jobs outside. They weren't the big issue. Our problem was Labour Party members and particularly the majority of three.

I don't have a recollection of being particularly concerned about the Conservative Party. We'd waited so long. We also had the advantage that once you've got the machine you have an enormous advantage because you're the people who set the agenda inside the House. You're better briefed than they are. When you've been in office for thirteen years, and it will happen this time, you have been very used to being spoon-fed and you suddenly find that the other guy's got the briefing that you used to have and you can't have it because only his department knows what they are going to do. The briefing is pretty impressive. So they will certainly take more than the first twelve months to get their breath back and get used to being in opposition, which is a different world – to do it properly.

RICHARD MARSH

✘ I don't think the Tories were particularly harassing. It was just that every single vote was one were you were living on the edge. Would you get the majority or not? If you had some people sick or away you were in trouble. We had lost the Leyton by-election. That was pretty bad, and then we had the constant economic crisis – 1965, 1966 – and also some very exciting things like George Brown's National Plan. In retrospect that sort of planning is old fashioned and was probably deeply mistaken but it was very exciting stuff at the time.

Postponing problems and stoking up the economy perhaps wasn't justified. I thought we had every chance of winning. Harold was doing a good job. There is no doubt that for Gaitskellites, that period was one where one had mixed feelings. There were questions about him. The man we didn't vote for was a very good opposition campaigner, ran an extremely effective opposition campaign, was the darling of the press, which was right on our side, and then in government handled things very shrewdly in a very tight spot and delivered a great victory. Oh that was very exciting. 1966, you really felt you were going to win. I thought we were going to win by a hundred seats and we damn nearly did, ninety-seven majority or something. I was much more nervous about the '64 election than the '66. We had everything going for us and Ted Heath wasn't a very effective leader. In opposition Douglas-Home wasn't either, so they exchanged him for Heath, but

Heath was such a wooden figure. Harold was a great success. So we all had to acknowledge that Harold was really rather good.   DICK TAVERNE

✗ In August of '65 I was invited to interview Harold Wilson. My previous attempts to interview him had been very laborious, but on this occasion I was actually invited to interview him. So I went along to No. 10 Downing Street and at the end of the interview he asked me to come and join his staff as political press officer. I was in some doubt as to whether to do that because the Labour majority of five had fallen to three because of the loss of the Leyton by-election the previous January. Labour were behind in the opinion polls and it didn't seem to me all that attractive a prospect to exchange what seemed to be a secure and interesting job for something that might be very insecure.

I was surprised at how small the political office was and how hand to mouth. There were very few people. There was Marcia Williams, one of the most brilliant people I've ever come across in my life, with an absolutely razor-edge brain in terms of political understanding, and she had a couple of shorthand typists. That was the political office and she'd fought like absolute hell to get that. All prime ministers, Labour and Conservative, who have come after have had political offices, and owe the ease with which they have been able to establish those offices to Marcia. She fought like a tiger, not only to have a political office but for the location of her own office next to the cabinet room, because the Prime Minister at that stage didn't have the study in No. 10 that Macmillan had and that Harold Wilson restored. He used to use the cabinet room as his office.

There was this very small operation. There was no catering or anything like that. If you were going to stay and have any kind of meeting with the Prime Minister the only food that would be available would be that Harold's housekeeper would scramble some eggs or something like that, and when we went through the 'beer and sandwiches' phase, when Harold was dealing with strikes by the railwaymen, etc., we had actually to send out for a sandwich. I was isolated. Marcia wasn't isolated, but I was very isolated. They wouldn't have me as part of the No. 10 staff. Derek Mitchell, who was the Prime Minister's private secretary, with whom I later became very friendly, made it absolutely clear that I was not welcome on the premises.

I was put into a room that was technically a part of the Prime Minister's flat because they had no control over that. They refused to allow me to have a No. 10 telephone, I had to have a House of Commons extension brought in; they refused to let me have access to 10 Downing Street paper. Derek Mitchell came in one day and saw a rack with 10 Downing Street paper (which I hadn't put there or asked for) and he picked it up and took it away with him. It was only towards the end of my period there, during the last few months, that I was allowed access to cabinet papers of any kind, and those were kept in a special tray in the Prime Minister's private office and I could go in and look at them there, but not take them away. This was by about 1969. Later prime ministers wouldn't have accepted any of that kind of nonsense, but Harold was very orthodox, very meticulous in abiding by the constitutional niceties, something which later prime ministers didn't seem so bothered about.   GERALD KAUFMAN

✘ We didn't feel temporary, I certainly didn't. I did say to my officials in '64 that this government can't last long, there's got to be another election, and I said I intend to achieve something during the lifetime of this government. In 1964 it was self-evident, it was the World Cup. I said, 'We're going to organise the World Cup,' and of course we did and it was a great success. The publicity is what the government wants.

DENIS HOWELL

✘ I was involved with keeping public expenditure down to agreed figures, which is hell in a Conservative government, and being Chief Secretary in a Conservative government is like falling off a log compared to being Chief Secretary in a Labour government. The pressures were just enormous. Especially the pressures for all social spending – for pensions, all those sort of things. They ran away with huge sums. We didn't start off with cutting. We started at too high a rate and had to cut later on. I've no doubt that Harold had planned an early general election to improve his majority from the beginning. I didn't discuss that with him but no doubt that's what he had in mind. So we had to make sure that the sort of thing that would cause one hell of a bust up in the headlines of all the newspapers didn't occur. We were under considerable political restraints because of the financial situation.

So it was a battle the whole time – a hard, hard battle. Whenever I had a disagreement I had to take my disagreement to cabinet. I wasn't a cabinet minister but that was the drill. So before I became a cabinet minister I was on average at every other cabinet meeting, sometimes three in a row, but that's how the average turned out. It was endless confrontation, trying to keep the lid of the kettle on. It wasn't difficult for me to know what I thought was right. If you're an accountant you can add up and that's all that's required, and at some point or other it goes over the top and there isn't the money there. The taxation figures have been agreed. That's the Chancellor's responsibility and you've got to work within that.

At a very early stage we had to reinvent the idea of a separate minister, a senior minister, taking the chair over a meeting at which the Treasury and the departmental chiefs would all assemble and put their various claims and try and agree a figure, as is done now regularly, but that was the first occasion that it was done and George was in the chair. After a long long time we got final agreement and then I piped up and made the simple point that in all my experience of business you can make your estimates but its given to no man to know the whole of the future. So you must allow for some contingencies to arise. A reasonable, modest percentage – perhaps 2% or 3%, whatever it is – but there is bound to be slippage. I shall never forget the look on George's face after they'd gone through hell to try and get the thing agreed all round the table.   JACK DIAMOND

✘ I did everything you'd care to name, and a great deal you wouldn't care to name. My main role was communicating with the press because Harold was absolutely punctilious on party political matters. Trevor Hughes, his official political secretary, was not allowed to have anything to do with party political matters. I had to deal with all of that. I had a desk at the House of Commons in the whips' office and I spent a lot of my time in the press gallery. I had to do with everything that Harold did on the Labour Party relating to the press.

Harold would consult me on almost anything political. Marcia and I were his two advisers who were always there. He paid a great deal of attention to what we said, using us as a sounding board but also asking for advice, except on rare occasions when he wanted to conceal from us what he was doing because he knew we wouldn't approve of it. He discussed reshuffles with us at length, and we had a great deal of input into reshuffles. He didn't do it when he appointed David Owen to the government, we read about that on tape, because he knew we would have tried to argue him out of it. I would go with him to his constituency when he did his constituency advice bureaux and other engagements. You name it, I was there to talk about it with him.   GERALD KAUFMAN

✗ There were few barriers between Transport House staff and ministers as there were no political advisers. In a sense those TH research staff with zing became informal political advisers. I was back and forth to ministerial offices. On one occasion I stood in for a junior minister and was given a copy of the departmental briefing – as well as police protection. This close contact between ministers and party machine was very good for morale and continued through to 1970, though by that time some ministers were suffering from ministerialitis – the symptoms: isolation from reality, exaggerated self-importance, too much time being driven round in cars and too little on public transport, and an exaggerated respect for paper rather than people.

Harold was a brilliant leader in the sense that he knew everybody's department better than they did. When I used to go and see him he always threw everything at me, it was like an interrogation as to what was going on so he could keep abreast of things. A great encourager.   TONY BENN

✗ We worked bloody hard at Transport House and there were nowhere near as many people as there are now. If you combine things, there were about a hundred and thirty staff probably, and there were very few staff in the PLP. We really worked hard. The relationship was much better because there wasn't the mistrust, we were all in it together, there were no advisers between MPs and ministers. It was just MPs and their secretaries and a small machine, a very small machine but it was madly dedicated. They were people who really believed in what they were doing in transforming society and weren't in it for anything else. The other thing was we didn't have the technology that we've got now. Photocopying you didn't have.

Things had to go to the printer's and come back in galley proof. Things then had to be checked by ministers. We were still feeling our way on that because we had not done it before. It was incredibly hard work leading up to that election.

ANN CARLTON

✘ Very wisely, Harold Wilson realised that the sensible thing to do was to get some political capital in the bank and win some credit in his first hundred days by things that would please, so that people could see that (a) he'd got a dynamic government (b) that he'd got competent people in charge and (c) that he was determined to fulfil his promises, thus creating the kind of climate which led to that smashing result in 1966.

One of the pledges that we had in the manifesto was to give pensioners an immediate increase. We all thought very strongly that this should be implemented. Margaret Herbison came to the party explaining with great regret that it was administratively impossible to give the pensioners an increase until the following spring. Some of us were very upset about this. So we went to see Peggy, and then we went to see Harold Wilson and eventually it was agreed as an interim measure that we would deliver a one-off Christmas bonus, £10 for all the pensioners that Christmas. Just because of the delay in implementing our election commitment. Of course give it once and it is then expected every year. The second year there was resentment because it was not being paid.   HAROLD WALKER

✘ The main focus of Transport House was on winning the next election and we were pushing out stuff all the time, pumping it out trying to get things done and acres and acres of propaganda and also party political broadcasts. Compared to now they were so true I still can't believe it.

That's what it was about. We'd just got to win the next election and when it came we did. That was partly due to opening the books. Partly it was giving money out and partly it was having a programme of what we'd done. We published a book, *The Go-Ahead Year*, giving each little area of what we'd done, and showing that Labour moves fast, Labour is action. We had this thing about action which went right the way through and right up until the '70 election, when it became Labour in Action, which was rather an unfortunate slogan.

ANN CARLTON

✘ George was put in charge of Prices and Incomes when he didn't actually want to be there. I would never talk about Prices and Incomes. I would only talk about Productivity, Prices and Incomes. What we were saying was, 'If you've earned it you can pay yourself.' But you couldn't get it across because the loony bins in the unions were demanding this, demanding that, and the nice guys wouldn't stand up because there was nothing on the horizon. The government wasn't producing anything. So consequently there was a tendency for the thing to begin to fall apart, basically because of the influence of the trade unions. The good ones were still good. The miners were still good in those days, and were holding the thing. There were still good people around. The other unions were the same but the loony-bin ones were making most noise. Then the MPs got all worried.   RON BROWN

✘ We were very fortunate. We were introducing in our first finance bill two major tax reforms: Capital Gains Tax and Corporation Tax, and I always remember one was known as CAT and one was known as CUT. The two of us handled these two halves of the huge Finance Bill which was introduced in '65. We had to argue that through on the floor of the House; at that point it was not the practice to send detailed taxation provision upstairs. The House wanted to know all about it. So inevitably we had all-night sittings. When it was all over, when the final bill was through, the three of us got up to go and there was a very warm 'Hear, hear' from all the Labour benches, and you remember things like that. They were very supportive of the tax measures and I should say they understood. The pressure wasn't from the back-benchers, the pressure was from the ministers.   JACK DIAMOND

✘ We came in encumbered with the National Plan. I'm not saying there's anything wrong with the concept of planning; obviously the more dissemination of information in an understandable way, the better, but the National Plan proved to be a great albatross. When George drew up the National Plan inevitably it was based on a retrospective snap shot and by the time it was produced it was considerably retrospective. They made projections of growth that it would be 3%. Then they decided that we were going to get more growth because we had a National Plan. So our 3% became 4%. So now we were able to plan ahead in a good socialist way on the basis of 4% growth. So all the spending departments put in 4% programmes and industry in the meantime were churning out 3% growth. There was a certain inexorability about what eventually happened. We then had to start trimming programmes, altering policy and so on over the whole period of government, up to 1970. The National Plan had been well intentioned. If they'd taken the figures on the basis of what it actually was, it might then have been useful. When I went to the DEA I clashed very early on with Sir Douglas Allan, who was our permanent secretary and who then went to the Treasury and became head of the Civil Service, because I said that no major firm could organise its budgets on the basis of a four-year static assessment, and that the only way forward if we were committed to planning was to find a way of updating it.   ALAN WILLIAMS

✗ To lock you out was the way the Civil Service worked. Harold had been a civil servant so he knew this. Mind you, he did allow discussion. He was extremely clever in committee discussion. We had excellent debate on East of Suez, on the question of the F111, even on devaluation. We had very good discussions. If he saw he couldn't get away with something he'd leave it for a week and then come back to it and try to persuade. If he couldn't get his way he'd bombard you with papers from the cabinet office to bog you down. When we were discussing cuts on one occasion, I said, 'Why don't we cut out the Think Tank and think for ourselves.' Not considered a very good show.   TONY BENN

✗ Very early on word came that Jim Callaghan, who was Chancellor of the Exchequer, would welcome the views of some back-benchers and I was one of a handful of back-benchers who were invited on two or three occasions to sit down with him over a drink and give him our views about the direction in which we ought to be going and what kind of thing he might include in the budget. Patrick Duffy, Brian Walden, John Macintosh, a number of others and I were included among them. Did he listen? Yes, I think he did.

I can remember other ministers taking us into their confidence. Fred Lee, who was an old mate of mine, was Minister for Energy at the time and Fred was always open to us. There were some ministers who were very aloof and

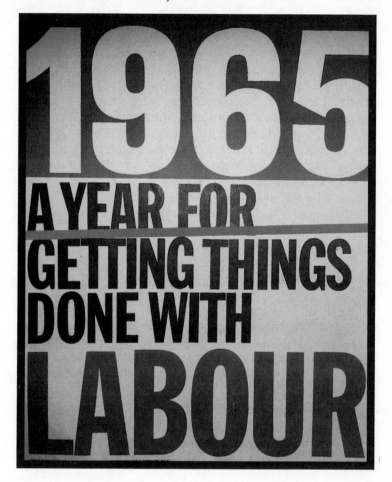

remote with whom you could never have any kind of dialogue; looking back, there were people with whom I never exchanged a word – Neil McDermot, Sir Frank Soskice, who was Home Secretary. I remember I hadn't been in the House long and I was in one of the gents' toilets and someone came next to me and immediately engaged me in very warm conversation saying how much people like me were needed and how we enriched the House. I was very flattered and felt very proud. It was Alec Douglas-Home. I thought what a bloody contrast with some of my own folk.

HAROLD WALKER

✘ I think it was basically left to Wilson. The people who felt they had been in the wilderness with him – which basically came down to Dick Crossman, Barbara Castle, Tommy Balogh – were constantly trying as all those diaries show to get Harold Wilson to see them, to get regular supper parties going or something, but Wilson was a loner. He was much happier sitting down and working things out for himself, probably with some input from Marcia Falkender who knew politics very well. The world is divided between those who think that Marcia was a bad influence and those who think she was a good influence. I am firmly on the side the latter. She had a very good political instinct and was a good influence on the Prime Minister. I think the person closest to Wilson throughout his government, until he retired during the second government, was Burke Trend who was head of the Civil Service and Secretary of the Cabinet. He talked to him more than he talked to anybody else.   TONY HOWARD

✘ He didn't believe in splitting the party over what he would call 'an arid theological argument'. He was right, of course. If you have clear policies, people rally round the policies. If you try and impose a single ideology, then ideology is itself divisive. If you say we want jobs, houses, schools, pensions and health, the people will say, 'Right, we're with you.' Harold Wilson saw that. He also saw that to keep people together you have to be moving all the time. He used to say, 'If the coach stops, people get out and fight. If the coach is on the move they'll stick with it.' A lot of serious wisdom came out of Harold. He was very perceptive.   TONY BENN

✘ As a reconstructed Bevanite he was haunted by the splits of the thirteen years of Tory rule which had kept us out of office. He was dedicated to party unity and that became a very profound principle with him. Anyone who says he was unprincipled doesn't understand the principles that can lead a man to castrate himself to keep a divided party together. He always used to promote his enemies. David Owen once said, 'All you have to do is attack him and you're in the cabinet.' We lefties, of course, used to get a bit miffed at this, though he gave us enough to do in cabinet to keep us quiet. But the key positions, the DEA, Treasury, Foreign Affairs were all in the hands of the right-wingers.

I used to say to Harold, 'Look, if we've got to do tough and unpleasant economic things, why don't we at least inspire our rank or file with something that doesn't cost money.' But of course he was a prisoner of his own appointments. His devotion to Gordon Walker was incredible. So we were excluded from even playing a part to help lift the idealistic tone of the whole government by some really radical liberty-loving foreign policy.   BARBARA CASTLE

✗ In those days – well, until fairly recently – there were two roads to power, via the party National Executive or via Parliament through the ministerial ladder, and of course there were those who saw that they would make progress in that direction: Eric Heffer, Tony Benn and one or two others. They made their progress through the party. But that was always one of the major problems, people striking attitudes in order to get on the NEC. It would mean that you couldn't get a rational approach on a central issue like devaluation and growth because it was cut across by all the other emotional issues.

In fairness, the constituencies were less interested in things like devaluation than Vietnam and CND, so these emotive issues took over, the interest in them usurped the more common-sense approaches to what you can actually do here and now. Striking attitudes was a better way to get on the NEC than dealing with the problems of inflation. The Tribune Group was quite good on economic policy but it was also pro-CND and opposing the Vietnam War became its major task which deflected it from exercising influence in other areas where it might have succeeded. Michael Foot was back in the fold. People had realised that, and Harold Wilson was very accommodating. He felt that a united party was crucial and he'd been through all the divisions of the 1950s and was determined that that wasn't going to happen again. In fact, he saw his role as a peacemaker.   ROBERT SHELDON

✗ Totally absorbing. An enormous number of hours of work. In the lightest day you were doing fifteen hours and there was one period, for three months, when I had to do eighteen hours a day. It takes a lot of doing. If anybody asks what are the prime requirements of a minister I would give the usual answer: there are three – the first is a good constitution, the second is a good constitution and the third is a good constitution. Physical stamina to get through. Look at Maggie Thatcher, tremendous physical stamina, that is the way in which our system is run. You've got to be a minister, you've got to run the department, you've got to be in the House and do all the legislation. You've got to be a constituency MP. But it's all very stimulating, you enjoy every moment of it. It all seems very important.

In my particular job in the Treasury you were at the crossroads of all the departments coming in wanting this, that and the other and you had a very full life. I remember going in to Jim's at No.11 one night at two o'clock in the morning to see if I could help Jim with his box. He'd done his first box, he'd still got the second box to do at two o'clock in the morning. I never got to bed before two o'clock. You develop the habit of, in my case, five and a half hours' sleeping and you can work on that. Yes I think there are times when you would have done better, you would have argued your case in the cabinet more freshly. I don't think you can put a lot of blame on a system which necessitates people working those hours. It has its advantages too. You cover a lot of ground. You are aware of what's going on. I would always divide my work so that decision-making was in the early part in the night.   JACK DIAMOND

✗ It was paralysed. There were some things it couldn't do. Jolly good thing too. The crazy plans to nationalise steel were put on hold because there were some Labour members who wouldn't support the government. I think when a government is in a minority situation and it has to be moderate and not come up with rash proposals, it actually gains support. Because it isn't doing very much, support then picks up. Perhaps because they weren't able to do much, they weren't a threat and a danger. People felt reassured and thought it would be safe to vote for Labour this time, and in 1966, the people who had been apprehensive previously did vote Labour and give Wilson his big majority.   GEORGE JONES

✗ Every now and then Harold would have flashes of his own, a sort of impatience with the orthodoxy which he was accepting. I remember once, when there was a terrible run on the pound, he stopped me in the lobby and said, 'I hate to be painted into a corner. Tomorrow at cabinet I'm going to propose something which will shock some. I'm under terrible pressure to raise rates. If we do raise them one per cent the run will intensify.' That was his analysis. So he said, 'I'm going to suggest that we cut them.' Well, even I was shocked. But he was damn right. The run stopped. Everyone said, 'He must know something that we don't know.'   BARBARA CASTLE

✗ I'd come into Parliament from ICI. I knew something about industry, and it was to me frustrating that there was all this nonsensical talk about what could be done. The irony was that because I appeared to talk knowledgeably in the House of Commons about economic affairs, on the Finance Bill of 1965 and so forth, because I'd been an ICI manager, I was put into the Ministry of Technology. My principal purpose was to tell my then bosses, first Frank Cousins then Tony Benn, that they were spending public money fruitlessly, counterproductively. So, in the field in which I was engaged, in the Ministry of Technology, in the Department of Economic Affairs subsequently, and then in the Board of Trade and the Department of Employment – I moved around with great speed in those days – I argued against the way industrial policy operated, and I was told, incidentally, that I wasn't a socialist.   EDMUND DELL

✗ Harold was always calm and confident, I can't remember a time when he wasn't. He was calm and confident throughout. He would never lose his cool. Only once in his whole career, and that was when the Rhodesians were starving people in prison, can I remember him actually losing his rag in any big way. He could remain cool. I'm very good when under pressure. An election campaign never worried me, I would take it as it came and just keep doing what had to be done. Make sure that everything gets done is the motto. Don't leave any loose ends. Don't forget to tell someone or ask someone whether they've done something because they won't have done it. So you'd better ask them or you live to regret it.

MARCIA WILLIAMS

CHAPTER SIX

The Great Unmentionable

The combined election and economic strategy of Harold Macmillan and his Chancellor Reggie Maudling had been a massive boost to growth as a happy prelude to the 1963 election. Once Macmillan had gone, the election had to be postponed and then prolonged into 1964. The result was a rapidly widening balance-of-payments deficit as an overheating economy sucked in imports. Concern about the scale of the problem grew throughout 1964, surfacing in the election campaign, but the full scale of it only hit Labour when the incoming ministers were presented with the books on the very first day. They were faced with a record deficit, then estimated at eight hundred million pounds, and a consequential loss of confidence in sterling.

The problem was addressed politically with tough actions, stern stances, and a touch of nationalism, as sterling was defended against foreign speculators and the Gnomes of Zurich. Yet the problem was not economic but the product of an overvaluation which had become ever more onerous through the fifties and into the sixties. By 1964, the overvalued exchange rate, fixed in 1949, was unsustainable.

Competitors had started after the war with undervalued currencies, which made exporting profitable. They built powerful exporting sectors and enjoyed all the benefits of scale, power and productivity which bring competitiveness and export success. Britain had started with an overvalued rate, getting more so by around 1% a year after 1949, pricing our goods out of markets, focusing manufacturing on the home market and opening that to more imports. So Britain's growth was slow, its balance of payments weak, its overvaluation more and more apparent. All this was clear by 1963. It was certain to be made worse by the balance-of-payments consequences of the Maudling 'dash for growth'.

Devaluation was the only answer. Without that the government was forced into endless deflation, putting up interest rates, and damping demand at home to check the tide of imports and ease the deficit. That increased costs, discouraged investment, reduced production, banished the growth which was central to Labour's strategies and effectively trapped the incoming government. If the promise to build a better, fairer society, sustained by a modernised economy enjoying the growth levels of competitors who were steadily overtaking and passing us, were to be kept, economic growth was central. Boosting production and exports and using the surplus for public spending permitted redistribution without pain and offered the prospect of the better Britain people had voted for.

All depended on economic performance. Labour proposed all sorts of supply-side measures to get it: a National Plan, better training and education, more investment, industrial reorganisation – all necessary but all futile unless the basic weakness of the economy was tackled. Slower growth meant lower profits, less investment, comparative decline and increasing vulnerability. Since the overvaluation wasn't going to go away, the deflation and the failure would be prolonged. Only devaluation could bring British prices in foreign-currency terms down to a more competitive level, boosting exports, taxing imports and allowing industry to generate the profits to invest and grow.

Devaluation could hardly be proclaimed, even mentioned, in a manifesto but a party committed to growth required the economic understanding to grasp the problem and Labour was inclined to the opposite view. Many thought socialist measures could make economic water flow uphill. The leader saw the exchange rate as a national virility symbol, so Britain could be proud when it was hard, filled with post-imperial triste when it drooped. Sterling was to be defended, and particularly by Labour, not devalued. Harold's mistake was to handle an economic problem as a political issue.

Labour's 'A' Team takes on the Gnomes

In power Labour faced the (then) horrendous balance-of-payments problem. The pound could have been devalued immediately and the blame put on the Tories, who were indeed responsible. Devaluation was one of the three options offered by the Treasury. But Wilson, Callaghan and Brown met on Saturday, 18 October and ruled it out. No one realised at the time, but the new government was marching into a fatal trap. Harold's finest hour was to become Jim Callaghan's worst.

✗ I wasn't very impressed by the run-up to the election in terms of the likely policy because it seemed to me that the most important decision we were going to have to face soon after getting into office was to devalue. I vividly remember a meeting of Labour's Economic Committee which was chaired by Jim Callaghan. It was Nicky Kaldor addressing us and arguing in favour of devaluation. He was totally convincing. He answered all his questions superbly. There was no doubt about it that everybody at that meeting was impressed by his arguments and thought they were right. These were Labour MPs that came to the Economic Committee. It was a well-attended meeting.

Jim Callaghan, Shadow Chancellor, was in the chair and here was our guru talking about economic policy. And Nicky was a brilliant man. He explained it all extremely lucidly. At the end Jim summed up and said, 'Nicky you were wonderful. You were extremely persuasive. You answered all the questions with logic. Thank you very much for coming. There is only one thing I want to say: Of course when we are in power we are not going to have any of this devaluation nonsense.' I thought, 'Jesus Christ.'   DICK TAVERNE

✗ Jim Callaghan, George Brown and the Prime Minister called a meeting at No. 10 to discuss devaluation. They said, 'First of all there is 1931.' The '31 devaluation was done by the National Government, in the September. Nevertheless, the economic crisis was when the Labour Party went out of office. They decided that with the devaluation of 1931, which was the saviour of this country, and with Stafford-Cripps devaluing in '49, quite properly, a Labour Party coming in could not devalue in '64.

So they decided not to. With a majority of only three or four, the idea that you could devalue out of the blue, given the political history of it, wasn't on. Not even a government with a majority of one hundred is able, out of the blue, to devalue. We are now in a situation where we devalue every five minutes and nobody notices. In those days, devaluation was edged in black almost as if the end of the world had come. So, it wasn't an easy time to come into power.   MERLYN REES

✗ Devaluation was handled by Harold, Jim and George. There's some dispute as to whether the decision was actually made on the Friday evening after the election. Certainly it was all signed and sealed by the Saturday, and those who wanted to take a different view, like Tony Crosland, were never given the opportunity of making their representations. He was told by George Brown it was over, settled, nothing to do with you. You are not to mention the subject again.   TONY HOWARD

✗ We were faced with a *fait accompli* when the cabinet first met. This private meeting had taken place before the first cabinet. Jim's great theme was: the strength of sterling will be our priority. I remember my heart sinking. We were crucified on that.   BARBARA CASTLE

✗ I don't think that on the economic side we realised – or at least Wilson certainly did not – that the only way of dealing with the problem would be to allow the pound to fall. Wilson refused to allow the cabinet to discuss the issue. He decided it with a tiny group of other ministers – the Chancellor Jim Callaghan and George Brown the Foreign Secretary, I think that was about it. They discussed it right away and decided that whatever happened they'd stick to the existing value of sterling, which was a disaster.

Of course, we had to surrender to the market forces and if we'd done this at the beginning, voluntarily, then we could have handled the economic situation much better. Economists disagree about everything. They didn't disagree with one another quite so much then as they do now, when you can't get two economists that agree with one another out of the hundreds of well-known economists there are in the country. At that time I think the bulk of economists would probably have supported Wilson's position at the beginning. Nobody was conscious of the problem of foreign exchange at that time and we attributed any problems that arose to some mythical creatures called the 'Gnomes of Zurich'.

Gaitskell was very orthodox on economic questions and he was a trained economist. Wilson was a trained economist. But they accepted the orthodoxy at that time and the great weakness of Keynesianism is that it almost totally ignored external forces. It also ignored domestic institutions, like trade unions and employers' organisations. Wilson was brought up in the Keynesian period. He was at Oxford in my time, just before the war. Gaitskell also was brought up in that tradition and it turned out to be really very unsuitable for the world we

were moving into in which the international markets were beginning to shape domestic policies in all countries. Andrew Schonfield was one of the very few economists who was watching the changes that were happening in the world which were going to influence the British economy. That's why he was in favour of devaluation. DENIS HEALEY

✘ The government was, in my view, damned from the start by the decision not to devalue. Indeed that was something that was discussed on the Saturday night between Roy Jenkins on the telephone, and George. But when we went round on that Saturday night, Roy, Tony Crosland, myself and our wives, a decision had been made not to devalue. I suppose we were all depressed by it, but not as depressed as we ought to have been. We all wanted to devalue. We thought it was right, but the decision had been made and we had to make the most of it. From then onwards you couldn't mention the word devaluation. What George would do, if he wanted to refer to it, would be to purse his lips and put a finger in front – and that meant devaluation. You just couldn't mention the name. It was banned from the language of government. All of us had to conform to that even in private gatherings with civil servants.

BILL RODGERS

✘ You must recognise the dominant world influence that the Bretton-Woods Agreement had on economic thinking at that time. The importance of world opinion on our economic and financial policy was especially strong, because of our position as the second leading world currency. It would be quite wrong to assume that we wished to cling to the reserve currency role. I would have been very happy to relinquish it, and talked to both the French and Germans about it, but neither of them wanted any part of becoming a reserve currency.

We still had real and genuine obligations at that time as a colonial power, and the centre of the Commonwealth in the matter of their reserves held in sterling.

Finally, we shouldn't underestimate the prevailing sentiment in the country about the Labour Party and devaluation. As a result of 1929–31, the general opinion fostered by the media was that a Labour government always leads to devaluation, and I see no reason to alter my judgement that whether we devalued in 1964, 1966 or at any other time, there would always have been very serious adverse political consequences for the government. Boosting the growth rate to solve our troubles does not take account of the fact that in 1964 the economy was already operating at a level of full employment – between 400,000 and 500,000 unemployed. Attempts to stoke up the growth rate even further would have led to a consumer boom, little or no increase in investment (because of the attitude of employers at the time), and a much worse balance-of-payments deficit.   JIM CALLAGHAN

✘ Not to devalue was a great mistake. An understandable mistake because of Labour being associated with the devaluation of '49 and it was thought it would look as if when Labour came to office they always devalued. Looking back it was a terrible error, though Douglas Jay used to say to me that he could defend the decision in 1964 not to devalue. What he couldn't defend was the decision in July 1966. By then he thought the equation was that you had to do it. But there were respectable economists who thought that in '64 it was a fifty/ fifty bet that you could get away without devaluation. Those did not include people like Roy Jenkins. Not that he's a professional economist, but Tony Crosland was, and there was a sizeable number who even then took the view that devaluation was the proper thing to do straightaway.   TONY HOWARD

✘ Harold Wilson had a great fear that Labour governments would be branded as governments that always devalued. There had been a devaluation in 1949, and a perfectly legitimate devaluation, but the Tories had used the fact that we devalued then in a scandalous way. Churchill especially. They talked as if it was a treachery almost to the country to devalue. That's all rubbish, of course. But all that was part of the lack of confidence of a Labour government in their own financial policies and their own financial outlooks.   MICHAEL FOOT

✘ Reggie Maudling had been Chancellor of the Exchequer. Jim had gone to No. 11 and said to Reggie, because they were mates, 'Don't rush out, Reggie. Take your time.' After two days, Reggie came down to that little office in No. 11 where the Chancellor usually sits and works. He came in carrying some suits over his arm and said, 'I'm finished, Jim. I'm off. Are you going to put up the bank rate? I was talking to Alec about it. We decided to do it. But Alec said, "Let's leave it for them to do." '

Jim indicated maybe, maybe not. Then within a couple of days, when we assembled, the bank rate was put up. All hell was let loose. The Labour Party putting up the bank rate!

MERLYN REES

✘ We knew we were inheriting a weak economy but we didn't realise just how bad it was. I don't think anyone really guessed how bad it was. Harold, within days of our getting into government, had gone public about the balance-of-payments deficit, which would have been multi-billions in today's terms. It was big, big money, and the balance of payments was so sensitive at that time because of runs on the pound. So Labour was in a quandary because the Tories had dubbed us the 'Party of Devaluation', though in a post-war situation it would hardly have been surprising if any government had devalued.

However, with a majority of just five when we got in, the cabinet found themselves in a very difficult position. The logical thing would have been to devalue straight away, get it out of the way and then hope that over the next four and a half years you could leave that behind with what you've built on the devaluation.

But he couldn't do that. He had a majority of five and he

didn't know when he'd have to go. I wasn't even aware of how serious the situation was until I got into government the other side of the election. I didn't know how much they had known. I went into the Department of Economic Affairs in '67. We were told a certain amount but some of the seriousness and the decisions that were having to be taken were concealed even from the members themselves.   ALAN WILLIAMS

✗ We had fought the election on an expansionist theme and immediately went into reverse under the triumvirate which Harold set up – Harold Wilson, Jim Callaghan and George Brown. The government's troubles started with Jim Callaghan's first speech as Chancellor. He switched the whole mood of the government from what had been an expansionist one to one of praising the Victorian virtues of paying your way and balancing your budgets. It was almost a pre-glimpse of the Thatcherite argument about having to balance our household budgets.   BARBARA CASTLE

✗ There was a feeling of crisis among the few who were pressing the government on the issue and I think Roy Jenkins was one at the very beginning. I think that we were much more worried about the scale of our domestic deficit, which we were very conscious of. We knew that a deficit was a thing you had to mend by borrowing and once you've borrowed you're in the hands of the lender. But that again, which is so obvious today, wasn't widely recognised then. I think again the few people who had enough economic knowledge to recognise the disasters which would follow if we had big domestic and external deficits, which we did in fact inherit from the Tories, were secondary figures in the party and to be perfectly honest they weren't so numerous in the academic world.

DENIS HEALEY

✗ What we didn't know in '64 was that the debt would be as large as it was. There was a balance-of-payments deficit much bigger than we had been given to understand. The books were not as open as they should have been. That was a big blow and put sterling under pressure. So Harold's first meetings with the Governor of the Bank of England were particularly hairy because he was told very firmly that he wouldn't be able to afford any of the plans for social security and health. There

'I think I'll put Income Tax up 6d' – Budget 1965

was one point at which Harold thought and said to the Governor, 'Are you telling me I can't raise retirement pensions? Then I will have to go back to the country and ask the people whether they will give us a better mandate, so I can do what I want without feeling nervous about that tiny majority.' I wish he'd done that because it would have been a marvellous election campaign, but sterling would have gone right down.   MARCIA WILLIAMS

✘ What we did was to put on an import surcharge. It was very difficult for our EFTA partners to accept. That was the first big foreign policy issue, and it was also an economic issue so it concerned the Treasury and George Brown's Department of Economic Affairs as well as the Foreign Office, and we went round all the EFTA countries doing our best to explain that we really found a situation in which there was no alternative. The only alternative would have been devaluation but we couldn't admit that – even think about that.   GEORGE THOMSON

✘ The moment I entered the Treasury I was given a piece of paper from William Armstrong who was head of the Treasury and later became head of the Civil Service. What a piece of paper! With one paragraph, just that, saying what the deficit was. No suggestion of how it was to be overcome, nothing like that. No policy. No doubt by this time he'd been talking to Jim about it but just wanted to make you aware what the situation was.That's what happened. It was a terrible mess. Just unheard

of, figures at that level. We'd been expecting some difficulties
but not such a mess as that.   JACK DIAMOND

✘ Sterling was the big problem linked very much with the
balance-of-payments deficit. That year we knew that things
were going badly wrong. We thought we would inherit a
deficit which in those terms was huge, about £400 million, and
it turned out to be £800 million. That was absolutely
monstrous. How did the Labour government deal with that? –
that was the interesting thing.

The first thing they did was to slap on an import surcharge,
a tax on imports to reduce them and then, as we later
developed it, through tax means, a kind of export subsidy to
correct that imbalance. It had a very useful effect which lasted a
couple of years. We were obliged to phase out the surcharge on
imports and the deficit was still too large and had to be
corrected.

Meanwhile there was pressure on sterling throughout this
period and we had to make arrangements with the United
States first of all and the Americans had their own interest in
this because in those days sterling and the dollar were really
the only reserve currencies. The Americans were very
concerned that if anything happened to sterling it would have
its repercussions on the dollar. So they were interested in
assisting maintaining sterling.

The truth is that the exchange rate was too high and
although these corrective measures were taken in the hope that
things would enable us to continue at the pre-existing exchange
rate, it wasn't possible. A number of our colleagues thought
that we should devalue from day one. Given the fact that we
had a majority of about four it didn't seem to be a totally
attractive idea and anyway we hadn't tried the corrective
measures – import surcharge, export rebates and so on.

                                                   PETER SHORE

✘ It is very demoralising to be faced with a problem of that
nature. It is demoralising because you have to look at all your
programmes. We didn't approach it by having a very careful
analysis of all the government's treasured programmes and
taking what we could spare. It was across the board. That was
the hardest thing to accept, that you had very little influence
on your programme. I fought very hard in the Education

Department, with some success, to say let's look at the whole of the programme in education and decide where we can have some movement. To protect one programme we've got to look at our other programmes, and that effectively is what we tried to do. You were just stuck with it. So school meals and school milk had just got to go up, and all you could do at the margin was to improve the entitlement to free school meals and milk.

DENIS HOWELL

X Once the decision had been made not to devalue, everything else was prejudiced as a result of that, and it wasn't just economic policy it was social policy. All those things which we wanted to do desperately were prejudiced and we saw the retreat from public expenditure stage by stage, first in the summer of '65.

BILL RODGERS

X I had some really close friends – Robert Sheldon, who got the seat for Ashton, Edmond Dell, who got Birkenhead. The three of us were very close, indeed we formed a coffee house in Manchester in a basement in Brasenose Street. When we came into Parliament we obviously hoped for big improvements. I had been absolutely convinced that we would devalue because it was so obviously needed if we were going to go for the kind of growth we wanted. The only person in the cabinet who agreed with us, when he was sober, was George Brown. George was a great guy. Harold had set up this Department of Economic Affairs, but it was a total disaster really. I don't think it can just be laid at the door of George Brown. Basically he had little influence over the Treasury. The Treasury was the most powerful department. They weren't prepared to listen to outsiders from the DEA.

Consequently, George had very little influence although I'm sure he was fighting tooth and nail inside the cabinet and with Harold and the Treasury. It may be that because we had a small majority at that time, in 1964, Harold was opposed to it. However, I think he was fundamentally opposed to the idea of devaluing, not just because of the size of the majority. There were different economic views even amongst serious economists. Harold was a serious economist, but he was Prime Minister and his major concern was to stay Prime Minister. It's not an unreasonable concern, as we see from current prime ministers. He had two reasons. One was the small majority, the other was that he genuinely wasn't convinced that devaluation would necessarily be a solution to our growth problem. But whatever the reason, we had no success in the many speeches and representations we made. Until the next Parliament.

JOEL BARNETT

✘ When you start talking about devaluation it could be misrepresented. But there is nothing to stop Harold feeling that way and discussing it with Jim and George Brown and deciding that's what they are going to do. By then of course he'd given his commitment to Lyndon Johnson. That was given probably '65/6. It wasn't given reluctantly. That was his view. That's my interpretation of it. Remember, when we came in we were at that tape everyday. You never passed that tape without looking at it to see what's the pressure on the pound. It was continuous. We made a big play of the eight-hundred-million-pound deficit and making that big play made people feel that our economy was shaky.

On the other hand, Harold wanted to pin the blame on the Conservatives. He should have done the job properly and devalued as well. You can blame it on the previous government. If you say, 'Look here, talking about devaluation labels us as the party that devalued twice.' I can see that and that's why I assumed he was waiting for a big majority and would then do it. But then in 1966 there was no sign of it, and bit by bit it dawned on me that it wasn't going to come. George Brown, Deputy Prime Minister, was in favour, Harold Wilson was against, and Jim was against, but not as enthusiastic as Harold. If Harold was uncertain then there'd have been a devaluation but Tommy Balogh, of course, played a part in that. Terrible advice.   ROBERT SHELDON

✘ Harold's veto on devaluation was tactical. A grave misjudgement. He said Labour had devalued in the '45 government under Stafford Cripps. If we were to devalue again people would say, 'Labour governments mean devaluation.' So those three met together and nailed the Labour Party on the cross of deflation and no devaluation. It was a forbidden word. It was almost the F word in cabinet. You weren't allowed even to mention it. And some of us were muttering on the sideline. This was not to be discussed. So you couldn't tell him in cabinet and it suited Jim Callaghan's

curiously hair-shirt mood. He had a sort of correctness of orthodoxy, a highly conventional mind. Harold hadn't. He had got an imaginative mind. BARBARA CASTLE

✗ Kaldor, who was the best economic adviser we ever had, and Robert Neild, whom Callaghan appointed as his economic adviser, both said, 'We have to devalue.' Donald McDougal said, 'We have to devalue.' The chairman of the European Community Monetary Committee came to Callaghan in the middle of November and said, 'You ought to devalue.' These were not secrets from informed people. But all this was ruled out because we'd said that we didn't want the reputation as the party of devaluation. Therefore, it was ruled out from day one. EDMUND DELL

✗ The PLP was told not to discuss devaluation, and so was the cabinet, particularly Mr Crossman. Crossman said he was for it, but on the other hand there were a lot of members of the PLP, and I was one of them, who thought it very unwise for a Labour government to jump immediately into a devaluation, because remember we were associated with devaluation and, had they done that, the impression would have been created that every time there was a Labour government there was a devaluation.   TAM DALYELL

✘ There was the occasion when Mr Pompidou came to visit us as prime minister, before he became president. We were all new to that sort of occasion and I dealt with the European side of things so I went with the Foreign Secretary, Michael Stewart, to the meeting with Prime Minister Pompidou in the cabinet room. We all had our big books of briefs tucked under the table and in front of us and of course we'd all applied ourselves seriously to them the night before. He didn't have a single bit of paper and he proceeded to give us a brilliant lecture on economics and the virtues of devaluation. The French had devalued and he told us how successfully he had carried through the French devaluation. A very egotistical performance but a very shocking performance to us. As a result there was a very serious run on the pound the next day and the relations between ourselves and the French were at rock bottom.   GEORGE THOMSON

✘ It's one of the awful things about a fixed exchange rate that inevitably it comes under pressure. Therefore those who are trying to defend the rate engage in a kind of psychological warfare with the speculators and the Gnomes of Zurich, as they were in those days. So Harold was increasingly driven to say, 'Over my dead body. I tell you we will not devalue.' When it does happen there is a tremendous loss of confidence.
                                                PETER SHORE

✘ There was a thing which was, if you like, the other side of the coin of devaluation. This was preservation at the price of great economic overstrain of our position as a world power. Keeping a worldwide military presence and avoiding devaluation was really part of the same piece in that it was associated with keeping the sterling area. That was thought to provide us with considerable influence but was, in fact, an albatross around our neck and an unsteady position so far as the world currency was concerned. We were all so anxious to be head prefect to Lyndon Johnson's headmastership, and it all went with an over-inflated view of the position in the world we could sustain.

'THE LABOUR PARTY IS LIKE A VEHICLE. IF YOU DRIVE AT GREAT SPEED, ALL THE PEOPLE IN IT ARE EITHER SO EXHILARATED OR SO SICK THAT YOU HAVE NO PROBLEMS. BUT WHEN YOU STOP, THEY ALL GET OUT AND START TO ARGUE ABOUT WHICH WAY TO GO.' — MR WILSON IN SEPTEMBER 1963.

That was part and parcel of the extreme reluctance to contemplate devaluation, as a result of which we turned what ought to have been a technical national monetary decision into a test of national virility. We paid a price for that when this relatively small devaluation, much smaller than some of the swings in sterling which took place in the 1980s without anyone else noticing, turned when it came in 1967 into a great national and party disaster. ROY JENKINS

✗ What the party realised at that stage was that there was this great deficit in the balance of payments but Wilson's dictum was that though we had this deficit, though we had this small majority (and though we would therefore need another election as soon as we could get away with it), nevertheless we must go ahead with all those things that we said we would do in the manifesto. But the two things were impossible. The only conceivable way of avoiding devaluation would have been if we had scrapped the manifesto. We probably couldn't have avoided devaluation even then but if we'd scrapped the manifesto, if we had taken very strong fiscal and monetary action, we might just have avoided devaluation. But without those things it was inconceivable.

I've often been regarded as insane. I am told that I'm not an authority on what is politically possible. I have frequently been characterised, in my brief political career, as not understanding politics. All I can say is this. We did have a majority. The Tories were burdened with a clear responsibility for the mess we'd inherited. If we had taken the steps that were necessary in the autumn of '64, that is if we'd devalued and we'd introduced very tough fiscal and monetary policies, I think we could have got away with it. I don't think the party would have rebelled against it. We'd just come into office and we wouldn't want to throw it away.

Instead we launched ourselves on a policy that was economically impossible and, therefore, though we won the election in '66 with a smashing majority, everything had been lost by 1970. If you look at politics from anything but the shortest point of view, it would have been better to be tough in 1964, to devalue not as a soft option but as a tough option. I think we'd have got away with it because we did have a majority and we could not have been thrown out as long as the party had stuck together. I believe the external influences that surround the Labour Party, like the trade unions, would have been saying, 'OK, we hate this, but for God's sake don't let the Tories back in.' Which, incidentally, is what they said in 1976. So I think, yes, we could have got away with it.   EDMUND DELL

CHAPTER SEVEN

Parliament as Hustings

The growth of government by party had transformed Parliament from the great controller of the Executive to its rubber stamp: a legislative machine run by the Executive through its party majority and used for its purposes. Parliament had settled into this role, providing a stage for party confrontation but always doing what the executive wanted because controlled through the party majority.

Labour's acquisition of power and its efforts to cope with it, the two problems of winning a new majority and grappling with an economic crisis, created a new scenario. With devaluation ruled out by government dictat and a forbidden topic for ministers, Parliament and party back rooms were the only forum in which advocates of this necessary heresy could gather to mention the unmentionable – if only to a small (but growing) band of Labour MPs.

The Commons also became the hustings for the new election campaign, which began immediately MPs gathered from the last. This was the emergence of the new role Parliament had been developing under the British system of government by party. The Commons was the stage on which the election battle between two parties was fought out. New MPs were electioneering just as surely as if they had never taken off their rosettes.

Both jobs were to be learned in unusually difficult circumstances. As the new MPs gathered, awestruck by their new surroundings, they faced a parliamentary situation which had occurred only once before, and that briefly, in the dying days of the post-war Labour government, from 1950 to 1951, when it had struggled through with a small majority albeit bigger than the five Labour now had. That majority meant tight discipline, late nights, frequent decisions, divisions, and intense harassment. The MPs in 1964, though younger, fresher and more enthusiastic than their tired counterparts of 1950, had a tougher job sustaining a new government engaged on a continuous election campaign and understanding why that government was imposing deflationary measures sharply opposed to those they had been elected to advance.

✘ I came in, put my coat in the cloakroom and went to look for my hanger. The fact that I was a marginal member.was bitterly rubbed in for me when I found that the hanger with 'Williams' on it had one set of initials crossed out and my initials written in . . . in pencil. They weren't going to waste a good label. I went into the chamber for the swearing in. You can imagine it. I was thirty-four; there was Harold and all the cabinet sitting just two rows below me, and there opposite, looking very dejected, all the outgoing famous Tory faces. Tudor Watkins, the Breconshire member, was sitting next to me – he would be in his mid-sixties at that time – and I turned to him and said, 'Tudor, it must be marvellous to be on this side of the House after thirteen years over there?' 'Yes, my boy,' he said. 'The sun gets in your eyes on the other side of the House.'

ALAN WILLIAMS

✘ When you first walk in as a new Member of Parliament, it's like walking into a new school as a new boy. You don't know any of the rules and everybody else seems to be dashing around and knowing were he or she is going. You yourself don't know the basic things and there is a certain amount of bewilderment. When we had meetings of the parliamentary party, the euphoria had carried over there and there was a tremendous feeling of going ahead. The first time we assembled in the House of Commons there was immense enthusiasm. It was only afterwards, when we came up against 'the problem' that it began to ebb.   STAN NEWENS

✘ I didn't even know how to get out of Parliament once I was in. They are much better prepared now. I didn't know the passages, I didn't know about parliamentary procedure, but I was a quick learner. I decided that since I seemed to know more about business than other people, although I didn't know much about finance bills, I'd make it up, and as it happened that became the big issue – Corporation Tax, Capital Gains Tax, the Finance Bill of 1965. There to my surprise I found myself with only another couple of people who knew anything about it. So you become an expert just by knowing a little bit more than one or two other people. So I devoted myself to that. When you've got to do that you're listened to on matters that really have nothing to do with it.   ROBERT SHELDON

✘ George Wigg came up to me and said, 'We want you to nominate Emanuel Shinwell as the chairman of the PLP.' I said, 'Good God, why me?' 'Because you're his successor.' So it was thought that I would be a good dogsbody, a good representative of the young members, to nominate this octogenarian whom they wanted as chairman of the PLP. He turned out to be the most disastrous chairman that the PLP has ever had because he really was mightily biased in favour of those that he liked, or most importantly, against those that he disliked. To have a chairman of the PLP thump the table and say, 'I'm not having that from you, Crossman,' is unbelievable.
          TAM DALYELL

✘ The question was, 'Who is going to be the Speaker?' because there was only a majority of four. So we said that it was really Horace King's turn to become Speaker because the previous incumbent had died. Naturally, Wilson wanted to have another Tory Speaker to take a vote away. But Charlie Pannell was on our side and we managed to carry it off. I'm not sure whether we had a vote on it but certainly we said we were going to do that. Horace King and not the Tory nominee got the job. So we reduced the majority that way.
          WOODROW WYATT

✘ The sort of general political management of the party – apart from the physical arithmetic which was difficult – but the political management of the party was very easy indeed, in spite of the fact that we had quite a lot of Mikardos and Sidney Silvermans and Bill Warbeys and people like that. But with that sort of majority they all played ball and nobody rocked the boat. Party management in the political sense was easy, until we got the big majority and then it was damn difficult.

We worked out a scheme for giving people time off and that worked very well because everybody saw that it was fair. In the whole party there was only one man who was difficult throughout, and that was old Bill Warbey.

Every day was alarming until ten o'clock, especially the Monday vote because they'd go off to the four corners of the kingdom every weekend, to North Wales and the north of Scotland, etc., and until we knew they were all back in Westminster it was always a headache.

The first vote we had on the first day. I was terrified and they weren't all in. I think that about twenty were late, but eventually we got them all in. There had been fog in Edinburgh and a lot of them had been stranded at Glasgow Airport. We got in touch with them and told them that Prestwick was clear so they went there. It was not a crisis exactly but it was quite an exciting time.   TED SHORT

✘ The whipping then would be almost inconceivable today. It took the '74 government without a majority to convince both parties you could govern the House of Commons without all-night sittings. I can remember on occasions my wife and I sitting until five o'clock in the morning, down in the cafeteria, and many times we were here all night. The Tories used to play games. They would go away and the place would be very quiet and then, at say two-thirty in the morning, cars and taxis would start flowing in through the front door and at a set time they'd call a snap division and see if they could ambush the government. It kept the Labour members and ministers very tied to the House of Commons. It was an horrendous period, and I'm glad I faced it at that age rather than the age I am now. Some of the older members found it very heavy going indeed when we had a majority of three.   ALAN WILLIAMS

✘ It was fun whipping. The party realised the dangers of a very small majority, only four, which people used to say could be carried in a taxi cab, and exercised a good deal of self-restraint. The left wing of the party, and indeed a large part of the party, wanted social measures which were difficult to provide in the economic climate of the time. Right at the start, Jim Callaghan, who was the Chancellor, was obliged to bring in austerity measures, a kind of mini-budget, and he balanced austerity on the one hand against alleviation on the other, especially in terms of things like old-age pensions. That mollified the party to some extent but it gave an uncertain message economically and, referring to some of Jim's rather gloomy speeches on the economic situation, one commentator said that, 'All Jim's clouds have got a silver lining.' So that there was always hope somewhere. It was fantasy hope. That kind of thing kept the party in tune.

It wasn't actually too difficult to keep the party in trim on the floor of the House and in votes. I can't recall many voting rebellions in the '64–6 Parliament. There was a good deal of noise generated in party group meetings and in the party meeting and there was a good deal of debate about discipline and Standing Orders at the time. The left wing actually took Standing Orders much more seriously than anybody else because they're ideologues and they believe things that are written down – a peculiar characteristic. They would feel that the Standing Orders were oppressive but only oppressive if you paid any attention to them. Although the whips have got things like Standing Orders at the back of them they're a bit like the nuclear bomb – you can't really use them. You've got to cajole people and comfort them, befriend them. That's really how some of us worked.

The Chief Whip was Ted Short, who followed Bert Bowden, a very upright, military-style figure. Ted was a schoolmasterly type of man. The whips' office was recast. The Labour Party and the Conservative Party use the whips' office quite differently. The Conservatives use it as the first rung on a ladder of promotion. The Labour Party has never really done that. Under Wilson, instead of having the old-style whips, Ted brought in people like myself, John Silkin, and others who were thought to be different, more humane, more intellectually accomplished. It was thought that we would be able to explain party policy with rather more subtlety than some of the old hands from the coal mines. We were trying always to explain policies rather than discipline them. Always, of course, with the reminder that the government's fate was in their hands.

WILLIAM HOWIE

✘ I remember there were people he brought in like Frank Cousins, appalled at the idea of having to stay on until ten o'clock at night because some squit of a whip told the General Secretary of the biggest trade union that he couldn't go home. So there was a restlessness but getting to camp beds in offices on a May morning at four o'clock was a very pleasant phase. There was no traffic on Westminster Bridge then.   JEREMY BRAY

✘ It was an entirely new role for me as I hadn't been involved in national politics except in relation to CND campaigns. It was all such a huge change for me and I felt quite lost being used to being leader of the council and that kind of policy-making. I can still vividly remember going down that staircase opposite the telephone kiosk in the upper lobby, suddenly stopping on the stairs and thinking, 'What the hell am I doing here?' It was a terrible feeling. You do adjust to it without even knowing it. The feeling in the party was very tense. All of us were there to do a job. That was to hold the government in. In those days, with procedures much more cumbersome than they are today, we spent many all-night sessions, voting very tightly to make sure we stayed. There was a feeling of getting things done. That's when the idea of a hundred days began to come into British politics. It had tremendous impact.   REG FREESON

✘ We were still in the honeymoon glow of victory and the feeling that we were just not going to let them beat us, and we were not going to let them get away with what they were trying to do. You almost wore your all-night sittings as campaign medals. When you went home at the weekend you'd go to your party and say, 'Two all-night sittings this week, and one five o'clock.' They didn't think you were idiots. They used to look at you in awe as at great fighters for the cause.

ALAN WILLIAMS

✘ Harold Wilson invited the newly elected back-benchers to a party at No.10 Downing Street where they could meet their betters and seniors, the cabinet and so on. So we're all there in the splendid drawing-room at No.10 Downing Street, over impressed, overawed by talking to our betters – the Chancellor, the Home Secretary – and it must have to got to about eight-thirty in the evening when the meeting was brought to order by someone banging some heavy object on a table. We all stopped in silence and looked up and there was Captain Bob, some distance away from Harold Wilson, saying,

'Colleagues, we all recognise the Prime Minister has very heavy burdens to bear and that doubtless he has a great deal of work to do and I think it would be appropriate if we allowed the Prime Minister now to retire but not without someone on your behalf expressing our gratitude,' and he went on to thank him. Harold Wilson was standing there goggle-eyed at this new back-bencher winding up his party.   HAROLD WALKER

✗ We were tied to the House because of the small majority. Very much more so than in the years later. Because of the majority it was easy for the Tories who did a lot of 'lying in wait', as the phrase was, in the bars and clubs around. John Silkin had an eye on where everybody was. He was the pairing whip. There had to be discipline, and it was a very sweaty seventeen months literally and metaphorically. It was a warm summer and the chamber was much fuller then. In those days you sat in your seat and you waited.   REG FREESON

✗ Having got power, people were exhilarated. I came into the House and it was really truly remarkable to see the chamber full, not just for the opening and winding-up but through the whole day, and people very anxious on our side to intervene to win the argument. That was the feel. We'd got the better argument and we were jolly well going to win it. People were enthusiastic to do just that and to contribute in debate, questions, interruptions and so on.

It wasn't noisy but it was very serious and purposeful. Also it was physically quite demanding with such a small majority, and that wasted away a bit after we'd elected the Speaker and the Deputy Speaker and lost a by-election. It was touch and go. I can remember many occasions when the Speaker had to give the casting vote in favour of the government.   PETER SHORE

✗ On one occasion in 1964, when it was Labour's first finance bill, I came from Manchester on Monday morning at about eleven-thirty and I left at five-thirty on Friday afternoon, never having left the precincts of the Palace of Westminster. I was very lucky because I had Room 56 where you could really rest at night. I remember the following day I went to speak for Fred Blackburn, who was then the very senior member for Stalybridge & Hyde.

I was speaking under the title 'The Week in Westminster',

and when I'd finished I was roundly condemned by a young man in the front row who said it was absolutely disgraceful for any new member to speak for thirty-five minutes and never to intone the words 'overseas aid'. Fred nearly burst a blood vessel. He said, 'He hasn't been to bed for about a hundred and six hours. He's come here because he was asked to speak about the week in Westminster, and this has been one of the very few weeks when there's been nothing about overseas aid.' He absolutely blew up about it.   ALFRED MORRIS

✘ As far as the party was concerned we were in pretty good fettle because we all felt extremely responsible. Each one of us thought that we carried the fate of the party personally. I remember going to Yugoslavia and being driven around by some of the hair-raising Yugoslav drivers and thinking that if they do me in the government will fall! It was really a time when the back-bencher felt himself to be as important as anybody else. We were very careful how we voted but I think we were in good spirits. There was very little division in the party. The narrowness of the majority made us concentrate on the whole business of survival, and you can't divide and survive with a majority of three.   HUGH JENKINS

✘ Night after night it was until three and four in the morning. It was all very well for me as a young, fit, person with no momentous responsibilities. It was a different matter if you were aged sixty-five, the Home Secretary. It was wearing when people in hospital had to be brought in on stretchers and the Tories were absolutely ruthless.   TAM DALYELL

✘ In those days there wasn't any sort of rush to make your maiden speech, as there is now. You were expected not to be too forward and pushy. I came into the House from being a shop steward in Oldham and it was on the occasion of the second reading of the Science and Technology Bill that I made my speech. It was on a Friday. I referred to my own relationships in the engineering industry which I had just left. 'Mr Speaker, I've listened to the Right Honourable Friend and the ministers speaking this morning about this bill, and using words like cybernetics and various other learned words. I spent a lifetime in the engineering industry. Six weeks ago I was working at my bench and I'd never heard of these words,

Published by the Labour Party, Transport House, Smith Sq., S.W.1.
Printed by The Compton Printing Works (London), Ltd. N.1. OCT. 1965

they're not part of the vocabulary that I learnt in the engineering industry. The reality of the engineering industry is much more like the good friend that I had, old Walter. He operated a grinding machine, and if there was a rush job which necessitated working weekends they would send for him in a taxi and return him home in a taxi the following day because

Walter was seventy-seven years of age and it was the only machine that was capable of producing that particular component. Only Walter could use it because it was the machine which he started work on as a half-timer sixty odd years previously. That is much more the reality of things.'

It brought the House down. On the following day the newspapers were full of the things I'd said and Frank Cousins at the next Parliamentary Labour Party meeting referred to my maiden speech and said it was the finest maiden speech he'd ever heard in his life. I instantly swelled with pride until a voice from behind me muttered, 'It's the only bloody speech he's ever heard.' That put me in my place.   HAROLD WALKER

✘ I was chairman of the PLP Education Group, and then subsequently the PLP Foreign Affairs Group. As chairman of the Foreign Affairs Group I was going to the Foreign Secretary every Wednesday night, I won't say with exactly the same regularity as the Prime Minister sees the Queen, but nevertheless, it was very often. It was the same for education. Tony Crosland, with whom I got on extremely well, was the Secretary of State and he took me seriously because I was careful not to say, 'These are my views,' but rather, 'These are the views of the group.'   TAM DALYELL

✘ We had to do a lot of all-night sittings. Much of the business we now send upstairs was then done on the floor of the House. For example, we used to do all the committee stage of a finance bill on the floor of the House. That meant if Clause 173 was a particularly controversial one which the opposition really wanted to hammer then their interest lay in delaying every single clause before and up to 173. That meant that trivialities occupied hours of debate in the House and the only way that the Chancellor could get his finance bill through was to sit all night, night after night.

There was a policeman who had the key to the blanket locker with blankets and pillows in it. You went and drew your blanket and pillow and kipped down. The opposition were running a tight pairing system: they were determined to pin us down; we would have happily paired if they had allowed us to do so. I remember when negotiating with our whips they used to say you need to have a firm pair. I said, 'What do you mean?' It was explained that they weren't prepared to consider you pairing with anyone who might not be there anyhow, somebody who was in hospital, for example; it was considered a bonus if one of the other side was in hospital and vice-versa or if somebody was going to be absent anyhow.

I remember Captain Robert Maxwell came in in 1964 with me and was forever absent. He wasn't one of those who did the all-nighters. When we kicked up a fuss it was explained to us that Captain Robert Maxwell with the encouragement of the Prime Minister was busy boosting our export earnings by his business deals in New York. It was suggested that we really ought to feel grateful that he was prepared to go over and sell his books over there.   HAROLD WALKER

✗ The Labour Party had nothing like the numbers we've got now in the Lords, so we were at the mercy of the Tories and it did need a good deal of skill to handle it. I'd been there for twenty years and made my mark, but I was never quite sure whether Harold Wilson was really pleased with it. I like to think that he was but he didn't make me chairman of any cabinet committee. I did a lot of speaking and Wilson was kind enough to say that I was very successful in those ways. I had the honour and glory. But in an impotent way. I did come to get very fond of him but you could never tell quite what was in his mind.

He told me that Albert Alexander was entitled to be Leader of the Lords but he was much older and he'd talked to Clem Attlee who said it must be me. It could be that the reason he wanted me as Leader in the House of Lords was that I needn't be given too important a role. The Tories wanted to win but they were concerned they would get into bad trouble if they were too nasty to us. I was, on paper anyway, skilful at getting things through. There was Attlee, Morrison, Alexander, people like that, Edith Summerskill. You can tell how few we were because we could get everybody into the Leader's room for meetings.   LORD   LONGFORD

✗ The first really rough water was a meeting of the Parliamentary Party before Christmas, in November. It was about pension rises. It took place in the Grand Committee Room upstairs. It was even darker, smellier and shabbier than it is now. It was absolutely packed. It was an adversarial situation and there were inflammatory, eloquent speeches

"TUT, TUT, SOMEONE'S WRITTEN A FIVE-LETTER WORD!"

about socialist belief from Jack Mendelson and a number of others who had not got jobs, and a very powerful intervention from Ian Mikardo. The feeling was of an enormous costly mistake, that Harold Wilson, because of his personal distaste, did not appoint Ian Mikardo.   TAM DALYELL

✗ I told my constituency party and the electorate in the 1964 election that I would not support the nationalisation of steel which I reckoned would lose at least a million pounds a day. It was totally pointless. The government already had sufficient control over it through their arrangement with the Iron and Steel Federation. I thought it was just a piece of nonsense, and they accepted that. Even the miners in the area agreed. I had a little local 'Gallup poll' and all the voters supported me.

When we won the election I was determined to see that they didn't nationalise steel which I thought would be bad for the country and bad for the Labour Party, one more albatross around their necks, very pointless. At the same time I'd made a deal with Jo Grimond who was then the leader of the Liberal

Party. I asked him if he would back us, me and two or three dissidents, in stopping nationalisation of steel. He said that he would. He came to lunch at my house and afterwards I told him I was going to write a letter to Harold Wilson and tell him what we were going to do to stop it. Jo Grimond said he was going down that evening so he'd take it with him and the silly ass, instead of putting it in a letter box, gave it to some Liberal Party messenger. So of course Harold, who was an extraordinary fellow who knew who was the Liberal Party messenger, knew immediately. When he replied to me he said, 'I notice that the Liberal Party delivered the letter for you.'

Wilson was awfully tricky. He was always intriguing. He tried to get me out of my seat. He sent people down to my constituency and said I should be de-selected and ran a campaign against me. However, my local constituency party stood firm. They were miners, and they adopted me again for the next election. After my arrangement with Jo Grimond we never voted against the government. I took a thing to the iron and steel people by which they would accept the kind of BP solution, 51% owned by the government and the rest by private industry, but run on private enterprise lines like BP. They said they'd accept that. So I told George Brown, Wilson knew it too. At the critical debate I was to get up and ask if the government would reconsider. So at the given moment I got up – just as he was winding up – and said, 'Would the government reconsider it?' and he said, 'Yes,' to the fury of a great number of the Labour Party. So we didn't vote against it because they had backed down. Some people thought we'd backed down but we hadn't, we'd made the government back down. That went quite well and for the whole of that Parliament we didn't nationalise steel.

Then the steel people themselves lost their heads because when the public opinion polls were showing against Labour they thought, 'We don't have to bother about this any more.' I said, 'You're a lot of idiots because you may well have to bother about it.' They said, 'Oh no, we're not going to go ahead with this idea of yours.' When the election actually came we got a much bigger majority and then it was all over. Everything which I had forecast about the disasters of nationalising steel came to pass. WOODROW WYATT

✗ George Brown resolved the conflict with Wyatt and Donnelly but there was something going on behind the scenes which the government didn't know about until afterwards. The vote was at ten o'clock as usual. At half-past nine or so the whips were doing the rounds as they do. We had them all ticked off on a great board in the office, but ensuring that they were actually present and could be seen. Just outside the Strangers' Bar I said hello to one of the policeman. He said, 'There's two of your men missing.' This is the thing about whipping. Your information gathering comes from all sorts of places. 'Christ Almighty,' says I. Or perhaps 'Oh dear.' He said, 'Chris Norwood and Dick Kelly' – both left-wingers, by the way. He said, 'I think Chris has gone across to St Stephen's Tavern.'

I rushed out to grab hold of Chris and I found him in what might be called 'party mood' in the middle of Bridge Street, the traffic zipping past him on all sides. I knew Chris well. He was one of these young Oxford intellectuals who was rather disappointed because he wasn't in the cabinet, though he'd only been in the House for ten minutes. I grabbed him and said, 'Chris, you get down that passageway there and don't stop running until you're in the lobby.' That was Chris sorted out.

Dick Kelly was another problem. I couldn't find Dick and I was standing just outside the Library door in the corridor and the ten o'clock bell rang. So I just gently nodded my head against the jamb of the door and Dick came out of the Library. He'd actually been sleeping it off in the Library. So although George was doing his great manoeuvre in the chamber, the whole vote actually hung on these two fellows. With that kind of majority there still remains a great element of chance. If these two guys hadn't got slewed at half-past nine, probably because they were bored, which was the major difficulty of keeping people happy . . . They had to be there all the time. Ministers liked it but back-benchers had very little to do.

WILLIAM HOWIE

✗ They kept at us. We made a mistake in the first session – we introduced new tax measures of a very complicated kind. Corporation Tax was introduced and Capital Gains Tax, but we had no hesitation in saying that we were going to have a Capital Gains Tax before the election and so on. That was part of our tax-raising intent but the Corporation Tax, which took the place of the old profits tax, was very complicated indeed, and in those days every bit of a finance bill had to taken on the floor of the House. So day after day, night after night, this Corporation Tax Bill ground its way through the House of Commons almost from the time we arrived until the summer recess of 1965. That was very taxing indeed on us.

PETER SHORE

✗ I was a great enthusiast for Capital Gains Tax and Corporation Tax. One of the great things Jim Callaghan said was that it was a great pity that he spent so much of his time on that. I think he was probably right. Nicky was the genius behind it. It was really brilliantly done, the whole concept. It was unpicked subsequently but the idea was first class and it would have given much more money for investment because of retentions. Most firms get their money for investment from retentions, that's the essential part of it, and Capital Gains Tax fitted in superbly. As Nicky devised it, it was a superb structure but once it started being picked at here and amended there, the thing fell apart.

ROBERT SHELDON

✗ There was an MP for Hartlepool, Ted Leadbitter. He was elected in '64 and we'd been in power about a week when he wrote to me. He said, 'I'm writing to complain about a telegraph pole that is outside the house of a constituent. I've decided to withdraw support from the government until the telegraph pole is removed.' We had a majority of four. I wrote to him asking him to come and have a talk about it. He said, 'I'm not coming to see you until the telegraph pole is removed.' So I told the Chief Whip. Ted Leadbitter is a lovely guy, former headmaster, and I said to him, 'If the government fell after we'd been out of office for thirteen years, and people asked why it fell, it wouldn't go down too well that it was because Mr Benn wouldn't remove a telegraph pole from outside the house of a constituent.' That's the sort of pressure there was.

TONY BENN

8 We had thirty, forty people used to meet in the Tribune Group and it was friendly towards the government in many respects. It was out to support the government, it wasn't out to destroy the government. We had quarrels with the

government, chiefly over Vietnam. There were other matters where there were differences, but that was the number one, and the left of the party was absolutely right. The other major anger was the question of incomes policy. We were at that time opposed to any kind of incomes policy. I think we were wrong about that. I don't think the government's own incomes policy was the right policy but I certainly don't think you can have a proper Labour government that hasn't got an incomes policy.

In '64 it was a narrow victory but Harold Wilson right from that moment onwards worked to try and get a good majority which all of us on the left wanted. We didn't think that we could carry anything that was worthwhile unless we did it. So we were eager to co-operate with him on that, even though the Vietnam War had just overlapped a bit. There were a few troubles too on incomes policy. Overwhelmingly, the left of the party wanted a new election and a good majority in order to get on with the job better. And I think that was the right attitude.

MICHAEL FOOT

✘ The left-right thing was still there but after a very long period in opposition people were anxious to make a success of the government. One didn't automatically line up on a left-right political basis as one had done in the days of Bevanite/Gaitskellite tribal warfare in the fifties. I think we were very much on tenterhooks. That was one thing that held the party together. I was on tenterhooks until well into 1965, certainly after we lost the Leyton by-election. Frank Cousins nearly lost the Nuneaton by-election and these were supposed to be two absolute rock-solid seats.

Most people would have betted quite heavily against our winning the next election. The Speaker died, if you remember, and we had to appoint a Speaker and that was going to upset the balance and take one of the majority. The nightmare was that we were forced into an election with the chances heavily against us and that was Wilson's tactical achievement, that he avoided our being forced into an election when we had this tiny majority. He played all that quite skilfully.   ROY JENKINS

✘ I was searching. What am I going to do here? I didn't understand these various procedures, but luckily I picked on the right one, the economy and my contribution to it, and the

East of Suez one. I went into that in great detail, as to the costs of keeping our forces East of Suez, and every time I wrote down the costs of that they rose, and it wasn't just the cost of having the troops there, you were producing weaponry to meet the requirements there in the jungles and things like that.

So every time you produced a design for a tank, it's how did it stand the tropical heat of Malaysia? When you produced clothing, can it be used in some other parts of the world? So everything was orientated that way. And if you take those things into account plus all the other costs directly attributed to having troops over there it seemed to rise. I got it up to four hundred million pounds, an awful lot of money then, and I got it beyond that.   ROBERT SHELDON

✗ Vietnam was one of Harold Wilson's greatest mistakes in my opinion still, because the Vietnam War was a disaster for the Americans, a disaster for the whole Western world and we on the left of the Labour Party were wisely saying, 'It's wrong, and we should be saying that to our American allies.' I've no doubt that that decision was greatly influenced by the economic situation. Harold Wilson didn't make his mind up on attitudes to the Vietnam War solely on the international grounds, as he should have done and all should have done, but that would have been in the interests of the Americans.

MICHAEL FOOT

✗ I was not much against many other things, although I was against them on matters of defence. We were always cutting the armed forces. We couldn't stretch the thing to go on being East of Suez indefinitely. There were various rows about it. Personally I think I was wrong on this issue at the time. Wilson was right, because he was in favour of keeping our troops in Kuwait and various other places. I said, at a party meeting, 'I suppose you're only doing this because the Americans are paying you to do it.' He got up and said, 'I want to make it absolutely clear that this is total rubbish and nonsense. We're not being paid anything by the Americans.' I got up again and said, 'If we're not even being paid for it what the hell are we doing it for?' Actually I was wrong on that issue. I took a different view in those days but I think, in retrospect, if we'd kept our troops in Kuwait the Gulf War would never have happened.   WOODROW WYATT

✘ I could do nothing. All I could do was what I did. I came into the House as one of the rare examples of an industrial manager coming into Labour Party politics and I knew two things. One, the industrial policies were terrible, and two, that the National Plan was a farce. There was a party meeting at which we discussed the National Plan, and I indicated what I thought about it. George Brown said to me, 'Is Mr Dell saying that we cannot do better economically than the Tories?' I said, 'Yes, I am saying that.'

This was not because of any special default in our ability to manage, it wasn't because the Tories were so good, it was just the situation which we'd inherited. The illusion was that we could suddenly up the rate of growth of this country by Departments of Economic Affairs and Ministries of Technology.

As to what I did. Who am I? I'm a back-bencher and nobody's heard of me. I happen to have a particular sort of experience which tells me this policy cannot work in this time-scale but there was little more that I could do. I criticised the industrial policy. I criticised the National Plan, but that was all I could do. I was in the government by 1966. I did not press for devaluation then, I merely said this policy is incredible. To get up in the House of Commons and press for devaluation at that time would not have been the most popular thing to do. Nor did I press inside the party.   EDMUND DELL

✘ I thought we should devalue right from the beginning, and I said so, in fact I wrote it in huge letters in the *Daily Mail* where they put it on the front page. Wilson was very annoyed about it but I was right and they had to do it. Wilson was doing what governments so often do and will go on doing until the very end of time. They stand like the boy at the dyke with their finger in the hole thinking they're going to stop the sea coming over their heads. There was a sort of veto on discussing it in the PLP. They'd say, 'We can't discuss this.' When government can't decide what to do they say it's much too important to be discussed! All governments, all parties say that.

WOODROW WYATT

✘ Before the election I had hopes for a resurgence of industry, this was the big thing. THE BIG THING, and about time it came. We'd just done nothing and we'd seen what was going on in other countries and I thought this really must be our number one priority, forget everything else. The sad thing was that to many on the left Vietnam became a more important problem than this. If they had spent all their efforts on pressing industry it might have been better. The Tribune Group was a very left-wing group at that time. I came near to joining it at one stage, but they spent their time on Vietnam where we could have little effect.

I realised that the problem wasn't being addressed. The Ministry of Technology was a joke, Frank Cousins and Lord Snow. Frank Cousins was scared stiff of the House of Commons, Lord Snow was busy thinking how his books were relevant to the political situation of the time, and he wasn't even in the House of Commons. I went to America in 1965 and met Douglas Wass who knew exactly how I was feeling and he intimated to me that he was completely sympathetic, which he was. He was a strong devaluationist from the word go.

ROBERT SHELDON

✗ I thought we would devalue straightaway. You take a difficult measure first and by the time the next election comes round you're well on the way to doing things that will be helpful to you to win it. I spoke about it in Parliament, but you have to speak in guarded terms. Everybody, now as well as then, feels that to talk about the pound is something you just don't do. It's a dirty word to talk about devaluation. The PLP itself was not the forum to discuss this. It was the Economic and Finance Committee which I basically became chairman of. Most of them agreed with us, but they wouldn't make any strong representations as a committee. So, one had to do it oneself. We started speaking to ministers. Individually. Bob and I were the group. We were making representations all over the place, including Harold. But nobody else seemed to be terribly concerned about it in 1964, apart from George, who was the strongest of our supporters. Indeed, he would argue that we were his supporters because he was really fighting against the cabinet. In 1964 we had no success.   JOEL BARNETT

✗ I think the 1966 election was held just in time. We couldn't have lasted much longer. We were getting very very tired indeed by the end of 1965. It was a shock as a new MP working those kind of hours, but the attitude was different from what it

ELECTION THRILLER No. 1

Will the sharp-toothed shark gobble up the floating voter – or will handsome Harold take the plunge and snatch the floating voter from the jaws of no return – or will the sharp-toothed shark wait for intrepid Harold to jump in and then gobble up both him and the floating voter – or will handsome Harold wait for reinforcements – or will . . . etc. Replies to No. 10 Downing Street, please.

is now. One was in there by conviction. Nowadays there is much more a sense of seeing Parliament as a career rather than as a vocation. Then it was something that you did because you badly wanted to do it.   HUGH JENKINS

✗ We were constantly tied to the House of Commons. It was terrible. Worse than the later experiences in the seventies, or when the Tories waged the war of attrition in 1950. I can tell you some horrendous stories. There were only ten doctors in both Houses. We used to be called on quite frequently, particularly during late-night sessions. In '64 to '66 we had some dramatic episodes. Lesley Spriggs had an embolism in his leg and he went to Manor House Hospital and he was looked after by one of my colleagues. Dr Kenneth rang me and said, 'Your mad men in the whips' office want to move this crazy patient of mine to go down in an ambulance to Westminster, stay in the ambulance and be counted as if he is going through the lobbies, and he is willing to do it. Dick, this fellow's got an embolism and I refuse to give him permission. But he insists he's going with or without medical permission. I've explained to him that the embolism could move and go right through his system to block his heart, but he won't listen. Can you do something?'

I said, 'Yes,' and I went up to see Lesley and argued with him, but I couldn't change his mind. I said to him, ' Lesley, you are being unfair to your wife.' He replied, 'The Labour Party is in difficulties. I must go and vote.' I described to him the difficulties of making the journey, going over bumps, emergency stops, any situation that could arise and how this could affect his embolism. I couldn't frighten him. So I went with him in the ambulance and he was counted through, he breezed through it and it never crossed his mind that his wife could have been widowed that night. There were other desperately ill members who agreed or even volunteered to come in to help to save the government. There was such passion about it because the Tories were hoping to hound us from office through illness. DICKSON MABON

✘ There was an old, very loyal party member, a man who must have been around seventy, which I then thought was rather an advanced age, called Frank Hayman, the member for Falmouth. He had a heart attack and we couldn't get him paired. So we did one of the sort of things that make your toes curl to think of. We booked a compartment in a train and we plonked Fred in it and his wife and an oxygen cylinder. We didn't put him through the lobby, of course. We brought him up and lodged him in one of the interview rooms below the chamber and there they sat; then he was wheeled back.

Needless to say he died shortly afterwards. That was towards the end of that Parliament. Norman Dodds died, and the fellow in Hull, Henry Solomons. The three of them died round about Christmas/New Year in '65. That was the majority to all intents and purposes gone, you couldn't really continue. We killed these three. That possibly over-dramatises the situation. Let's put it this way: the pressure we put on these three to attend the House when they were extremely ill was a contributory factor in their deaths. WILLIAM HOWIE

CHAPTER EIGHT

On to Victory

	1965				1966						
	Sept	Oct	Nov	Dec	Jan	Feb 4	Feb 25	Mar 4	Mar 13	Mar 20	Mar 27	Mar 31
Lab.	43	41	42	41	39	41	41	43	41	43	44	44
Con.	37	37	36	34	37	37	35	33	33	35	36	34
Lead	+6	-4	-6	+7	+2	+4	+6	+10	+8	+8	+8	+10

(all polls from Gallup)

The long election, stretching from late 1963 up to March 1966, beginning in the media then transferring to the hustings then to the 1964–6. Parliament and finally back to the hustings, was Harold Wilson's finest hour. The best part of it was from mid-1965 to Labour's triumphant election victory in March 1966.

The whole eighteen months were a period of frenetic activity, endless initiatives, driven by a dynamic new prime minister demonstrating his greatest skill: that of the high-wire artist. Yet the loss of the Leyton by-election and the fall in the Labour vote when Frank Cousins was brought in for Nuneaton were warnings that the electorate could not be taken for granted. Through the early months of 1965 support as measured by the Gallup poll fell away. By August the Conservatives were in the lead. What transformed the situation was not Harold Wilson's skill in wrong footing the Tories and their new leader Edward Heath, but the apparent toughness and determination of his stance. On the economy, he defied the speculators and the Gnomes and invoked a

Dunkirk spirit he had once deplored. On Rhodesia's unilateral declaration of independence he stood firm against rebellion. This allowed Wilson to dominate the stage, rally the nation, and divide the Tories.

Labour moved back into the lead. As it did so the time became ripe for a new election. Harold Wilson always claimed that he planned things in advance and knew crucial dates, such as the timing of the 1970 election, and his own retirement in 1976, well ahead. He said the same about the 1966 election, claiming that everything, from his entry into Downing Street in October 1964, was planned on an eighteen-month agenda.

Perhaps it was. Yet it was clear by the last quarter of 1965 that everything was moving Labour's way. The time was becoming ripe but it took the death of Henry Solomons, the MP for Hull North, in November 1965, and the resulting Hull North by-election in January, to prove it. If Labour was confident it would win the by-election, and the general election which would follow, then that confidence didn't show, for every stop was pulled out, from Barbara Castle's promise of a Humber Bridge (which eventually cost £70 million) to by-election campaigning on an unprecedented scale. Everything centred on Hull.

When Labour won Hull North, the 1966 general election followed automatically. It lacked the revivalist atmosphere and the energy of 1964, being fought in dark suits and from office almost as a process of predestination rather than the cliff-hanger of 1964. Labour won: a percentage lead of 6% over the Tories, an overall majority of 97 and a mandate for a postponed new start. R. H. S. Crossman asked himself, 'Can we get that new start twenty months after the government came into power? Of course we have a majority of a hundred. Of course the cabinet has a good deal of experience. But are we doomed to a bout of deflation?' In fact they were. The majority to do anything was marched straight into the bunker.

✘ In the first six months we were so pleased to be there; we knew the minority was slender but Harold Wilson always behaved with very great skill and appointed unknown people to be Deputy Speakers and so forth. So I don't think for the first six months I felt it was very precarious, or that we were just looking to the next election. But then if you're new into government it's an exciting experience, you're buoyed up by it. Never underestimate the thrill of holding office, whether you're new into government with a precarious majority or have been in government for donkey's years with your party falling apart. It isn't just your car, it isn't just your power. It's an orderly life where you've got people working for you of high quality and you're making decisions. I enjoyed it and I was very busy so I didn't think there was an ominous threat. And also I think I took the view that when the election came, unless we made a total mess of it, we were bound to win. The country having by a narrow majority opted for a Labour government was going to give a good endorsement the second time round; this is what one would expect, I think, in any comparable circumstances. Second time round if you're on the rise you do better. If you're on the fall, as in '50/'51, it's quite different.   BILL RODGERS

✘ Harold enjoyed it. During the Tory Conference he would go to Balmoral to see the Queen so that the speculation would be, 'Will there be an election?' The whole Tory Conference would be utterly ruined. He was very clever at that. TONY BENN

✘ Patrick Gordon Walker lost in Leyton and that was an absolute disaster because we then had a majority of four, less the Speaker, and by losing this one seat Wilson now had a majority of two after only three months in office. At that moment it did look as if Labour would not win the next election but Ian Smith did Wilson a wonderful turn with his UDI in November 1965, enabling Wilson to play the kind of patriotic card – 'Think again, Prime Minister,' this kind of thing, and flying up to Balmoral the week of the Tory Conference. Everyone thought he was going to ask for a dissolution. He wasn't at all. He was just consulting the Queen about Rhodesia.

The whole Rhodesia thing dragged on for years and was a terrible embarrassment. Wilson used his fateful phrase about weeks not months for bringing them to heel. None the less, in the short term, in terms of the 1966 election, Rhodesia was a wonderful bonus. It enabled him to play the national leader

and no one really could be against him. There were wild right-
wingers in the Monday Club who were pro-Smithy and kith
and kin and all that but even respectable Conservatives had to
condemn it. He was on a winning streak there. UDI was 11
November 1965 and I think from that moment on it was pretty
clear that Wilson must win the election.   TONY HOWARD

✘ The thing that governments are most guilty of is self-
deception. We all have to deceive others from time to time but
don't start off by deceiving yourself. If you do that I think
you're more likely to go desperately wrong. The self-deception
on Rhodesia was that sanctions were going to work. I saw the
telegrams. As a junior minister in the DEA I saw a lot of things
that junior ministers wouldn't have seen. I was absolutely
convinced from the beginning that sanctions wouldn't work.
We knew the policy would fail. I would have taken the view,
probably wrong in retrospect, that we could have gone in and
got rid of Smith. But Denis Healey wouldn't have done it at
Defence. The Ministry of Defence is a very difficult department
to move. It really believes it's got to have everything going for
it to go in and they won't go in except with everything which is
almost certain to guarantee a victory several times over. But
I'm not making an issue of that, and I did not make an issue of
that then, I mentioned it to one or two friends but I wasn't
outspoken about it and I am quite prepared to say I was
wrong. What I didn't like was the extent to which we were
deceiving ourselves.

In the beginning of 1966 the economic situation began to
deteriorate very seriously. That was when a new committee
was set up. I think it was called SET. It was an inner cabinet on
economic policy which hadn't existed before, and it came into
existence largely from pressure by Tony Crosland and Roy
Jenkins, neither of whom was an economic minister but both of
whom of course were concerned about the economic situation.
In the early part of 1966 the economic signs were so distressing
that we would have been in a desperately difficult situation if
the election had been postponed and, indeed, we were
afterwards when there was something of a delay before the
economic measures of the summer of 1966 – which everybody,
especially George, hated but which by then were inescapable.

BILL RODGERS

✗ Harold had already decided before the Hull North by-election to have a general election on 31 March. I know that because I was there with him. I'd arrived in the October and he kept nothing from me. We discussed everything, and I know that he'd decided the date of the election, just as I knew long before his resignation in '76 that he was going to resign. So it came as no surprise whatsoever to me, and all those extraordinary theories which have arisen have always earned my scorn because I knew he was going to go, I knew why he was going to go, I knew he was going to call a general election on 31 March 1966. But of course he was very encouraged by the result of Hull North, and once we'd got to that point it was clear we were going to do very well and that we were going to increase the majority substantially. As we did. GERALD KAUFMAN

✗ The majority at Hull North was roughly a thousand. It was crucial for me because it changed the whole of my life, but it was an interesting win for all sorts of reasons. Firstly, because it had only been just won in '64, it had been a Tory seat until then. In 1959 it was the only Labour seat that had been put down to be won in that election, and it was the only one at that time that wasn't.

How and why did I win? Well the favoured candidate for the constituency was a man called Guy Barnett, who became quite a close friend of mine. Guy had won the South Dorset by-election in '62. He lost the seat in '64 and, therefore, appeared on every list for by-elections and he was the one that the Labour Party wanted. But I fortunately had the nomination of four wards and the support of the Transport and General Workers' Union. This was the last selection in which – to be delegate to the party – you did not have to be an individual member of the Labour Party. So you had roughly twenty-five T&G delegates, thirty-seven USDAW (it had been an USDAW seat), eighteen engineers, quite a number of electricians, eighteen GMB as well as the wards. I could understand why the people at Transport House wanted Guy Barnett. They didn't know me. Somehow my reputation had gone before me. I don't know why, but much of Harold Wilson's letter to the candidate in the by-election was of the advantages of the Irish Free Trade Treaty and that with my finest public monument a statue of William of Orange and about six Irish people living in the constituency.

The PLP adjourns to Hull

The regional secretary of the TGWU told me to go down to the office at once. He wouldn't tell me what it was about so I got on my bike and went down to the T&G offices, sat down and he said, 'Sign those.' It was a big stack of nomination forms. 'Nobody speaks to me like that,' he said. 'They came up to me and they said they didn't want anybody from the Transport and General Workers' Union, and in particular they didn't want McNamara.' Anyway, I just filled in the forms and he said, 'That's it. I'll get the delegates,' and that was it. They got Frank Cousins, who was then in the cabinet, to ring him up to pressure him about supporting me and say, 'What's going on, Bob?' Bob said, 'He's a good T&G lad.' So Frank said, 'That's all right then.' That's all I was asked to do. As far as I can gather they put all sorts of pressures on not to have me. Fortunately, I was selected at the end of November and, apart from a brief period up to Christmas, after that my feet scarcely touched the ground. I was up at 6.30 a.m. and went to bed at 10.00 p.m.

It was the most highly organised election I have seen for the Labour Party. It was amazing. There were paid agents, not in every ward but in nearly every polling district. The turnout was I think something like eighty-eight per cent, certainly approaching the nineties, on a register that was fifteen months out of date. The degree of organisation was fantastic, the meetings were phenomenal. At first, John Anson, who was the agent, refused to allow me on television. Then I spent an hour or so being grilled by Anthony Howard in the new television room in Transport House; I came out feeling like a damp rag after he'd finished with me. After that Anson said, 'Go on as often as you like.' But they wouldn't let me on – afraid of the Gott factor.

It was an election that gripped the imagination. People understood the national significance of it. You went from ward to ward and they were all there, George Brown, Jenkins, Barbara Castle, Tony Benn, Thomson, Michael Stewart, packed meeting after packed meeting. I think that was probably the last time streets were decorated in Yorkshire by-elections. The strange thing was, though, that everyone thought we were going to lose because the Tories did a brilliant PR exercise. They took over a couple of empty shops and in every window you had people busy at typewriters for the agent. Longbottom, a Tory who was member for York, which was then a marginal seat, and Jopling, and Kitson, did a fantastic PR job from the Royal Station Hotel. Champagne for everybody, that sort of thing.

The place was flooded with Labour people coming down. Thirty years on I keep meeting people who tell me they were in Hull that day, knocking on the doors. It was amazing, and because it was so programmed, I was doing things all the time, I was so exhausted at night that I didn't have time to lie down and think, 'Oh my God, what happens if I lose.' I never anticipated losing. I just got so carried away with it.

KEVIN MCNAMARA

✗ I expected to win the '66 election hands down. I never lost faith. We were going to win, we were winning. We'd lost Leyton in '65 but we won Hull North and that was a signal. There is an interesting story about Hull North. It was down to a bridge. You have to be smart enough to know the right time to close or open a road, or a bridge, or a new railway line. Civil servants won't do that for you. You have to do that for yourself, and you have to make a case to justify it, which we know, as politicians, will not be the real reason why you are advocating it. It is the economic reason for political advantage, disgraceful though that is from the point of view of civil servants. 1966 was more dignified, and we also knew our stuff, we knew where we were going. We were really ready in the winter of '65 and the spring of '66 to put forward our programme. More ready than we had been in '64.

DICKSON MABON

✗ If you ask me was there any doubt about the 1966 election I will tell you that the odds at Ladbrokes were 9 to 1 on Labour. I was in America and I hadn't got much money in those days. But I had a friend called Ron Pollard in Ladbrokes and I rang him up from Washington and said, 'Ron, I want to put £1,800 on a Labour win,' and he said, 'Have you got £1,800?' and I said, 'Yes, I've just got £1,800.' He asked me if I was sure I wanted him to do it and I told him, 'Absolutely.' Sure enough it was money for jam. It seemed to me so clear that even with attractive odds of 9 to 1 to have lost that bet it would have required Wilson to have been found in bed with Christine Keeler.

TONY HOWARD

✗ Donations received to help us were so tiny people would burst out laughing now if you told them. That was the case throughout all of Harold's years. Despite any of the publicity that came later on, they were tiny tiny tiny sums. There was never any funding. We never had any money so you could not appoint people to help you who were on top of their job. You had to settle for someone who was near retirement or someone who was dedicated to the party or someone who was second or third rate and we ended up with people who might not have been what we needed but we had to make do because we didn't have the money to spend on that.

One of the nicest things Harold ever said to me was, 'We never made any mistakes. I never saw us on the front page of

any paper having said something that caused the headline'–
and it's true we didn't. It was a massive operation because there
were thousands of letters coming in. We did have the clerks of
the Parliamentary Labour Party during the election campaign of
'64 and '66. Through the three weeks of that campaign they
went to Transport House because you were not allowed to work
in the Palace of Westminster and they worked there answering
all our letters for us. That was very, very helpful and they took
calls coming from the general public. Otherwise it would have
been quite unmanageable. It was just for that three-week period
and I think they didn't do anything before that and then after
we'd won they were not allowed into No.10. You've got to be
vetted and it's such a complicated procedure, at least it was
then. I wouldn't have thought everybody walking in is going to
be a KGB agent. That's the sort of talk we had when we first
went in in '64.   MARCIA WILLIAMS

✗ One of the things we did do for the '66 election was that we
started our early-morning meetings where for the first time a
small group of us sat down and we had all the newspapers, we
assessed all the issues, we assessed the reactions to what we'd
done the day before. That was the first time that we did that.
We got more system into things. We got more objectivity. We
got more rationality. Compared with today, there wasn't
manipulation in that sense. I don't think you could have called
us spin doctors because it wasn't what we were doing. Until
the '66 election the Labour Party didn't take us seriously. There
was still a strong anxiety about it, even in '70. Then we would
go into the campaign committee and there would be very open
arguments. We were just setting up and the rest of the
campaign was purely about policies, issues, and what the
Labour government could do. We didn't have the control of
television parties now have. We didn't have much time for
television. We didn't have the money which was a very
important limiting factor. We had to accept we were in an
environment in which the media wasn't going to support us.
Therefore we had to take that into account in the way we
positioned ourselves in what we did. The personality factor
was certainly there with Harold but it was still very balanced
with issues and clear statements of issues and policies. I don't
think we've got that at the moment. Sadly. I wish we had.
                                                   DAVID KINGSLEY

✘ In the campaign we were very much reacting to the newspapers because the agenda was being set by the newspapers, not the television. So every morning at 6 a.m. we had to read them and then you would have the campaign meeting downstairs, which was always held in the General Secretary's room at 8 a.m., where they worked out the strategy, then maybe you would alter your briefing notes.   ANN CARLTON

✘ To fight the 1966 campaign the political staff had to move over. We were given the women's officer's room at party headquarters, nothing grander than that, and in the '64 campaign we also had to move out – and we were not welcome in Transport House either really. They put us in some not terribly good accommodation and we had to make do and mend there; we were not very welcome at our party headquarters or at No. 10, so in two election campaigns we were a bit like asylum seekers. You were exhausted but no way could you stop. You had to go on and you ploughed on with your health being damaged as a result because you had no sleep. When we got to the '66 campaign I had shingles and the doctor said, 'Don't tell anybody, just grin and bear it; just get on with it,' and I went round the country with terrible shingles. I was in such agony, being in low health. It was the hours that were being worked, unsocial hours and no wasting time.

To a certain extent, though, your part is smoother because you're with the Prime Minister. He doesn't stop being Prime Minister, going round the country to address meetings. So it was easier in that sense and you had the official machine with you the whole time and so there is a certain amount of unseen and unspoken help that you get even if it's small and so in that sense it was easier. By then we had more staff; I'd already been able to add other people. Transport House became more co-operative in that they allowed us two girls, by the time we got to '66 I think we were allowed two secretaries, so that was great and meant there were then three of us plus Gerald, making four. So we were quite well staffed by the time we got to the '66 election, compared to the '64 when there was just me.

It was easier to organise. Train arrangements, everything was easier; the atmosphere was different. You were coming and bringing the office with you. It was one of the advantages of winning, getting in there, and the next time you'll be able to get your next election under your belt with a better majority because you have every advantage of being the prime minister. People want to see you, and in that '66 campaign we noticed that people wanted to touch him. It hadn't happened in elections before but ever since it's been the case; with other people they want to touch royalty or pop stars but in those days it was mainly politicians, because politicians were much more highly regarded. They had a much more glamorous look about them than they do now. It was a great event when a prime minister suddenly came down or the MP turned up. It wasn't just any old body; now they probably go on eating and chatting away and don't notice you're in the room. But it was a big event. We arrived and they were all wanting to touch him; they would knock you out of the way just to touch him. We noticed that young people particularly were absolutely excited beyond belief that he was there amongst them. So it looked good but even looking good didn't convince me until it was there and I could see it and somebody said, 'Right, you've won.'   MARCIA WILLIAMS

✘ In 1966 I was part of the team writing *Today* – the briefing notes for candidates. These were six pages of short sharp journalism, or so we thought at the time. *Today* was sent to candidates to arrive next morning. The pages were short and sharp on the grounds that candidates should be canvassing not reading in offices. The fax had not been invented so *Today* was the main way of influencing the campaign out in the constituencies. I suspect many of them never read it, but we lived in hope. There was no photocopying. Everything had to be produced on Gestetner skins, then rolled off in the general office and collated there. Consequently we had very little writing time. We came in at 6 a.m., read the papers delivered by the paper shop in Horseferry Road – which also delivered to Conservative Central Office – decided what we wanted to write about that day in the light of the papers, and any other issues we wanted to promote or defensive points we wanted to cover, started writing while somebody went downstairs to the 8 a.m. strategy meeting to tell them what had been decided. The strategy meeting attendee would then come back upstairs and tell us whether our items had been approved or if new ones were to be covered.   ANN CARLTON

'. . . and I know why' – Jim Callaghan, 1966

✘ We didn't doubt that the party nationally would win in '66. We were sure it would win though we didn't have the polling process in those days so it was much more guesswork than it is now. Not that the polls are always right but we do have a much better idea about trends nowadays than we did then, when it was much more a case of guesswork really. The '66 election was much more an organisational job than in '64; mind you, the people still came over, but it wasn't so much an unexpected result as it had been in 1964. The result in '66 was obtained, I think, partly by better organisation and partly because we still carried the enthusiasm. I had become the MP. Once you are the MP it's much easier to stay the MP, particularly if the party as a whole is in a winning frame of mind – which it was in '66. I remember saying that: 'Now Putney has gone socialist and we are a socialist constituency and will remain so.' I could see this to be a permanent situation. HUGH JENKINS

✘ We went back in with a song in our hearts in that we are here and we've come back and we are the government and we've won. It is a Labour government. That was our '66 slogan, 'You Know Labour Government Works', I remember it clearly because I had gone to one of the northern seats to check out the hall for Harold. Our press officer was hanging it upside down from the rafters and I looked up and there was the message, 'You Know Labour Government Works', but it was upside down. So I said to him, 'You do really have to hang it up the right way.' It was a good slogan. People really did believe it, they actually accepted that that was the case. It was a jolly good campaign slogan. It worked.   MARCIA WILLIAMS

✖ I think, looking back, I was in a bit of a daze. Everything is new at your first election. You're hyped up and you're making speeches and you're rushing around. I remember walking into the House of Commons. It's different today, with security. I remember going in through St Stephens Yard and a bloke said, 'Hey, what are you doing here?' and I said, 'I'm coming to work.' He was a bit numb. He thought I was a painter or something. He said, 'You're not a new Member of Parliament are you?' I said, 'I am.' 'Oh,' he said. 'Go in.' And I wandered in and I went through that door and got in the first lift and finished up in the press gallery. It was most bizarre and I went around asking naïve things like, 'Can I have a plan of the place?' You can never get a plan of all the corridors in the House of Commons for security reasons. I went home again, having met nobody (as you wouldn't in recess time) and waited for something to happen. Unconsciously, I expected to be thrown out every now and again. What was I doing there? I was aware that some of my colleagues who had just been elected were talking about which junior ministers they were going to be. I thought, 'You bastards!'   JOHN ELLIS

✖ We didn't feel the world was our oyster because we knew with an inward groan we were going back into politics. Remember, this is still the time of Vietnam, still the time of Rhodesia – two world events that were hanging there like black clouds. And the economy. We knew we'd actually been able to make it look good and be very convincing in the election campaign but there were problems up ahead, particularly with the Trade Union Movement, over wages and the prices problem. There were difficulties. We knew that they were there. We could feel them. Harold came back into No.10 and we all went up in the lift together to the flat. He said, 'I

All dressed up and nowhere to go – victory night 1966

think we'll just mark time for a little while to recover our strength,' meaning just let it tick over until we can re-group and work out what we want and where we're going. But by the time he'd sat down to work that out, God knows what happened and all hell broke loose.   MARCIA WILLIAMS

✘ Just before the '66 election, and after it as well, his health was deteriorating. It wasn't Harold of '64. He was lack lustre, depressed, he couldn't be bothered to do things. We had one cabinet meeting late one afternoon, about revising the legislation on secrecy. I've never known a meeting get into such a tangle in all my life. It was as though a cat had got into a ball of wool and tangled it all up. People all around the place were putting different points and there was nothing to pull it together. It was an absolute tangle and for the first time he couldn't draw it all together at the end, he had to leave it at that. I used to go to see him and whereas previously he had been bright and lively and joking, and was a great man for gossip – he knew all the party gossip about people – he now seemed to lack interest in anything at all. I think it was the beginning of his illness. Not the Alzheimer's but the other thing, for which he had a major operation later. It was a great tragedy. This bright, lively man who was thought by everyone to be devious – but he wasn't devious, he was just very clever and could think more moves ahead than most people. When a chap can do that he often gives the impression of being devious. He was the kindest man imaginable. Too kind, as a matter of a fact. He supported his friends through thick and thin. And he just sort of went down. It was sad. I loved the man.   TED SHORT

CHAPTER NINE

The Power to Fail

					1966					
	May	June	July	Aug	Sept	Oct	Nov	Dec	Jan	Feb
Lab.	48	46	42	37	38	34	35	41	39	43
Con.	32	35	36	38	36	38	38	37	36	32
Lead	+16	+11	+6	-1	+2	-4	-3	+4	+3	+11
					1967					
	Mar	Apr	May	June	July	Aug	Sept	Oct	Nov	Dec
Lab.	35	34	34	34	37	33	35	30	29	26
Con.	35	40	40	39	37	36	38	38	40	42
Lead	—	-6	-6	-5	—	-3	-3	-8	-11	-16

(all polls from Gallup)

Labour now had the power to carry through its programme of economic regeneration to build a new Britain and the better society for which it had been elected. It had a massive majority of enthusiastic new MPs. It had an experienced team of ministers who had shown that Labour government worked. It had a Prime Minister who had risen to new heights of popularity.

Yet within months all those advantages had been thrown away, and the government's popularity had collapsed. Harold Wilson, exhausted from his successful campaign, relaxed – but the impossibility of Labour's position was now suddenly brought home. Labour had to get growth but had committed itself to deflationary policies to defend sterling. Now a widening balance-of-payments deficit and another sterling crisis exacerbated by a seamen's strike showed that the policies of 1964–6 had not worked. So devaluation again came to the fore. Once again Wilson rejected it despite the fact that it was now politically straightforward and he had a majority to do anything. He did allow a cabinet vote on the issue, but he made it a question of confidence in himself.

So the government again chose deflation in the July measures. Soldiering on into futility ruled out growth and lost George Brown, who left the Department of Economic Affairs and killed the National Plan; all was a prelude to sixteen more months of doomed rearguard action against the inevitable.

That came in November 1967 when the forces Wilson had been attempting to damn up became irresistible. Labour was forced to devalue. Too little and too late, but deeply damaging and discrediting because so long delayed. R. H. S. Crossman wrote that this was the 'destruction of the Wilson myth in the public eye and even more in my own private eye. It's amazing how his luck ran up to a certain point and suddenly stopped. I suppose it is the most dramatic decline any modern prime minister has suffered.'

From finest hour to worst, in a year and a half. Labour plumbed the depths as party and leader tumbled in the polls. That fall and the losses in council and by-elections were worse than any modern party had experienced.

✘ Some of the things done by that government were good, but the great weakness of it, the thing that broke that government and has broken many other Labour governments and every Labour government has to prepare against, was the financial crisis. In '66 when we had that hundred majority, that was the greatest moment the Labour Party had had since 1945 and the greatest opportunity we've had for a real, settled long-term achievement by a Labour government led by pretty capable people – not only Harold Wilson himself but Callaghan, Roy Jenkins, Barbara Castle and Dick Crossman and the rest. They were pretty highly skilled.

So 'Why did this happen? people may say. It was chiefly the failure to understand the full scale of the economic blizzard

Waiting for Black Rod . . . or devaluation – State Opening, 1966

that was going to hit us and to know how we should stand up to it. Some of us on the left of the party would have had, I think, a better way of standing up to the blast than Harold. You had to have a more deliberate Keynesian plan for dealing with the blight of economic crisis, and we didn't have it. At the first signs of the economic threat Harold Wilson gave in. He and the government were so bitterly hostile to any idea of devaluation that they just closed the door to what would have been the remedy. They made the big mistake of thinking that devaluation would have been the biggest crisis ever, and then we'd robbed ourselves of the means of escape from it.

When the crisis came even Harold Wilson, who had a good strong majority, showed signs of being so much knocked off course he could never get back on it again. The Treasury is the place we've got to get under control if a Labour government comes in. In that case the Treasury was allowed to get away with it. I'm sorry to say that it doomed the whole government. It wasn't all doom, of course. It isn't the case that that '64 to '70 government didn't achieve anything. If we'd had earlier control over the economic situation we could have achieved a lot more and indeed not have suffered the defeat that we had in '70. The majority of one hundred was the golden moment which was somehow thrown away. We'll have another golden moment before the end of the century. If you look back at all these Labour governments, each one was destroyed by a kind of economic crisis or economic enemies in the country.

MICHAEL FOOT

✘ Everything suddenly went right and equally suddenly it went wrong. The day that it went wrong was the 20 July 1966, when there was this statement on the pound, and it was partly that Harold had absolutely relaxed from his big election victory. He'd done very little from the election victory right through that May and June, and taken it easy. Then, suddenly, the deluge. I also think it was something else that happened. He had lived by the press and television. He then got the question, an artless question, from a man, Sir John Langford Holt who was the MP for Shrewsbury, who had never hurt a fly. Harold started on this question and went into a long tirade against Colonel Sammy Lohan and D Notices, and in twenty minutes at the despatch box absolutely infuriated the press whom he had previously enchanted. Those who live by the press have their problems.

DAVID MARQUAND

✘ Things got more difficult after the election. The first reason was that the self-imposed restraints were relaxed. Left-wingers would no longer go through the lobby in tears – I've actually seen that. One of my group came out of the lobby in tears and he said, 'I gave that vote for you, Will, not for Harold Wilson.' It was really gut-wrenching for some of them to go through the lobbies during that period. So that was relaxed which meant they could relieve their consciences a bit and perhaps make up a bit of lost ground. That was the first difficulty.

The second difficulty was that the new intake was a bit odd. The intake of '64 consisted to a large extent of quite old hands, even the new ones. They'd been around. You would meet them in the party in various places and you would know who they were and they would have fought elections themselves, sometimes several, so they were far from callow. They knew about politics and they knew that whether they wanted to or not things couldn't be done immediately.

The new intake had a certain element among it of rather

academic, very clever, youngish men who were in a bit of a hurry. There were people like John Mackintosh, David Marquand, Stanley Henig, Jimmy Dickens, they were all bright, clever people with bright, clever ideas, an eagerness to get on, an eagerness to press the government; some of them were pressing very hard to get into Europe. Some of them were pressing very hard for what you might call socialist measures. And some for devaluation. Oddly enough the most interesting comment I heard in those days about devaluation was from Bob Maxwell. He said he didn't think we should devalue, it would only make him richer!

They were more difficult to handle, they were more argumentative and the majority was big. The young bloods didn't take quite so readily to the constraints of whipping. They assumed that whips were unnecessary. It wasn't that they were ill-disciplined but they were individuals. They were eager. Their eagerness was really their undoing. Whips are men of balanced, compassionate nature. They've seen things before and they don't rush madly into enthusiasms, whereas these young people on both wings of the party were enthusiasts. They would press for something and the whip would say, 'Oh Jesus Christ, am I hearing this? Is this true?' The new group were, in the nicest sense, amateurs. They lacked that cynicism which is the most delightful characteristic a politician can have. He's got to be seriously cynical, and they didn't have it. That made it difficult.   WILLIAM HOWIE

✗ It fell apart quicker than anything I've ever known. The high-water mark of Wilson's political career was the night of 31 March 1966 when he'd won this majority. He'd proved that he was a master politician. He now had the biggest majority Labour had ever had, with one exception in 1945. The world was at his feet and from that moment on everything went wrong. Everything turned to dust, really very very quickly. The seamen's strike came along. All sorts of accidents happened. Frank Cousins was getting all het up about incomes policy and he walked out of the government, not that he was a great asset to the government but none the less it was a bit of an embarrassment. Really from that moment on, with the July measures of 1966, I don't think that Labour government ever recovered.   TONY HOWARD

✘ All sorts of things were beginning to go wrong then. There was a lot of unease in the Parliamentary Party, a lot of restlessness, and if you are a junior minister you share that restlessness. A junior minister is a political eunuch because while a back-bencher can carry influence, can affect policy and be bloody minded, a junior minister carries collective responsibility for the government. But you aren't in cabinet. You can talk to your own minister – and I influenced George quite often – but you do not have access to the cabinet itself and quite often they make decisions you don't like but you can't be outspoken.

The Treasury wrote a paper on devaluation during the '66 election. Wilson had every copy burned because he wasn't prepared to allow devaluation. He was a great sterling man. When I was put in the cabinet in July 1966 the first meeting I attended was the meeting at which devaluation was considered. I voted for it, with George Brown and Roy Jenkins, and Marcia said to me afterwards, 'Harold was very disappointed with you for voting for devaluation' – because for sterling, the Commonwealth, there was a touch of old-fashioned pride in Britain in him. In the summer of '66 the National Plan went down the pan and George Brown left the DEA and threatened to resign. By the summer of '66 we were in a bit of a mess.   TONY BENN

✘ I think the case by the summer of 1966 was pretty clear. It was a great pity that we didn't devalue either then or even after, by February of 1967 or something like that. The trouble was that by accepting a kind of crude damping down of the economy in the summer of '66 the National Plan lost all meaning and with it a lot of Labour's planning policy.

PETER SHORE

✘ In 1966 when the government was faced with the choice, deflate or devalue, they deflated. That was the real catastrophe. There is no question that they should have devalued in 1966. In '64 it was more evenly balanced. They had just won the election. I can understand them not wanting to be tagged as the party of devaluation. After all the last devaluation before that had been the Labour Party in 1949. So I can understand them not wanting to have the label, but that's a political argument not an economic one. I suppose I can understand them saying, 'Well, maybe it's a gamble. We don't know if we need to devalue or not. There is obviously a case for it but lets hope for the best and not do it because the political costs are so obviously high.'

That might have been a reasonable choice in 1964, given the information they had at their disposal. But the very fact that the crisis came back again in '66 proves that that was actually the wrong choice in '64. I think the political arguments could have been made to cut both ways. They could well have said in '64 – which it was too late to say in '66 – this devaluation is the result of the Tory policies. We had to do this awful thing because the Tories left such a mess. They couldn't say that in '66.

I don't think it was Callaghan. It was Wilson. I think if Wilson had wanted to devalue Callaghan would certainly have gone along with that, no question. Whether Callaghan argued for it or not, I don't know. That's one of the 64,000 dollar questions about Callaghan. It is alleged that in the summer of '66 he did want to move. In 1966 it was clear that either they were going to devalue or they were going to have a very massive deflationary package. This time they chose the deflationary package. This was the great tragedy of the whole thing, the more Wilson staked his authority on not devaluing, on maintaining the exchange rate of the pound, the bigger would be the cost to him in authority and reputation if in the end there was a devaluation. It was like he was a general throwing new armies into the battle. Each new army he threw in made it harder for him to retreat and so by '66 he had already committed an awful lot of himself, of his own political capital, to not devaluing.   DAVID MARQUAND

✘ I personally was one of the people who wanted the cabinet to discuss the thing but I didn't have a very strong view. I know it was a central problem and I did of course press very hard for it later on when it was clear we were going to have to devalue. In the end Wilson put me on the committee he finally set up which decided in favour of that while Callaghan was Chancellor. But, as I say, in those days movements of sterling were regarded very much as virility tests. If it went up, it went up, exactly like a virility test. 'Rich men keep their women in beautiful golden palaces but the steadily declining profit rate exposes their worn-out places.'   DENIS HEALEY

✘ Harold as Prime Minister had an obsession with the politics of everything. The economic considerations always came second to him. It may be that if you are the prime minister, you take a different view than if you are a back-bencher or the chairman of the Economic and Finance group. In fairness to him one has to say that although he took a different view from me, almost all the time, it didn't mean he was a bad prime minister. It may have been that I was wrong. How do you define a good prime minister? Margaret Thatcher was a great prime minister, she won three general elections. I wouldn't like to say that Harold was necessarily a bad or a weak prime minister. But when you become obsessive, above all about remaining prime minister regardless of the consequences and the economic considerations, I think it does make you a weaker prime minister.

We had a one hundred majority after 1966 and there was no need then to be obsessive about winning the next election. The concern one should have been obsessive about was making sure you had the right economic policy. The Chancellor and the Prime Minister worked very close together, the relationship between Denis and Harold was much weaker. Between '64 and '66 it was a strong relationship because they both fundamentally agreed. They both thought George was useless and always drunk – so why should he be right? The Department of Economic Affairs therefore had no impact on anything economic. Yet there were some very good people there. I don't know whether anybody really thought about the National Plan or believed in it, but I doubt if it had major impact on what the Treasury were doing. George believed in it. He had nothing else to believe in. But the last thing in the world the Treasury would be concerned about was a National Plan. They were concerned with running the economy.

BARBARA CASTLE

✘ Tony Crosland was in favour of devaluation. He was the best economist there, I suppose. It was called the unmentionable thing. You mustn't mention it in cabinet. In 1966 that was the moment, because the issue was raised in the summer of '66 and the question was whether to devalue then or not. I was Leader in the House of Lords but I hadn't got any economic advice at all. I was on economic committees, and had been chairman of a bank, but no one ever consulted me about economics. Then it came to the point where there was going to be a vote on it in the full cabinet. I thought, 'I've got to vote one way or the other,' so I went to see Jim Callaghan and he said, 'We must support Harold.' He then said, 'See Douglas Jay,' who was President of the Board of Trade. So I went to see Douglas Jay and he was very strongly against devaluation, in a sort of British way like he was against Europe, 'these bloody foreigners needn't think they can get the better of us' sort of thing.

So, what with the Chancellor of the Exchequer and the President of the Board of Trade both being against, I also voted against at that time. I sat next to Tony Crosland in the cabinet at that time, saying that I was the only intellectual who had voted against devaluation. But Douglas Jay and Harold Wilson were both intellectuals and they both also voted against it. He was a brilliant man. The likes of Tony Crosland, Dick Crossman, the advanced intelligentsia in the cabinet were, in favour of devaluation.

It wasn't a close vote that I remember. I don't know what advice the civil servants gave them, but it was very much the City and the Bank who were against it. The City was very much against devaluation – a blow to the reputation of London.

LORD LONGFORD

✗ Devaluation was such a serious subject that you wouldn't dream of talking about it. But in the tearoom and privately some of us talked and it just seemed to me that we were overpriced. It is the same now. We've still got shades of the British Empire. This is always the difficulty with politics, realising where you are now – and it is not where we were yesterday, let alone twenty-five years ago. We still, at that time, believed that we were a mighty empire on which the sun never set. But we were in the real world and sterling stood on its own merits and it was overpriced.

We had a national lack of humility about our place in the world. We were overvaluing ourselves politically, talking about us being there with the big four. What were we talking about, for God's sake? I remember once at some debate about foreign affairs. One of the old men said to me, 'When you go in there look up at the distinguished Strangers' Gallery. At the time of the British Empire that would have been full of the plenipotentiaries and his excellencies and her excellencies, the foreign ambassadors, to report back every word that was said.

You go in and listen and they're still talking in the same way and the bloody gallery is empty.' It was. That was a very graphic way of describing the whole thing.   JOHN ELLIS

✗ It came back in July 1966, the famous weekend at Mrs Anne Flemming's where the plot was meant to have been agreed against Wilson. Wilson was in Moscow at the time. Then he came back into the argument. For a moment, and this he's confessed to me, Callaghan, who was Chancellor, was converted to devaluation. He allowed himself to be pulled back by Wilson, but if he had not had his own doubts and fears overall we would not have wasted the next fifteen months until November 1967 when it eventually happened. They nearly had a majority in cabinet for devaluation.

That's why Wilson saw it as a plot against him. They had people like Barbara Castle in favour of devaluation, and Tony Benn. They also had Roy Jenkins and Dick Crossman in favour of it. They had Tony Crosland and, for obvious reasons, because he was paying the price for it, George Brown, because he was still at the DEA. Indeed, he had to be bought off in the end, becoming the Foreign Secretary to stay in the government because he realised that there was no future at the DEA once he had had those terrible July cuts of '66. His whole programme of 4% growth was just cut up in shreds on the floor.   TONY HOWARD

✗ You did have an atmosphere of disillusionment which lasted right up until November 1967 when Jim was obliged to devalue. The whole of that period was one of disillusionment and distress. When devaluation happened, people's natural response was, 'Well, what the hell was it all for?' and what were 'they' playing at? 'They' were the cabinet. We've gone through all this battle of the Somme and we haven't actually gained two yards of ground, we've actually gone backwards. That made whipping both harder and easier. I came out of the whips' office about six months after that.   WILLIAM HOWIE

✗ George Brown carried a great deal of clout, not only because he was Deputy Prime Minister, but because he had a very good mind and was a very powerful arguer. It was only really when the prices and incomes policy collapsed in the summer of 1966 that George's morale collapsed too. I remember the day he said to me, 'Bill, it's downhill all the way.' When we had failed on these two central questions of what we were going to do, he knew that it would affect him and that was very close to the end. He carried on for another couple of years in government, but it was effectively the end of him as a major force in politics.   BILL RODGERS

✘ Harold's best years were '63 to '66. Everything else was difficult, and we all know what happened in the end. But those were brilliant years. He was a marvellous leader of the opposition, and he was a great prime minister in '64, '65 and '66, until we had the seamen's strike. Then he came unstuck. I think the beginning of the paranoia set in after the seamen's strike. Maybe it was the pressures of office. I do think he was badly served by his assistants. Gerald Kaufman was a good assistant, I wouldn't blame him at all, but Harold had many fears. For example, he used to confide in Lord Goodman and he would call him up and mention the latest news he'd heard of some country-house party which Roy Jenkins had attended, and Goodman would say, 'I was there and Jenkins wasn't,' but it fed his paranoia which was beginning. I would blame Marcia most of all, and to some extent Joe for feeding his paranoia – instead of calming him, they fed him these things which disturbed his judgement a lot.   DICKSON MABON

✘ Obviously things were starting to go wrong. It was not very long before I was questioning myself about why I was there. Judges' salaries, for example. I was going to abstain. It's the most traumatic thing when you vote against your own government; it becomes progressively easier, but the first time it's pretty traumatic. I had not even been to university or mixed in those kind of circles. When I became an MP, it was the first time I had even taken a taxi. I thought it was greatly daring. Could you be so right and they were so wrong. There was that business about it. It was a very strange period. I certainly didn't go there to do some of the things that we were doing. The judges' salaries were only one thing but we were doing others against the left. Then the dreadful seamen's strike. A load of bloody waffle saying that they were Communists and fellow travellers and evilly motivated men. There was a group of us meeting them down below and they were ordinary decent blokes. They had no democracy in the seamen's union. There were no delegates among the ship's crew and they were objecting to being sold out. They had been well sold out by their leadership who were just there taking the money and getting their peerages or whatever. The July measures. Here we were going to have to cut down on everything.   JOHN ELLIS

✗ We paid a very high price for not getting a substantial majority in that '64 Parliament. I was a little forgiving thinking there's an election coming and as soon as it comes we go with a proper devaluation. I was chairman of the Economic Policy Group and bit by bit we got together a group of people who were in favour of devaluation. It was called the Snakes and Alligators because there was such a wide range of people. We thought the politician to chair that was not myself but Eric Heffer. He became chairman. John Ellis was the one who gave it the name Snakes and Alligators, and we were going for devaluation. We spoke in a debate in '64 when nine back-bench members spoke in favour of devaluation. It wasn't reported.

If we'd had it in a back-bench committee meeting it would have leaked and it would have been front-page news. But the message got across to those people who were concerned. From 1965 onwards I went with Joel Barnett to see every member of the cabinet to let them know there was an alternative to deflation. We went round them all and informed them and Harold Wilson wasn't very happy about that. They just listened. They weren't going to commit themselves. They wanted to be friends with us because we were very influential people.

The great thing, if you want to get things done, is to look as if you're ready to go beyond the pale. To look as if you're moving in that direction. Then there's hands ready to pull you back. Once you're over the pale you're finished. But if you look as if you're going in that direction you can exercise quite a bit of influence. That's the role I took. Harold Wilson never forgave me for it. I made a speech on that in '65 against the nonsense, and he replied to that by saying that our frontiers were in the Himalayas. He forgave me for East of Suez but never for the devaluation one. But the interesting thing is he appointed me to the government. It wouldn't happen today.

                                                  ROBERT SHELDON

Still a band of brothers – some of us – Conference 1966

✗ There is about one third of the House whom I call House of Commons men. You go in there and you listen to the stones talking. There were some of us who really did this all the time. If you listened and talked you knew what was going on. So I heard about this group meeting on devaluation soon after I arrived. It was put together very quickly, as I remember it. It was on an interview floor right down in the bottom. It was one evening about six o'clock. Somehow we got to know about a group of people who were interested in this question of economics and thought it was serious we should meet together. But it had to be deadly hush-hush because the press mustn't know. I can remember Joel Barnett and Bob Sheldon and possibly David Marquand and some others. I looked around. I said, 'We're a right group of snakes and alligators,' because we were such a diverse group. Somebody said, 'Are you a snake or an alligator?' I thought, 'Oh well, I'm an alligator'– I didn't fancy the snake image. But we were certainly a very mixed group.

We had a general chat. There was no argument or deep analysis. Presumably the word had gone out, overheard in the tearoom, and I don't know who put it together quite frankly. It was people who were unhappy about the economic trend and believed that we should have devaluation. We had to be very circumspect. We all swore a great oath that we would not reveal a word about it. In fact it's not in any books that I've ever come across. It was agreed that one or two people – and I've a feeling that it was Joel Barnet and possibly Bob Sheldon – would go and see the powers that be. We left it as loose as that.

It was right at the point when it was teetering on the edge. The seamen's strike led to the downturn. That was when there was a real chance of devaluation but then things began to improve for whatever reasons and of course it melts away doesn't it. So it must have been the actual day when it was at its lowest ebb. Subsequently I found out that there were supporters in the cabinet and they were talking about it as well. But where the cabinet is unanimous you never get to know as a back-bencher what is going on.   JOHN ELLIS

✗ There was pressure. Edmund Dell, Joel Barnet and Bob Sheldon came to see me privately and they said that this conversation will not pass ever from us, but we've come to tell you we ought to devalue. They went to see other ministers one by one and they used the power of argument to try and inject into our minds what we had to do.   TONY BENN

✗ Splits happened largely because there was a big majority. That's a paradox in the parliamentary system. If you have a big majority it means you can get your legislation through and in a way the opposition doesn't really count. But at the same time, the fact that there is a large majority means that the party itself can afford the luxury of division. There isn't the same sense amongst the Parliamentary Party of hanging together or else we'll hang separately. If there is a small majority, every member of the Parliamentary Party has the feeling that they daren't rock the boat.

Apart from anything else, in the '64–6 period they knew there was going to be another election very soon. The only question was when. After '66, it's obvious that Labour is going to be in power for a whole Parliament. It is a long time before the next election so there can be revolts inside the ranks without bringing the government down. So it is much more tempting for different groups within the party to revolt, and that is exactly what did happen. There was the Tribune Group, which was almost a party within a party, with regular meetings, with its own offices, its own sort of ethos and to a certain extent its own ideology. The legacy of the factional struggles of the 1950s was very much alive – deep suspicion on the part of the left, a fairly organised left, for the right. I don't see any sign of that now. DAVID MARQUAND

X We couldn't get anything moving which was going to build the achievements we wanted. We had a whole mass of things coming up which were causing divisions in the party. Wherever you went you couldn't talk about the broader issues, you were got on to one issue. Westminster Hall, was crowded day after day. I used to go out and meet all these people and you'd see the same lot on different issues. It would be on Vietnam one day, anti-Vietnam, then you'd see them on the Greek Colonels, then you'd see them on Apartheid and they were all scruffy women with their boobs hanging out. So we were breaking up into a one-issue thing. You were no longer a cohesive Labour Party with a plan for the future. We were assuring people this, assuring people that. But we never did it. We never actually achieved it.

We stopped it going from bad to worse but what we didn't do was to make it good, because we never had the wherewithal to do it. There was nothing in the coffers to do it and it never got better, although Jenkins began to turn it around. By '69 things were beginning to look good but too late. Rather like Douglas-Home, you run out of time. RON BROWN

X Joel and I went round all the cabinet ministers telling them that there was an alternative. By that time there was strong opinion that we should devalue. At the end of all this, we went to see Harold Wilson, July 1966, to tell him. We just got a lot of waffle. Unknown to us, he had given this assurance to President Johnson so he was not going to go back on that. This is one of the problems. You give an assurance and you find yourself caught. Whenever there is devaluation in the air, naturally one's creditors or one's financial partners want to make sure that you are not going to do it. So they ask you for your personal assurance. Having given your personal assurance, particularly to the president of the United States, then it becomes very hard to say, 'Oh I was only joking.' You have to be forced by circumstances so that it's inevitable then it's accepted by the friend or the ally or the lender of money that you really haven't got any choice. That may be very good for the standing of the PM concerned. It's not very good for the economy.   ROBERT SHELDON

✘ The government tried to get support and, because I have Dutch connections and speak Dutch, they suggested that I should go on a short tour of Holland and speak generally about what was happening in Britain and see a lot of the Dutch politicians, which I did; I had a briefing and my brief was to support the stance of the Exchequer. There was not going to be a devaluation. I suppose this must have been a fortnight before we devalued. I was briefed, because here I was, Home Office Minister, not concerned with Treasury management at all and I saw a man from the Treasury who was supposed to brief me. I said, 'But aren't we going to have to devalue?' And he said, 'That's a trendy view amongst economists which is contrary to the realities.' So I went round saying we weren't going to devalue. God it was embarrassing! I remember having dinner with some Dutch journalists. One of them just pooh-poohed it and said, 'Well, that's what you say, but it's absolute nonsense, isn't it?' And it was!   DICK TAVERNE

✘ When I was going off to conduct some Western European Union negotiations in Paris, I was warned by the news department in the Foreign Office that I would certainly be asked questions about devaluation. I was sternly told by the Treasury and by Jim Callaghan that there was absolutely no question whatsoever of any devaluation. So when I was asked in Paris what was the possibility of a change in the sterling exchange rate, I said, 'absolutely none'. No possibility of any change whatsoever. As I was having my coffee after dinner I was passed a note from the Foreign Office saying that sterling had been devalued that day. That didn't go down awfully well.
                                               ALUN CHALFONT

✘ What Jim is given to doing, and still does to a certain degree, he was a great one for calling you to his room in the evening and testing ideas with you. Close to him at that time was Tony Crosland and he would talk with Tony, and he certainly talked with me. The first time it really went badly wrong, and one could see the writing on the wall long before it broke, was July '66. In '67, he said, 'We can't hold it. There is no way, given the development of events. We are going to have to devalue.' When he had decided, he said to me, 'I shall resign. The buck stops with me.' My memory is that when he did offer his resignation to Harold I think Harold discussed it with him and Tony Crosland was going to be Chancellor. Tony was at Education. Now Harold thought, as I understand it, 'I don't want a strong member of the cabinet on the back-benches,' and it was then that he changed his mind. Why he changed his mind about Tony I don't know. Tony had taught at Oxford. He had all the academic qualifications. My own view is that Tony was a buccaneer. You don't want buccaneers at such a point in time. The situation is too difficult. That's my reading of it. Roy Jenkins was to be Chancellor and Jim was going to be Home Secretary. It was as well, because Ireland broke shortly afterwards.   MERLYN REES

✗ The inducement that Harold offered Tony to move as a secretary of state from a department in which he was utterly engrossed, Education, to one that he regarded with a rather chilly eye, the Board of Trade, was that as President of the Board of Trade he would be one of half a dozen men who were on the steering committee for economic policy. Thus Tony got into this position that he hadn't been in before of being able to influence economic policy. As the push for devaluation from him and several others then was intensive, he could push directly. But Tony was one of the few people who hadn't talked to Harold Wilson directly. Harold Wilson, who was a very canny man, wanted to break this log jam. So he asked Tony to lunch in the apartment at the top of No.10. The subject of the lunch was Tony's sending his papers on to all his colleagues about devaluation, and Harold said he was not convinced by Tony's argument but he had an open mind. This was in October '67 and it was the first time that he had said that. Tony said, 'The trouble with Harold is, one hasn't the faintest idea whether the bastard means what he says, even at the moment he speaks it.' Then, early in November, was when the decisive struggle took place in SEP. Tony once again put the case for devaluation and reluctantly, highly reluctantly, the Prime Minister accepted.

Early November, the Belgian prime minister was here. Just before this meeting Callaghan had told Tony that they were going to devalue, I think it was to be the following day or the next week. Wilson pushed across the table these two little bits of paper. One said, 'Happy?' and the second said, 'It is terribly important nothing be said to *any* colleague. A few of us are meeting today, including you of course, but others off SEP will not be there. We have to keep things very tight. H.' I asked Tony when we had our evening gossip what was happening, and he said, 'It's happening on Saturday,' and I said, 'Are you excited?' he said, 'After three years it's somewhat anticlimactic.'

It was then my spectator role began changing abruptly because he came home and said, 'Jim may resign as Chancellor at the end of next week.' I said with utter dismay, 'Oh no, not that soon.' When he saw Jim on that Sunday, he came home afterwards and he was grey, he was breaking the news to me very gently and in tears. He got out of his chair and walked up and down the study and then he said, 'I think I should tell you that Jim talked in front of the others about my being Chancellor in a week or so. He says that he and Harold have agreed that the odds on this are ninety-five to five.'

I realised that as this public responsibility intensified, because nothing could be more intense that the post of Chancellor of the Exchequer, how much of our own private life would slip away. I was sick at least once a day in the loo. I said, 'I don't want you not to be Chancellor, I just wish it could be postponed for a couple of years.' So, Tony goes to see Jim, tells him, 'Don't make up your mind, go out into the country this weekend and get some sleep, and then decide.' In telling me all this, Tony said to me, 'If I find next week that I've just talked myself out of a job it will feel very odd.' Jim went to his Sussex farm for the weekend, and decided to stay in government and swap with Roy Jenkins.

Roy had been around to see us on that weekend because he felt so out of things, he didn't know what was going on, and at the beginning of the week when I got home the telephone was ringing as I walked in and it was the principal private secretary for Tony at the Board of Trade, and what he said was, 'The President is in a meeting but he has asked me to let you know that the six o'clock news will announce the appointment of Mr Jenkins as Chancellor. I understand that you'd expected the President home for dinner but because of today's changeover he's been asked to deputise for the Chancellor in Paris, so he'll be taking the 7.30 flight. Could you have an overnight bag ready for him?' When Tony came home to fetch his overnight bag, he said, 'It's the greatest fall I've ever had in my life.' Then he forgot the bag.   SUSAN CROSLAND

✗ The final crisis came when the pound was clearly under enormous pressure in the autumn of 1967. I went to see the Speaker to tell him how important it was. There came on the tapes the loan from France, about one billion pounds. I thought that will really finish us. Once we get that loan, it will be bound up with conditions which will obviously be very unfavourable to us. That will rule out devaluation and that would mean very severe cutbacks here. So I was against that strongly. I put down a private-notice question. In fairness Harold Wilson gets it right in his book. Roy Jenkins gets it wrong. He says that the cabinet instructed John Silkin to get me to withdraw that private-notice question. I was never asked. I wouldn't have been able to withdraw it. There is no precedent for withdrawing it.

My question was, 'Is it true that we are going to accept this loan that's going to affect our economy for years to come?' An easy question to answer. If they had told me they'd already decided to devalue it wouldn't have happened. They couldn't stop Sam Orme asking wouldn't it be better to devalue. That was the real question. Then he said, 'I've nothing to add or to subtract from what I've said on it before.' That was a very weak answer to the question of whether or not he was going to devalue. He should have denied it like Stafford Cripps did. But Callaghan was an honest, straightforward fellow. He couldn't tell a lie. Of course, the markets realised what it was about, and sterling was sold. If I'd thought they were going to do it, I would just have been delighted and shut up. They'd already decided. In fact, on that same evening, Dick Crossman came up to me and said, 'You musn't assume that we don't play a part in these things.' That was after the question.
                                                         ROBERT SHELDON

✗ Curiously there was something of a relief about the actual devaluation. The party had become very shaken by then. There were a combination of reasons. Ted Short was the Chief Whip from the beginning of the government through to May or June 1966. He was a Chief Whip of the old school, the only thing a Chief Whip can be in that particular job. He must be a martinet of great integrity, and Ted Short fitted that description. He was absolutely straight. He was succeeded by John Silkin, who was an absolute disaster because you never knew where you stood. The Silkin regime, plus the increasing disillusion with the failure of the government to make progress, the undercurrent of feeling that devaluation was the only way and the failure to find a solution, meant that morale was very low. So when devaluation took place I think there was a lot of relief.

I wrote a note to Jim Callaghan. I liked Jim when I first met him in the Fabian Society in the 1950s but I'd always supported candidates other than him, and he knew that. I'd been with George when George and him had clashed. I felt that it wasn't his fault, he was on the wrong side in devaluation but I didn't feel bitterly about him personally. I sent him a note to say I was very sorry about it. But there was great relief in the PLP as a whole. I think it was a relief that we'd got devaluation and that we'd got a new face at the Treasury.   BILL RODGERS

✗ We were still uncertain that we'd win the day – until George came into the chamber and indicated that we had won. I remember vividly George coming into the chamber the day it happened and he put his thumbs up to Bob. So we knew. To say won, to see the pound go lower, is a strange kind of victory in many ways because it would be better if you could have a stable pound and a strong economic situation. But it broke the jam and enabled us to make some progress. But neither the Prime Minister nor the Chancellor was in favour of it basically. They were forced into it.   JOEL BARNETT

✗ Devaluation was a great shock to everyone. I'd gone into the DEA literally a matter of weeks before devaluation took place. I'm inclined to think it was a mere coincidence and that there was no causal relationship between the two events! I think, even to most junior ministers, when it happened it came as a shock. It was kept very close, through a limited number of cabinet ministers, and when it took place the party, like the country, hadn't expected it and, equally, hadn't expected the consequences. It was the wrong time to devalue. For a devaluation to work you have to have slack in the economy, otherwise you get no benefit out of it and it actually becomes inflationary.   ALAN WILLIAMS

✗ In effect the decision was taken at a private meeting at Chequers, and then after that I had this awful business of knowing a great secret, not that you're tempted to leak it, just afraid you'll wake up in the middle of the night and say we're going to devalue and someone might hear. Then the decision was taken and then of course it did assist. But devaluation by itself without micro industrial measures doesn't actually solve the problem. After devaluation the general Treasury view was that you didn't need any more micro economic measures, it could all be done by the trade from devaluation. They used that to destroy all the micro measures that had been used by George Brown, Peter Shore and Michael Stewart.   TONY BENN

✗ It was shattering, of course, and Wilson felt it badly. My own feeling was that we didn't devalue enough. Fourteen per cent wasn't enough. I would have wanted to have seen about twenty, twenty-five. I never said that, because once you've devalued, you've got to make the best of it, and fourteen did have its effect eventually but it would have been easier with more. After that, of course, came demoralisation. Of course, the Tories made a big thing of it, 'The pound in your pocket,' was a rather unwise thing to say. I expected Roy to take action straightaway. To my astonishment he did nothing! He did nothing! It was three months. I found that astonishing, I still do.

Roy called me in to see if I had any views because he could see that I'd been right. I didn't have much to tell him, except that it was a pity and that it was now history and that I wanted to take action straightaway. To my astonishment he still didn't. He should have converted things to exports after devaluation. That's when we had a marvellous opportunity.

We had two and a half years left. It would have been better in 1966 with a whole Parliament ahead to get things right. We'd lost a year and a half out of the five years, but it could still have been done. In fact it was nearly done. We nearly won.

I think that, looking back, Mendès-France got it right. Devalue and blame it on the previous government. De Gaulle was right, devalue and deflate to force it into exports. We, having those two examples before us, were wrong. If he'd got it right the balance of payments which was an obsession would have ceased to have been an obsession. Industry would have been able to export. The stop-go cycle, if not ended, at least the fluctuations could have been much less. So we could have had manufacturing industry much better placed. That was all gone. It was terribly sad. We only got one proper term.

ROBERT SHELDON

✗ Morale didn't collapse but it got very turbulent. There was a feeling that things had gone pretty seriously wrong. What happened was a good many members found themselves in an uncomfortable situation in their own constituencies with their own local parties. The local party would say, 'What are you trying to do?' You would try and explain it to them as best you could but in a sense what you were saying was inexplicable. There are two things you can do. You can either just join your local party and become a subversive critic of the government, or you can attempt to defend the government and explain what it is doing, admitting misgivings and all that kind of thing.

It's not an easy situation to be in. Especially as I was in the government as a whip, admittedly a fairly junior cog, but I couldn't express misgivings, or not very loudly. Morale didn't quite collapse but it certainly slumped and what was very noticeable was that when members came back after a visit to their constituency where the Labour members had perhaps been round the pubs as well as talking to their party, they would report this kind of feeling back to the whips.

WILLIAM HOWIE

✗ My thought was, 'Oh we've got a chance at the next election.' Most of the party were rather shattered and Harold was totally shattered, largely because of the reaction to his famous broadcast. It was perfectly true. The power of the pound in your pocket wasn't devalued. It was the way he put it. Interestingly, it had the same sort of immediate reaction as 1992. Roy Jenkins came through with the budget of 1968 which was just before he brought me into the Treasury. It was a terrific performance. He was raising tax after tax after tax, and leaving the House waving order papers. They thought it was the most brilliant budget of all time. They were absolutely delighted because they felt that at last there was an attempt to get hold of it. The feeling was very high and then Cecil King wrote that editorial at the *Daily Mirror* saying, 'We must have a change of leader.' In effect saying, 'Roy for leader.' Roy Jenkins was on a rising tide of support.

DICK TAVERNE

✗ There were people who were constantly seeking to replace Harold. I'm not saying that many of the people whose names were being suggested as alternative leaders were themselves engaged in that activity but there were other people on the back-benches forming groups and pressing for change. That undoubtedly had its effect. Then there was the undoubted failure to really deal with the trade unions and to enforce prices and incomes. The policy was really abandoned in 1968 and there was a very poor substitute policy, the so-called 'In Place of Strife' proposals.

Harold had all the guts in the world. He really achieved what he could and went out on a limb on many occasions. His dealing with the trade unions was far more forceful than that of any previous Labour leader. But the resistance to him was also more formidable than ever it had been before.

The big thing was the difficulty about getting the economy going, and the late decision to devalue sterling really was quite crucial. We needed to do it to get that competitiveness and without that the economy could only stay rather frozen. Of course, at last, it began to move towards the end of that Parliament, when it would have been so much better if we'd got it going near the beginning rather than the end. There was a major turnaround but it came too late to be secure or to be really convincing. If we'd had a few more months it would have been obvious because the country had in 1970 one of the biggest surpluses it ever had. PETER SHORE

✗ Once your party's in real trouble it is backs to the wall. You're almost stoic by then. Jim Callaghan was very bitter after the devaluation. Crosland and Jenkins didn't like each other. George was very difficult to work with. I worried about the bloody party and letting down the people that we were supposed to be there to go and help. The terrible things we did. We got into this goulash about Concorde and then decided that we couldn't abandon it. Terrible meetings at Bristol. Then there was the whole thing about the cuts. The National Health Service. I voted against the half-crown prescription charges. Teeth and specs was dreadful for the party. Ministers had all been told by the Chancellor that they had to cut.

We were a tough lot. We became like stoics. Then the Nationalists won the by-election in Scotland and I remember joining some Scottish Labour MPs in the tearoom. 'We'll all lose our seats,' they said. I said, 'What about me?' They said, 'You're all right – you knew you would lose yours!' The effect on my local party was pretty bloody awful. I had to explain things to them as best I could. The party don't understand things like that. They are concerned with their jobs and their livelihoods and their general standards and they don't expect it in the Labour Party. It's an inevitable downhill ride. Our councillors were all losing their seats. The trade unions and party members were all fed up. We were being wiped out. Rather like what the Tories are going through now. One becomes very stoical. You know, 'Hit me again.' JOHN ELLIS

✗ By that time Wilson had committed even more political capital to not devaluing. He had repeated it and repeated it and repeated it until he was blue in the face. So had Callaghan. Callaghan in a funny way was able to escape the personal political sacrifice because he left the Treasury and made the swap with Roy Jenkins so that he became Home Secretary and Jenkins became Chancellor of the Exchequer. So in a way Callaghan sort of expiated his errors in not devaluing.

Wilson, of course, couldn't do that and I think Wilson's reputation never recovered, at least not in the lifetime of that Parliament. So it was a classic tragic thing that the first three years of that government were spent defending an unsustainable exchange rate and in the end they lost, causing an enormous loss of authority and reputation to the Prime Minister. The remaining three years of the government were spent undoing the damage of the first three years. Some of us had argued for it publicly which made us very unpopular with the leadership. So in a sense we belatedly claimed a certain credit for being right, although it was not a very pleasant credit.

Those of us who wanted devaluation earlier didn't want it to happen like this. The fact that it did happen proved that we were right, but it wasn't a very pleasant kind of proof, because we had wanted the government to make a conscious decision and devalue. We didn't want them to be forced into it against their will. So although we were in one way proved right, I don't think we derived very much comfort from that. It was manifestly a huge defeat for the government. There is no getting away from that. Those of us who had said, 'Look, if you don't devalue, in the end you'll be forced to and that will be a

'What can be forgot?' – Conference 1966

defeat,' all that we could now say was, 'Look, yes, we told you so.' Not a very pleasant position to be in and the people who didn't want to devalue of course couldn't say anything else but that it was a defeat. Everybody knew it was a defeat. I think the cloud left by that defeat hung over the government for the rest of its term in office. There was a tremendous swing against the government in the opinion polls and some very very bad by-election results, devastating losses in the local elections and so on. So maybe if the public at large had not turned against the government in the way that they did, the Parliamentary Party would have been less depressed, but as it was I think it was a pretty demoralised outfit after '67.   DAVID MARQUAND

CHAPTER TEN

Epilogue and After

					1968					
	Jan	Feb	Mar	April	May	June	July	Aug	Sept	Oct
Lab.	32	23	24	23	21	21	23	26	29	33
Con.	37	43	38	45	45	41	42	38	39	40
Lead	-5	-20	-14	-22	-24	-20	-19	-12	-10	-7

	1968		1969							
	Nov	Dec	Jan	Feb	Mar	April	May	June	July	Aug
Lab.	26	23	25	24	27	25	24	27	25	27
Con.	42	43	42	42	43	41	42	40	45	38
Lead	-16	-20	-17	-18	-16	-16	-18	-13	-20	-11

	1969				1970					
	Sept	Oct	Nov	Dec	Jan	Feb	Mar	April	May	June
Lab.	30	36	34	32	33	34	34	35	42	40
Con.	38	39	38	42	40	40	40	38	38	39
Lead	-8	-3	-4	-10	-7	-6	-6	-3	+4	+1

(all polls from Gallup)

A party seeking to reform Britain and chart a new course must first change itself and test its own assumptions. It needs a clear and prioritised plan, going right to the heart of the problem, and must implement it boldly and quickly, doing the necessary dirty work first to get it out of the way.

Harold Wilson's Labour government failed all three tasks. The party was changed but a leader balancing factions didn't clear out dead assumptions and ideology, rather he projected a new set and never examined either his own assumptions, many of them dead orthodoxies, or those of the party. Harold Wilson was a fox not a hedgehog. He had many brilliant insights but no strategic vision and a party struggling to get a majority was in no position to act boldly on the key economic problem but prone to dissipate its efforts in trying to do too much else too quickly. In such circumstances the dirty work was left until it was finally forced on the government. The wisdom of hindsight makes this clear now, but it was clear to many at the time. R. H. S. Crossman thought it implicit in democracy:

> When I look back over these three years I realise how much better we could have done and how everything we've done has been too little and too late. The main disasters are our own fault, but one has to look deeper and seek the cause for our inadequacy. Why was it, for example, that when the Labour government came in after thirteen years the men who took charge of foreign policy and defence – Wilson, Brown, Callaghan, Stewart – all believed that it was their role to prove that Labour could run Great Britain as well as the Conservatives? Not one of them admitted that the job of a socialist government was to scale Britain down to an offshore island, to accept devaluation, to accept the winding-up of the sterling area and to do these things voluntarily and not under compulsion.

The 1964–70 government was far from being a failure. Britain emerged as a better, more civilised and richer nation. Labour built 300,000 houses a year, maintained full employment, improved the welfare state, introduced comprehensive education and expanded higher education. All this was success, but less than had been promised and less than hopes had been aroused to expect.

Recovery was too little and too late to rescue either Labour or Harold Wilson's reputation. Yet beating heads against brick walls does teach lessons. A better, more experienced, more realistic, and wiser government emerged from the débâcle. Parties can transform themselves in power, though they find it far more difficult in opposition. Labour had disappointed and failed to become either the natural party of government, or the inevitable majority in the new society which Harold Wilson had set out to create. It wasn't trusted. It hadn't delivered. It had failed at the two crucial jobs of government: to maximise the living standards of the people and to win a second term.

> In view of what has happened in the last fifteen years I suppose we did achieve something, but at the time it didn't seem so. We were retreating. All my time in Parliament has been a great retreat. I was always the one that was trying to protect things, like the National Health Service, either in national government or in local government. It's sad.
>
> JOHN ELLIS

The rearguard action lasted over two decades of defending the world Labour had built. It is now over. A new party means a new beginning and the failures of the last move forward offer lessons to the government about to come to power after an even longer period in opposition. Those who experienced last time are keen to point out the lessons for next.

✗ I think the first thing – and it's so much easier with modern technology – is to have a game plan for government which you could adapt depending on how big your majority was. With modern technology you could work out a game plan for majorities of eighty, forty, twenty, etc., and you could build in ways to deal with all sorts of eventualities. I think you've got to know what you want to do and take a strategic view of the time you've got to do it.

Secondly, you've got to face up immediately to the unpleasant things and get them over with. It's no good saying, 'We've said these things in our manifesto so we'd better start implementing them at once.' It's mainly a question of economics. If, when you open the books, you find things are worse than you expected, or if there are skeletons in the cupboard, drag them out, deal with them straightaway, even if your own supporters will feel a bit bruised. Get it out of the way so that you are on an even keel and dictating your own terms.

Thirdly, though I'm in favour of proportional representation and the reform of the House of Lords, for God's sake don't get bogged down in too much constitutional change, particularly local government reorganisation. It's the most time-wasting expensive thing you could ever do, and it doesn't make friends, it makes enemies. So look very carefully at the issues. On constitutional reform I think there are things that have got to be done quickly so mark those out and don't get too far down the road in doing other things.

Don't forget that what the people want is first prosperity, good education and good health. Provided you face up to the economic situation you inherit, which may be difficult, don't take your eye off the ball. These are things which a Labour government is there to give the people if they possibly can. Desirable social change. The Labour Party if it's anything should still be the party of the underdog, and that should be in the forefront of that government's mind.   BILL RODGERS

✗ Don't be bounced. I've got some very good advice for any new minister taking office under Mr Blair. Don't take any decisions for three days, use that three days to find out where you are, to think about what you're being told, to consult at all stages and get your feet under the table. It happened to me time and again that people tried to bounce me.

DENIS HOWELL

✗ MPs have many more opportunities now to find out what's going on, I mean all the stuff that they get now and the relationship with the House. They come in with different expectations, but once they come here they can quickly grasp what can be done. Expectations are always going to be greater than the reality. I hold that the greatest thing that ever happened to me in my life was to become a Member of Parliament. When I came down those steps at the Town Hall in Manchester, I had the Hallelujah Chorus ringing in my ears. The greatest achievement of any living Englishman was to become a Member of Parliament. I hope it still is.

Some of them are much more knowledgeable but the population as a whole is more knowledgeable because of television and so on, so they're more likely to come in with more realistic expectations as to what is happening – not so much expectations but detailed knowledge of the way it works and possibly the way in which they might be able to influence things. The grand themes are probably no longer available in the way that they were. So people coming here are now looking at small improvements here and small improvements there, to an extent they weren't many years ago.

ROBERT SHELDON

✘ Things are much better; you are better briefed now, you have research assistants. Maybe I'm exaggerating and I have the wrong impression but they seem to me to know more about going into government than we did. They may not know the options but we're not talking about that, not about what you can do but about what you want to do. How are you going to reform things quickly. I like the way Blair is working towards the idea of a ten-year stretch because there's going to be a lot of disappointment among ministers and would be ministers when they go in and they find that they cannot do certain things.

I think that it is not nonsense to have a legislative programme cast in your mind for ten years. Ten Queen's speeches. That should be an incentive for people to make really good bills even though they are not going to get them this year or next year. For a minister I would say that a rule of thumb is to give them three years – a year to get used to it, a year of creation and then, in case he's bored, a year to move up the line or into some other job, or to prove the fact that he has fully realised his potential. Two years is too short, and one year in a department in nonsense.

DICKSON MABON

✘ I think the biggest problem our government will have is that we shall have been out of office about eighteen years probably when the election comes. There'll be one or two ministers who had junior jobs under the Callaghan government but most of them have had no government experience ever and I think everybody has got to be prepared for people to work themselves in. Then Blair will have to have, as he certainly has, the courage to remove people pretty fast if they are not up to it and replace them with people who are. It is a very important job and one great advantage Wilson had was that he had been a cabinet minister for several years before he became prime minister and he was in a better position to do that than perhaps Blair will be initially, though I think Blair will learn very fast.

DENIS HEALEY

✗ I suppose the good lesson is not to promise too much, and we're not doing that. I just hope that while we're not promising too much we will deliver something rather more than we're promising. If we have a big enough majority I certainly hope that will happen because sadly I don't see us having growth at the levels that will enable us to finance all the things that I personally would like to see happen, and I'm sure Gordon and Tony would like to see happen. The major lesson was that if you come into Parliament with a big enough majority for God's sake stop worrying about winning the next election. Think about what you are in power for and what you are in politics for – to do something. The fact that the present shadow cabinet have never been ministers is irrelevant. When they get there the first day the leading civil servants, including their private secretary or PA, are bright people and they will have read the manifesto.

In every department they will be ready not to try to defeat the minister but to help him achieve his targets. If the targets or plans are crazy, as they see it, not from a party political point of view but if they simply think they are bad plans, then they will tell him so. If, on the other hand, he is a strong minister, he will say, 'OK, I take the points you are making but I still want you to do this, this and this,' and they'll do it. There is no way they are going to stop their new minister from doing what he wants to do, as long as he doesn't allow himself to be diverted.

I never had a problem. I'd never been in government before and I hadn't had the training they are having now, going to Templeman Hall to be taught how to be a minister. You don't need that. I went straight in as Chief Secretary to the Treasury never having been in government, and I never found it a problem, so they shouldn't find it a problem. They should stop worrying about it and just carry on with what they have in mind to do. But what we have learned from 1964 is, I hope, that the major priority must be to increase growth in the economy because unless you do that you're never going to have the resources to do the things you want to do, and getting that growth must be the centre of everything you want to do, and not to be diverted by the pressure on the pound, or interest rates, or anything else. Keep that in the forefront of your mind, that you want economic growth in order to do the things you are in politics to do.   JOEL BARNETT

✘ Now it's the party that is seen as alien to New Labour. The whole party. Every day you see something that doesn't come through the mechanism. Wilson was very meticulous about the benefits of discussion. You had working parties where you put ideas about anything from home policies to international affairs. Now the policy trickles down from above and doesn't necessarily relate to what people are feeling. That's the biggest change of all: the sense now that the party isn't needed, isn't important, and that, I think, explains a lot of the early emotion. Even if you agree with what's being done they don't make you feel part of it, and if you don't share in the decision-making then the triumphs aren't yours and the failures aren't yours.

TONY BENN

✘ You must recognise that in many areas of policy the unexpected will happen and you have got to be prepared. Although you've got to plan what you're going to do you've got to know that events will disrupt the plan. Then you have got to adjust it and not imagine that you can go on with the old plan when the situation is different. You've only got to look at some of the external factors. It's possible that you may have a major war in the Far East between China and Japan and the South Asian countries over the oil. It's possible you could have war on the fringe on the old Soviet Union. You've got little wars now. They could turn into big ones. It's possible you could have war in the Mediterranean involving Greece and Turkey or involving also Bulgaria and Albania and Serbia. All these things will affect your economic situation as well as your political and military situation. So you've got to be ready for the unexpected and by definition the unexpected is something you can't be expected to foresee. DENIS HEALEY

✘ I think in fairness we've learned the lessons surprisingly well. They are that you don't make too many commitments before you know what the books are going to show. We shouldn't allow ourselves to be pressurised by the Tories into producing any detailed policy until it's essential to do so. Maggie went to the election on the broadest manifesto commitments you could think of, nothing detailed but a broad sweep that enabled her to justify the reforms that nobody had ever envisaged which were met within these casual terms. So we've done the right thing in recognising that we must set our own agenda and we must time it ourselves, and we have to recognise that there is going to be – as there was in '64 – a hole in the bucket when you get in there. Ken Clarke is a very formidable politician. He won't do a Roy Jenkins because that didn't work but they've probably been borrowing right, left and centre, and we're going to find ourselves in the most enormous difficulties when we get into office. I actually feel rather sorry for whichever ministers are going to have to try very quickly to work out the implications of the shocks that I think will be waiting for them the other side of election day.

ALAN WILLIAMS

✗ What we should learn is that industrial policy is not a practical business. Through industrial policy, if you can work it out and be very sensible about it, you might improve the performance of the economy by .0001%, if that's what you mean by supply-side measures, but it has no greater significance than that, and the trouble with industrial policy is that it leads everyone to do stupid things. Well, that's what we did after '74, we bailed out lame ducks, and that's the cost of industrial policy.

Even if you can devise a sensible industrial policy, and that's difficult enough, the trouble is that once you have the power to intervene, once you have these industrial organisation corporations, and industrial development executives, you are tempted to do all sorts of things that cost more than any benefit that arises. So if the Labour Party is to learn anything from previous experience I think it must decide right away that it cannot do anything about the economic growth of this country in measurable political time. Economic policy is not about speeding the rate of economic growth. We don't know how to do it. Economic policy in my view is about maintaining in this country a reasonable standard of life and a reasonable relationship with the rest of the world.

EDMUND DELL

✗ The Civil Service can be a magnificent institution if you know how to use civil servants, and you don't get browbeaten by them. I gave them no alternative. I'll tell you a little homily. The Permanent Secretary to Education was another posh-spoken chap, a man named Herbert Andrews. After about a month of being in office, this was in '64 when I was establishing myself, he came in and said, 'Denis, do you mind if I say something personal? You don't know how to use the Civil Service, and I'd like to put you right.' I said, 'How's that?' He said, 'You're an initiating minister, creating new ideas. Don't tell the Civil Service how to do it. If you tell them what your policy is they'll advise you on the best way of implementing it, because that's what they're here for.' That was a lesson well learned, so after that I always used to say, 'This is the policy I want to pursue. Can I have a paper very quickly setting out the means of achieving it' – and it worked. That's a lesson for incoming ministers. To understand how to use the Civil Service. I think when people fall down it's because they don't want to use the Civil Service any way, and they're not up to the job.   DENIS HOWELL

✗ One of the things that you have to remember when you get into office is that the country doesn't expect miracles. If they expect miracles then that's your fault, because you've promised miracles. Most people want the government to behave sensibly and do the right thing. That's my view, but it may be because I'm conditioned by living in Yorkshire for thirty-five years. But it's certainly within my political experience. Just govern the bloody place. Winning the election is a different thing from what they expect when you're in government. Make it clear that you can't do it overnight. I believe that the moral of '64 was over-expectancy and that is fatal.   MERLYN REES

✗ Once the Labour government is in office then the degree of acquiescence that exist today in order to try and ensure that we end sixteen or seventeen years of Conservative rule will I think dissolve fairly quickly once the Labour government has to face the very difficult decisions. Goodness knows what they will find when they come in and open the books. Goodness knows what will happen between now and the election. Government is just very difficult and so there will be much more debate inside the Parliamentary Labour Party once the Labour government is in than there is now. I am a general fan of Blairite policies since I was originally a Gaitskellite and therefore I hope he will do well. Since I've become part of that bit of the Labour Party that went off into the SDP, now Liberal Democrat, I've no great differences with Labour policies today and wish them well and hope there will be some form of partnership between the Lib Dems and the Labour Party in government.   GEORGE THOMSON

✘ All I can say is that I hope they haven't forgotten the poor. I hadn't been to a local party meeting for some time but last May I went to one in Chelsea. I said, 'When I became Labour I went to see King George VI and he said to me, "Why did you join them?" So I said, "I'm on the side of the underdog." George said, "So am I." He felt he was on the side of the underdog.' Anyway, at the Labour Party meeting last May I said, 'Is the Labour Party still on the side of the underdog?' The candidate was a very intelligent man and his candid response was, 'Well, yes we are but you've got to win the election first then we can do justice to the underdog society.' I presume that's the stock answer – are you still on the side of the underdog? Without the redistribution of wealth I don't see that you can really be. Not Labour that's with any meaning to it.   LORD LONGFORD

✘ I'm a great admirer of Blair. He is doing everything that I wanted doing years ago. His dropping of Clause Four, the dropping of socialism, the renaming of the party, were all things we wanted in the late fifties. His whole approach, being extremely moderate, not making promises, not being specific, is exactly right. He is playing it absolutely right. He is firm on defence of the country, so there is no nonsense about disarming and trusting our enemies. The big difference is Europe. He could come unstuck over Europe. Gaitskell was sceptical about Europe. The mood of the British public at the moment is to be sceptical, whereas Labour and Blair are very pro-European. The Conservatives could portray Labour as being ready to allow Brussels to rule us. That could be damaging. Blair is doing his best but there are still some people who want him to make rash promises. You mustn't have specific clear policies because there is sure to be somebody who disagrees and you will alienate them. So far he has been absolutely spot on. I only wish I was thirty years younger.
                                                    GEORGE JONES

✘ There are things we can learn from '64 and '66. There is the question about the need for the government to be in contact with the Parliamentary Party, and the activists. The problems that eventually emerged so much later under Callaghan, with the National Executive, appeared because the Executive was assumed to be a rubber stamp. The activists were disillusioned by the cuts that took place, by the refusal to devalue, by the lack of explanation about what was going on, then by the failure to take a tough line on Rhodesia and the flirting about whether we should or should not sell arms to South Africa, and the attack on the unions over 'In Place of Strife'.

Those sort of things were not explained, not talked about, there was no real relationship, and what did emerge, particularly under Wilson and Callaghan, was that things were better when ministers bothered to bring people into their own rooms and talk to them. There wasn't a formal structure to enable them to do that, and the committees that existed tended to be places which ministers who bothered about them used, rather than places in which there would be discussion and where people felt they could get changes. The only time people felt they could get changes was when the government was in a difficult position, and that is not a happy situation in which to be.   KEVIN MCNAMARA

✘ I think a lot of the lessons have clearly been learned. First of all, as I understand it, there is a serious open involvement between the Civil Service at top level and the Labour Party members, so that's a good thing. I think there is a major problem, which may be an even bigger problem now than it was previously, in having a whole echelon of people who have either been academics or they have been lawyers or they have been full-time politicians by way of coming straight in as advisers; it's happened on both sides over the years. I think there was a greater proportion of people in that Labour government at that stage who had done other things, some of them as trade-union officials – real ones, not branch officials but full-time union officials; indeed, there were people like Ray Gunter and Tom Bradley, who were still union officials, around.

My worry about this advisers thing is that the ministers don't overestimate the political ability of people who have never been seriously in politics. It sounds terribly pompous, but the track record, whether its businessmen or scientists or whatever, in my view is pretty consistently bad, they don't adapt and go to the top, just as very few professional politicians make it seriously to the top in business or get out of politics and go into business. They are different animals. Likewise, if you go back to John Davies, David Young, Frank Cousins and Geoffrey Robinson, for example, who had probably more practical, more serious senior managerial positions, they didn't shine as major political figures. It doesn't seem instinctively to be there. I may be over egging this but I've got a bee in my bonnet that politicians have too great a deference. They believe that it is all terribly difficult. Most jobs are about common sense basically and if there is some technical information you need to know, or some bits of specific advice you need to have, you can actually get off your arse and get it. It isn't that difficult.   RICHARD MARSH

✘ I would be a lot more at ease about people, less worried about trying to make them into something that they may not be. I had a man called Stanley Hyland who used to do a lot of training. Stanley would always say all you can do is draw out what a person is. You must help them to understand what they are and then let it come out, and I still subscribe to that theory. There's too much commentary going on from minute to minute and hour to hour and this is adding to confusion. I don't think there's a lot of clarity. People are getting very frustrated that no political party is actually putting a set of proposals down. I don't mean to say a programme which you can swear by, but it's difficult for people to find out where a party is. I think this is a great difference. We could still tell where the parties were and where they were coming from. It would be good if we could go back to more clarity.

DAVID KINGSLEY

✘ We have a very different leader now from Harold Wilson. Harold was a man who agreed with everybody and thus got that character at the cost of his own reputation, though looking back on that one can see that what he was up to was holding the party together, and he succeeded in doing that. This is not the case at the moment. At the moment it seems to me we are heading strongly in the wrong direction in some respects and the tone of the party is what worries me. We seem to be over anxious to please our critics. We are, for example, probably at this moment more in favour of nuclear weapons than the Tories are.   HUGH JENKINS

✘ Don't be over attentive to official advice. Harold was very good at that in the beginning. It's well known about how he refused the huge swinging cuts the Governor of the Bank of England tried to impose upon him when the first of numerous sterling crises arose shortly after the Labour government was elected in '64. Labour is an over-conventional party. The Tories are much more adventurous and in the end the Tories will do whatever they like. If we had devalued in '64 or '66 the whole future of this country would have been entirely different. But Labour were too orthodox and they believed devaluation was something they must never talk about.

When the Conservatives came in they just floated sterling and nothing happened, the skies didn't fall in. I've been giving a lot of lectures at the Templeton, seminars, and I've been saying to them over and over again, 'Listen to advice. Pay attention to advice, but in the end make your own decisions, because if things are going to go wrong – and things will go wrong – at least let them go wrong because you decided rather than because somebody else decided. Make your own mistakes rather than somebody else's.' I think that's very important and obviously the key example is Denis falling for Treasury clap-trap in '76 and calling in the IMF when he never needed to. The Labour Party has been over-respectful towards political advice in government. Far from being reckless and unreliable, Labour governments have been prudent.   GERALD KAUFMAN

✘ Every encouragement was given to invest, we introduced not merely a very generous sort of tax arrangements but investment grants, actual cash payments to firms who would invest, and those who invested in development areas in the regions were very generously treated. That worked, no question. The regions did very well indeed, the gap closed quite substantially during the period of Labour government. We also then controlled the location of industry, as IDC policy was then called, very vigorously. The housing programme worked. The education changes undoubtedly worked. But the general reluctance of industry to invest, in spite of the Ministry of Technology's encouragement via investment grants and so on, left in most of our minds the question, 'How do you motivate British industry to a policy of sustained industrial expansion?' I'm not sure whether any of us yet knows the answer to that.   PETER SHORE

✘ Remember you're the bosses. That's key. You're the minister. You've been elected. All of these people in the departments, clever, helpful, they are there to do what you say. You are not there to do what they say. The next thing is: remember you're Labour. Ministers get hidden away in their departments. It's happened to the Conservatives after this long period in office, and I fear it will happen too soon to the Labour people. Which is why I went to Tony Blair and said, 'You've got to do something to give your front-benchers induction courses, otherwise they will just be swallowed up in the Civil Service mêlée from day one in those huge cocoons. You are in one cocoon which is No. 10 Downing Street, even more of a cocoon since those terrible gates went up at the end of the street. You are in one in an enormous historic department like the Treasury. Or you're in all these other departments with dozens of people, hundreds of people, thousands of civil servants, at your beck and call.

You can forget that out there there is Parliament and the Labour Party, and if you do that you're finished. You're Labour and you've been elected because you're Labour, and you ought not to have scorn for or disregard for the party out there, or for your fellow members of the Parliamentary Labour Party. Even in opposition too few members of the shadow cabinet, except at shadow cabinet election time, go into the tearoom or the cafeteria, or smoking- or dining-rooms to talk to their back-bench colleagues.

They will have the excuse of being very busy when they are in government – well, they don't have to be very busy; being a minister is an extraordinarily easy job compared with being in opposition. The amount of back-up you've got is so huge that life is one long doddle. Therefore, if they're going to start being really uppity and sticking in their departments and saying, 'We're too important,' then they're going to start planting the seeds of destruction. I'm not saying they'll do this; what I do say is that they need to be warned not to do it.

GERALD KAUFMAN

✘ I think you need to operate as a sort of chairman/chief executive of a conglomerate because ministries are that big normally. You see your parliamentary secretaries and probably the Civil Service as almost a management group and you have a discussion so that you know what is happening, you know what the issues are. It's quite easy to understand the objective; that's the easy bit. It is impossible for you to understand the detailed process of getting there because there is too much of it and you are dealing with too many factors. You've a conglomerate in a ministry of a size which makes Hanson look simple in its complexity.

What you can do is to keep an eye on the extent to which each of those functions is clear where its going and is it getting there? So that you know if there is a serious problem. A civil servant is perfectly happy to put the political line, as long as he is being told that is what he is doing. He'll not find a problem in that; he'll enjoy it because it gives him status and experience.

RICHARD MARSH

✗ First they must be ready and they must not imagine that being taught by civil servants what it will be like in No.10 will necessarily equip them for coping with how it feels when they're there and how they have to perform the duties that they are responsible for. If you are going to be integrated into policy-making and the governmental machine then maybe that's being helpful and you'll know the right people to seek advice from when you are in there. If you are political and you're going in there, you'd better be prepared because there will be no help there for you just because you happen to have a nice face. You have to have influence in the right areas. That will be difficult. If you want to establish how you are going to be as a party not just as a government you are going to have to make that known from day one.

It's no good expecting it to come to you two or three months later. From day one you have to start in there and know what you are going to do. We knew we had to have a political office. We knew whatever else happened the party had to have as much access to the Prime Minister as the civil servants had. That we achieved. I don't know whether it could be done now; as they don't have any access in opposition I doubt if they will have any access in government. You don't come risen from the waves like Venus. You are a party-supported person, you are there by virtue of being a member of the party, new or old Labour, and you owe your allegiance to the other members. You owe them the respect that they deserve and they get very offended and upset if they don't get that and they're right.

They are right to expect that if they're working themselves to a standstill for you all the time that when you are a Member of Parliament you won't just disappear into the blue yonder and not even leave a note on the pin cushion for them. That's too much, they will become disaffected. Equally the Prime Minister musn't disappear, he must be there so that either he or someone close to him will listen to your grumbles – and I've listened to more grumbles . . . I could fill a library full of books with grumbles, masses of grumbles from disaffected members of the Parliamentary Labour Party wanting the Vietnam War stopped or saying pensions should have been increased more dramatically, or complaining the party was not behaving properly. Its endless.   MARCIA WILLIAMS

✗ I don't think the economic situation is nearly as bad. It seems to me that there is much more realism about. Forget about tax cuts, we need tax increases. We need a tight fiscal policy and a loose monetary policy, good for investment, and keep consumption down. The government has done quite well doing that for the last few years. There has been quite a good recovery. Don't throw it away now. Whoever is in government will probably have to increase taxes. So don't make the mistake of going for easy popularity straightaway, play it long. I would have thought Blair would, and Brown will. I am much more confident about this lot than the last lot. Maybe that's because I'm outside now.   DICK TAVERNE

✗ Wilson did very quickly become a victim of paranoia and there is no doubt that having had this wonderful honeymoon with the press, they were eating out of his hand. He was treating them like human beings. He called them by their Christian names. He didn't treat them like tradesmen as the Tory Party and Home and Macmillan had done. They were conned by him and when they found that they were conned they turned against him in a very vicious way.

I don't say that there is any danger of paranoia with the present leader of the Labour Party. I don't think there is. But I think there is with Mr Mandelson, and I think Mr Mandelson may feed whatever element there is of that in Tony Blair. It's a very bad thing to have a conspiracy-minded person. So I think there my advice would be like Mr Attlee's, don't read the newspapers. Don't bother with them. Whatever you do don't listen to Radio 1 and Radio 2 disc jockeys – which Wilson used to do in the small hours of the night and then address the cabinet the next morning about the most terribly grave crisis that had arisen over this disc jockey who would have to be reported to the chairman of the BBC and this kind of thing and they sat there not believing their ears and their eyes. Nobody else had heard the programme and nobody gave a damn about it.   TONY HOWARD

✘ I think if I had one single lesson to draw from this period for now, it would be a rather curious one. It would be that you simply cannot predict from opposition what government will be like. There is simply no way of telling. You do not know from the record of opposition leaders whether they will be good prime ministers or not. The skills that are needed to be a good prime pinister are quite different from the skills needed to be a good opposition leader. They may go together, but they don't have to. You cannot tell from the standing of shadow ministers and their apparent competence what they will be like when they are in charge of departments. They may be good, they may not be good. You just don't know. You do not know what the issues will be that you will face in government.

Nobody in 1963 thought that the great problem facing the Labour Party in 1964 was going to be the overheating of the economy. They thought it was going to be depression. Nobody in 1944 thought that the great problem facing the Labour Party in 1945 was going to be inflation and overfull employment. People were worrying about a return to what happened after World War I, the mass unemployment. The past is never a guide.

That's what I would say and in this present world that we live in now where old ideologies have disappeared and it is no longer clear whether there is such a thing as socialism, and if so what it means, it's even more difficult to predict. Look at the socialist party in France or the labour party in New Zealand or the labour party in Australia or, for that matter, the present Olive Tree coalition in Italy, the main constituent of which is former Communists. What they are doing doesn't remind you very much of anything which used to be called socialism, does it? So all bets are off.   DAVID MARQUAND

✘ I don't think it is true of Tony Blair, but politicians can be divided into two categories – those who want to be someone and those who want to do something. I'm afraid at the end of the day, though he wasn't vain, Wilson just wanted to be the boy in the superbox. He just wanted to be there. He had no conception of any strategy that he wanted to follow. This was his fatal weakness as a politician. Very good on the footwork and the day-to-day tactics. No idea of where he was going or what he wanted to do.

Ted Heath did the exact reverse. Ted was frightfully bad on tactics, frightfully bad on footwork, but he did come in, for better or for worse, with a clear objective of what he wanted to do in the country. A lot of the economic side went wrong early on but the supreme objective he achieved – which was to take Britain into Europe. That's what he wanted to do. None of that with Wilson. I hope that Blair knows what he wants to do because I don't think it's enough to be prime minister and just to think it's a nice job to have – and that's the ultimate indictment of Harold Wilson.   TONY HOWARD

✗ This time round they're making no promises at all. I don't think the two situations are very comparable. In '64 the campaign was basically thirteen wasted years. We were going to have a planned economy. We would raise the rate of growth. We would be able to afford high levels of public expenditure, better levels of public provision, a more egalitarian society. All of this was going to come out of the proceeds of a high rate of economic growth. That was the basic assumption in 1964. Nobody questioned that the Keynesian paradigm was still in existence and nobody questioned that they could plan the economy effectively. 1966 was, in a way, the continuation of '64. Now the slogan was 'You Know Labour Government Works'. In other words, we've won, we've been in power for eighteen months and we're doing what we said we would do. I don't think that it's like that now. I think the big difference between then and now is that Wilson went round the country in '64 making incredibly boring speeches explaining exactly what he was going to do with this, that and the other. Well, Blair has started doing a little bit of that but today we're in the politics of low expectations and in the sixties it was still the politics of high expectations. This was the Kennedy era. It's the same all over the Western world and not only in Britain. Government can deliver. That's what people thought then.   DAVID MARQUAND

CHAPTER ELEVEN

A New Beginning

Much is different from 1964 yet much remains the same. Tony Blair is not as far ahead of his Tory opponent, John Major, or of his own party as Harold Wilson was, but Labour is further ahead of today's Tory government, which looks much more demoralised. That government has eighteen years on the debit sheet, rather than the mere thirteen of 1964. Yet all these differences are trivial against the fact that Labour is poised for power now, just as it was in 1963–4.

Then Labour came to power in a period of expansion and rising expectations, holding out the prospect of boosting growth to build a better society, proposing for Britain the kind of economic miracle European competitors and Japan were enjoying. Labour did many good things, improving society, education, the welfare state and industry, but failed to get the higher growth rate Britain needed. So politics became more bitter, sectional and mercurial, and more importantly the people felt little sense of satisfaction for Labour hadn't delivered it.

It failed to fulfil the expectations it had held out because its leadership lacked the necessary single-minded dedication to a central objective and didn't grasp the importance of down-sizing Britain's great-power status and ending imperial overstretch. Cutting our coat to suit our cloth was the essential prerequisite for transforming Britain into a classless society and a competitive, modern economy capable of fighting a commercial war for markets to provide the good life for its people.

Growth was central. The failure to deliver it was the key to other failures for 1964–70 was in many respects a last chance for Britain to enjoy what our competitors had had through the fifties. When it was lost Labour and the nation had to embark on a long rearguard action to avert worse, rather than build better. The days of hope were over. The days of difficulty and down-sizing began. Because the cake wasn't growing fast enough, arguments about shares intensified. Because growth didn't raise living standards, trade unions struggled and struck for higher wages. A complacent sense of superiority gradually became a defensive inferiority complex. Labour's next period of power in the seventies became a struggle to keep an increasingly rickety show on the road, keeping spending up by taxation, because there was no growth, and inflation down by incomes policy, and discrediting itself, taxes, and the unions in the process. This dug the gulf which now lies between Labour Wilson-style and Blair's new version.

Everything seemed to have failed: British management not up to its job. British civil servants not technocratic. British industrial relations chaotic. British trade unions Luddite. British people lazy and under-motivated. So Europe, and hitching our growth to someone else's engine, became the all-purpose solution and Labour's role to defend what it had achieved, rather than boosting and bettering it, as we had hoped to do in the sixties. One by one the foundations of the post-war settlement – welfare state, Keynesian economics, corporate management and the historic compromise between capital and labour – were questioned, then undermined or destroyed. Had Britain enjoyed the same success as the fast growing European economies, had it satisfied the electorate by delivering the higher standards of living, welfare and work they did, then Thatcherism could never have been thought to be the answer to a national problem, just as anorexia would never be prescribed to an ailing athlete. A richer country made strong by sustained growth, high productivity and investments would have been more altruistic, happier and simply better than a poorer one made anorexic by long years of cutbacks, where cuts compounded problems to justify more cuts in a downward spiral.

Today at the end of that New Labour moves to power to clear up the consequences of the counter-revolution which last time's failure made inevitable. It does so cautiously, offering a sparse agenda, few new departures, more a return to stability and the prospect of gradual change as the levers of power are moved progressively to the people. This national regeneration programme is paced over two Parliaments, not a short sharp dash or a dramatic hundred days. It has been developed by a cautious leadership for a nervous electorate and sets out aspirations rather than details, making it more a strategy for winning than a prescription for governing. Labour's almost asking a doctor's mandate rather than offering a radical new departure such as Margaret Thatcher embarked on after 1979.

The approach is the best our best brains can devise and more relevant to new times than 1964's boldness. Then Labour faced a do-nothing-very-much Conservative government, Today we face the failing fag-end of a radical government which has destabilised everything over eighteen years. Today's electors choose as consumers and must not be frightened. Today's Labour Party is less confident, more apologetic, ever ready to tie its own hands, talk down expectations and damp its own instincts, a political Puritanism which makes Harold Wilson and his party look like naïve revivalists.

Old Labour look positively ideological compared to today's political pragmatism. C. A. R. Crosland asserted that socialism is 'about equality'. Now we hardly mention 'socialism' and Labour is about managerialism, empowerment and simple responsibility. Little to enthuse. Less to answer for. No promises. No packdrill. All this may be less than an electorate anxious for change is now ready to accept and less than party members desire. 'Enough is Enough' is a good slogan. Yet a touch of 'Let's Go with Labour' would bring an adrenalin boost.

Our caution combined with 'Time for a Change' should allow us to master the first of the two great lessons of 1964–70, that power comes neither easily nor quickly to Labour. In 1951, 1970 and 1979, Tory governments came in with majorities to last a Parliament, and in the first and last cases bases to build bigger on. In 1964 and 1974 Labour won narrowly, or hardly at all, and had to go to the country again shortly. So 1964's transfer of power took the form of a big drop of 6.0% in the

Tory vote, and a smaller 1.5% in 1966, but a small increase in Labour's share of only 0.3% at the first but 3.8% as suspicion abated, a crab-like progress which combined to give a 5.8% swing. Bigger than we now need for a majority to govern, though this time a disintegrating Tory Party is doing far more to help us reach power in one stride than Sir Alec Douglas-Home ever proffered.

The second lesson – can Labour deliver? – is more difficult. Labour's programme and approach are well calculated to win power but so heavily focused on doing that that they hardly provide a prescription for what lies beyond when we must deliver at Labour's crucial task: maximising the living standards of the overwhelming majority. Then, as now, doing that does not depend on the supply-side measures which always preoccupy Labour, for proposals for investment, training, upgrading, are usually running out of our ears. Yet supply does not produce its own demand. Success depends on economic competence, on knowing and mobilising the dynamics of growth and demand, on understanding the crucial role of the exchange rate. This was, and is, much too high, ensuring that domestic production is not profitable enough to sustain the investment and the expansion which allow the real economy to be strengthened and expanded. Unless it is made profitable the natural dynamics of the economy work against us.

The economic circumstances of 1997 are different from those in 1964. Then exchange rates were fixed, now they float, though still kept too high by high real-interest rates and by the dominance of the financial interest in British counsels. Then Europe was expanding, now it is deflating to fit into the Maastricht straight-jacket. Yet in both cases the real problem lay not in the world but in ourselves: our lack of courage and understanding of the real economy, our conditioning to orthodoxy, financial then European now, our deference to finance and our naïve belief that we can make water flow uphill. Tories pursue the self-interest of their people ruthlessly. Labour is usually inhibited about doing the same, and far readier to ask the people for sacrifices to defend the orthodoxies of others.

The key test of success or failure for Labour governments is neither respectability nor acclamation from a Gaderene media herd but simple ability to deliver. That means growth, maximising the living standards of the British people, lifting all the boats, and allowing the painless redistribution through growing public spending which builds a fairer society. Labour delivered that between 1945 and 1951, less well between 1964 and 1970, for growth then came too late and was not on the scale the people expected. From 1974–9 we merely struggled to stop things getting worse. Today, at long last, opportunity is opening up again. With a programme in which neither increased taxation nor redistribution play a part, everything now depends on economic growth to create jobs, to widen the tax base and to generate more public spending. The chance to get it has been a long time coming. It mustn't be thrown away.

Those Who Took Part

Lord Barnett (Joel Barnett)
MP Heywood and Royton Division, Lancashire
(1964–83)

Rt Hon. Tony Benn
MP Bristol SE (November 1950–60, August 1963–83)
Postmaster-General (1964–6)
Minister of Technology (1966–70)

Jeremy Bray
MP Middlesbrough West (1962–70)
Parliamentary Secretary, Ministry of Power (1966–7)

Ron Brown
MP Shoreditch and Finsbury (1964–74)

Walter Brown
Regional Assistant Organiser, Southern Region (1964–6)

Ann Carlton
Research Assistant, Labour Party Head Office (1965–6)
Local Government Officer (1966–74)

Lord Callaghan (Jim Callaghan)
MP Cardiff SE (1950–83)
Chancellor of the Exchequer (1964–7)

Lady Castle (Barbara Castle)
MP Blackburn (1955–79)
Member of National Executive Committee of Labour
Party (1950–79)
Minister for Overseas Development (1964–5)
Minister of Transport (1965–8)

Lord Chalfont (Alun Chalfont)
Minister of State, Foreign and Commonwealth Office
(1964–70)

Susan Crosland
Wife of Tony Crosland

Tam Dalyell
MP West Lothian (1962–83)
PPS to Rt Hon. Richard Crossman (1964–5)

Rt Hon. Edmund Dell
MP Birkenhead (1964–79)
Parliamentary Secretary, Ministry of Technology (1966–7)

Lord Diamond (Jack Diamond)
MP Gloucester (1957–70)
Chief Secretary to the Treasury (1964–70)

Lady Falkender (Marcia Williams)
Private and Political Secretary to Harold Wilson
(1956–83); at No. 10 Downing Street (1964–70)

Rt Hon. Michael Foot
MP Ebbw Vale (1960–83)

Rt Hon. Reg Freeson
MP Willesden E (1964–74)
PPS to Minister of Transport (1964–7)

Lord Glenamara (Ted Short)
MP for Newcastle upon Tyne (1951–76)
Government Chief Whip and Parliamentary Secretary to
the Treasury (1964–6)

Lord Healey (Denis Healey)
MP Leeds E (1955–92)
Shadow Cabinet (1959–64)
Secretary of State for Defence (1964–70)

Anthony Howard
Political Correspondent, *New Statesman* (1961–4)
Whitehall Correspondent, *Sunday Times* (1965)

Lord Denis Howell

MP Birmingham, Small Heath (March 1961–92)
Joint Parliamentary Under-Secretary of State,
Department Education and Science (with responsibility
for sport) (1964–9)

Lord Howie of Troon (Will Howie)

MP Luton (November 1963–70)
Assistant Whip (1964–6)
Lord Commander of the Treasury (1966–7)

Lord Jenkins of Putney (Hugh Jenkins)

MP Wandsworth, Putney (1964–79)

Lord Jenkins of Hillhead (Ray Jenkins)

MP Stechford, Birmingham (1950–76)
Minister of Aviation (1964–5)
Home Secretary (1965–7)

Professor George Jones

Contested Kidderminster 1964
University of Leeds, Lecturer in Government (1965)
London School of Economics, Lecturer in Political
Science (1966)

Rt Hon. Gerald Kaufman

MP Manchester, Ardwick (1970–83)
Political Correspondent, *New Statesman* (1964–5)
Parliamentary Press Liaison Officer, Labour Party
(1965–70)

David Kingsley

Publicity adviser to the Labour Party and Government
(1962–70)

Lord Longford

Lord Privy Seal (1964–5 and 1966–8)
Secretary of State for the Colonies (1965–6)
Leader of the House of Lords (1964–8)

Lord Lovell-Davis (Peter Davis)

Managing Director, Central Press Features Ltd (1952–70)

Rt Hon. Dickson Mabon
MP Greenock (December 1955–74)
Joint Parliamentary Under-Secretary of State for
Scotland (1964–7)

Kevin McNamara
MP Kingston-upon-Hull North (January 1966–74)

Professor David Marquand
Contested Barry (1964)
MP Ashfield (1966–77)

Lord Marsh (Richard Marsh)
MP Greenwich (1959–71)
Parliamentary Secretary, Ministry of Labour (1964–5)
Joint Parliamentary Secretary, Ministry of Technology
(1965–6)

Lord Merlyn-Rees (Merlyn Rees)
MP South Leeds (1963–83)
PPS to Chancellor of the Exchequer (1964)
Parliamentary Under-Secretary of State, Ministry of
Defence (Army) (1965–6)

Rt Hon. Alfred Morris
MP Manchester, Wythenshawe (since 1964)
PPS Minister of Agriculture, Fisheries and Food
(1964–7)

Stan Newens
MP Epping (1964–70)

Lord Rodgers of Quarry Bank (Bill Rodgers)
MP Stockton-on-Tees (1962–74)
Parliamentary Under-Secretary of State, Department of
Economic Affairs (1964–7)

Rt Hon. Robert Sheldon
MP Ashton-under-Lyne (since 1964)
Chairman, Labour Parliamentary Economic Affairs and
Finance Group (1967–8)

Rt Hon. Peter Shore

MP Stepney (1964–74)
PPS to the Prime Minister (1965–6)
Joint Parliamentary Secretary, Ministry of Technology
(1966–7)

Dick Taverne

MP Lincoln (1962–72)
Parliamentary Under-Secretary of State, Home Office
(1966–8)

Lord Thomson of Monifieth (George Thomson)

MP Dundee East (July 1952–72)
Minister of State, Foreign Office (1964–6)
Chancellor of the Duchy of Lancaster (1966–7)

Beryl Urquhart

Committee Clerk, Parliamentary Labour Party (1954–74)

Rt Hon. Sir Harold Walker

MP Doncaster (1964–83)
An Assistant Government Whip (1967–8)

Ann Ward

Professional photographer and photo journalist for *Daily
Mail* (1962–7) and *Daily Mirror* (1967–70)

Rt Hon. Alan Williams

MP Swansea West (since 1964)
PPS to Postmaster-General (1966–7)
Parliamentary Under-Secretary, Department of
Economic Affairs (1967–9)

Lord Wyatt of Weeford (Woodrow Wyatt)

MP Bosworth Division of Leicester (1959–70)

ABOUT THE AUTHORS

Austin Mitchell has been the Labour Member of Parliament for Great Grimsby since 1977. A former official fellow of Nuffield College, Oxford, he was elected after a career as a political science lecturer in New Zealand and as a broadcaster and journalist with the BBC and Yorkshire Television. Author of several books on the Labour Party, New Zealand and Yorkshire.

David Wienir, prior to this publication, was the host of the political commentary broadcast 'Estonia Today' on Estonian National Radio. Educated at Columbia, Oxford and the London School of Economics.